T0360668

Consumer Optimization Problem Solving

Consumer Optimization Problem Solving

Alfred L Norman

World Scientific

NEW JERSEY • LONDON • SINGAPORE • BEIJING • SHANGHAI • HONG KONG • TAIPEI • CHENNAI

Published by

World Scientific Publishing Co. Pte. Ltd.

5 Toh Tuck Link, Singapore 596224

USA office: 27 Warren Street, Suite 401-402, Hackensack, NJ 07601

UK office: 57 Shelton Street, Covent Garden, London WC2H 9HE

Library of Congress Cataloging-in-Publication Data
Norman, A. L. (Alfred L.)
    Consumer optimization problem solving / Alfred L Norman, The University of Texas at Austin, USA.
        pages cm
    Includes bibliographical references and index.
    ISBN 978-9814635288 (hardcover) -- ISBN 9814635286 (hardcover)
    1. Consumer behavior--Econometric models. 2. Consumption (Economics)--Econometric models.
I. Title.
    HF5415.32.N67 2015
    658.4'03--dc23

2014039632

British Library Cataloguing-in-Publication Data
A catalogue record for this book is available from the British Library.

In-house Editor: Philly Lim

Typeset by Stallion Press
Email: enquiries@stallionpress.com

Printed in Singapore

Acknowledgements

This book could not have been written without the able assistance of the members of my research group: Michael Aberty, Ansh Agarwal, Ali Ahmed, Jeffrey Berman, Yodit Beyene, Drew Bloom, Katie Brehm, Jacklin Chou, Mridul Chowdhury, Michelle Eisbrenner, Aparna Dalal, Michael Drake, Audrey Dyer, Gita El Kadiri, Kenneth Fortson, Amy Folmer, Jordan Frisby, Mandara Gabriel, Charu Govil, Sheetal Gour, Casey Gribble, Brian Gu, Jessica Hart, Lon Heuer, Carolyn Hinchey, Nancy Hite, Kyle Hood, Mukti Jindal, Julia Ke, Samarth Kejirwal, Samuel Keyburn, Katherine Kuang, Madhura Kulharni, Chris Kurz, Hunter Lee, Greg Leneord, Samuel Ler, Leigh Linden, Colleen Mattingly, Nina Mehta, Kara Meythaler, Kim Murray, Leeor Mushin, Herb Newhouse, Kirsten Powers, Kendall Payne, Alex Raff, Mukund Rajan, Sharanya Rajan, Rebecca Rando, Ben Rice, Ashley Roberston, Jiten Sanghai, Jason Scheick, Chris Schulz, Prateek Shah, Vivek Shah, Kevin Sheppard, Hui Sub Shim, Yaso Sivakumaran, Eric Sublett, Andrea Surratt, Jason Sussman, Anisha Sutaria, Lilian Tan, Melodie Tang, Nancy Tantzen, Andrew Tello, Chris Tillmanns, Rachelle Wang, Ingrid White, Kan Yan, Frank Zahradnic, Tlek Zeinullayev and Michael Ziegler.

These "with" authors were members of my economic research group for one to four years between 1995 and 2012. They are coauthors on the various papers we submitted to journals and presented at conferences as a tag team where each member spoke for 2 to 5 minutes. Much of the research of the group involved questionnaires and experiments, which required much effort to clarify the large number of details. Students had a much better idea what undergraduate subjects were thinking than I and were very creative in resolving the details. They also helped with the editing the papers upon which this book is based. In addition, students were encouraged to use the skills that they learned in their courses, such as econometrics. It was rewarding working with them and I believe that they also profited from the experience. Students not listed on the Norman et al references worked on one or more of the questionnaires in Chapters 6,7,8 and 9.

I would also like to thank the editors for the book: Chester Polson, Andrew Hoffman, and my wife Noreen. I would also like to thank Tom Wiseman for his helpful comments.

Contents

Chapter 1

Introduction

1.1 Introduction

What algorithms are tractable depends on the speed of the processor. A cell phone processor can execute millions of instructions per second. Solving the consumer optimization problem is known to be tractable for a digital processor. In contrast, the System 2 (conscious) processor of the human brain is known to be very slow. For example, a human can take several seconds to make one binary comparison between two pens. Given the slow speed of the human conscious processor we argue that solving the consumer optimization problem is intractable for an unaided human.

We study the simplifications consumers employ to solve the consumer problem. Consumers search for goods and services item-by-item, which greatly reduces the number of alternatives to consider. In addition, consumers have operators that can process a set in a single operation. Finally, consumers budget by incremental adjustment.

In considering consumer performance we focus on how close to optimal is consumer performance and not whether consumers optimize as a yes/no question. Given the ordinal nature of utility theory this creates a basic measurement problem. We review the literature on consumer performance.

This is an opportune time to study consumer procedures because decision aids presented on the Internet can make substantial improvements in consumer performance. We create software for digital camera selection that we demonstrate with a field experiment provides better advice than the advice of sales people.

We now discuss the organization of the book in greater detail.

1.2   Computational Complexity and Consumers

Chapter 2: Computational Complexity

In this book, formal models of consumer procedures will be specified as algorithms that will be defined in terms of the specified elementary operations, which, as will be discussed in Chapter 2, are defined as System 2 (conscious) operations. These will include psychological decision rules, information operations, as well as arithmetic operations that will be treated as black boxes with execution costs. We will not consider the details of how the human neural network performs these elementary operations. There is a precedent for this approach in that [Huber (1980)] and [Johnson (1988)] proposed studying decision strategies by their elementary information processes.

Algorithms can be analyzed by computational complexity, which is a measure of the difficulty in solving a problem asymptotically. The analysis focuses on determining how the cost function of an algorithm increases with respect to one or more growth parameters. An example of a growth parameter would be the number of alternatives for the consumer to consider. Given the large number of alternatives and astronomical number of corresponding bundles in the marketplace, this type of analysis is appropriate.

A basic overview of these techniques used in the book is presented. We also present our analysis of the computational complexity of a discrete consumer utility optimization model and a review of the subsequent literature.

How difficult a problem a processor can solve depends on the speed at which the processor executes an elementary operation. Problems which a processor can solve in a "reasonable" amount of time are called processor tractable. Let us first consider DC tractable, which is tractable for digital computer processors. A computer with a processor capable of computing 1 billion floating point operations a second could complete a linear program over 1 million alternatives executing 1000 operations per alternative in 1 second. This is clearly DC tractable. Given the speed at which digital computers execute operations, algorithms for which the cost function increases as a polynomial of the growth parameter are considered tractable in that it could be executed in a time considered economic. Nevertheless, the discrete consumer utility optimization problem in the general case is not DC tractable, unless we impose an additional condition on the problem.

Now let us consider a human as a computational agent executing System 2 (conscious) operations. Compared with a digital computer, an unaided human is generally very slow in executing an operation. For example, we determined that subjects took about 3.2 seconds to execute a binary comparison involving two pens, [Norman *et al.* (2004)], and we are 90% confident that is is greater than 1.5 seconds. A linear human algorithm requiring 3.2 seconds to compare two alternatives would take 889 hours to process a million alternatives. This is not tractable for unaided humans. Human tractable will be abbreviated to H tractable.

Theories of human procedures must not require more computational resources than humans possess. Faced with the number of alternatives that a consumer encounters in the marketplace we assert that **sublinear** algorithms are H tractable and that algorithms linear and higher are not except for a small number of alternatives. This defines Simon's concept of bounded rationality in terms of computational complexity. Computational complexity analysis is useful because if a consumer model created by economic theorists is not H tractable then the researcher should ask how does the consumer simplify the problem to obtain a H tractable algorithm, and what is the performance of such an algorithm relative to the optimal solution of the theoretical model.

We consider how consumers simplify the consumer optimization problem in order to obtain an H tractable problem. In the theoretical model consumers maximize their utility by evaluating alternative bundles of goods subject to the budget constraint. But, in the marketplace consumers purchase their goods item by item. In order to intuitively understand why this is the case, let us consider two models of a grocery store. The first model is the traditional grocery store where the consumer traverses the aisles filling the shopping cart item by item. An item-by-item grocery store organizes close substitutes such as brands of cereal in the same aisle.

A second model is a bundles grocery store that enables the consumer to compare bundles of groceries. In such a store the consumer walks down a single aisle comparing shopping carts, each loaded with a basket or bundle of groceries. In addition to the current practice of listing the price of each item, assume the store lists the price of the entire bundle on the shopping cart. Also, assume the store organizes the giant line of shopping carts containing all the possible bundles in ascending order by bundle price.

To obtain some perspective of the number of alternatives that must be considered, let us assume that the two grocery stores each carry 30 categories of goods and 10 alternatives in each, for example, 10 types of cereal and 10 types of bread. These numbers are very conservative for a modern grocery store. In this case the number of shopping carts that the consumer must consider in the bundles grocery store is $10 \times 10 \times 10 \times \cdots \times 10 = 10^{30}$. If it only took 10 seconds to make a binary comparison between two bundles of 30 items, it would take 1.59×10^{23} years to find the preferred bundle using the linear procedure of comparing the first with the second and the preferred with the third and so on. If each bundle were placed in a 3-foot-long shopping cart then the consumer would have to travel 5.68×10^{27} miles just to view all the bundles.

To drastically reduce their display space, sellers organize their goods for item by item acquisition, and consumers acquire goods item by item to drastically reduce the number of alternatives they need to consider. In the case above acquiring groceries item-by-item reduces the number of alternatives to consider from 10^{30} to $10 + 10 + 10 + \ldots + 10 = 300$ that is the number of alternatives increase additively not geometrically.

We assert that humans achieve sublinear algorithms to solve their consumer optimization problem by making the following simplifications:

1. They search for goods and services item-by-item. These searches are sublinear because as we shall show, humans have operators that can process a set in a single operation.

2. They budget using an incremental adjustment process.

Consumers make sequential item searches for goods and services all their lives. While consumers may not be optimal in their searches, they do have an incentive to improve the efficiency of their searches. This raises a basic question: How do consumers improve the efficiency of their item searches over time?

1.3   Component Studies

Before examining how consumers learn to be efficient in repeated searches, we present preliminary studies of some components of the consumer problem in the next three chapters.

Chapter 3: Ordering

We use experiments to show that humans can order a small number of items using a linear procedure. Binary comparison operators form the basis of consumer set theory. If humans could only perform binary comparisons, the most efficient procedure a human might employ to make a complete preference ordering of n items would be a $n \log_2 n$ algorithm. But, if humans are capable of assigning each item a utility value, they are capable of implementing a more efficient linear algorithm. We consider six incentive systems for ordering three different sets of objects: pens, notebooks, and Hot Wheels. We establish that subjects are using a linear procedure by performing regression analysis, observing the hand motions of the subjects, and talking with the subjects about which algorithm they used. What makes regression analysis possible is that a binary comparison takes seconds not nanoseconds.

This research demonstrates a case where being able to create a utility value leads to a more efficient algorithm than just using a binary comparison. The fact that humans can order a small number of alternatives such as stores, products, or attributes using a linear procedure is useful to develop efficient search procedures over time.

Chapter 4: Computational Complexity: Decision Rules

A consumer entering a new bookstore can face more than 250,000 alternatives. We then consider the efficiency of using various known psychological decision rules in search procedures. In this analysis we assume that the cost of creating such decision rules is fixed and that a consumer uses the same decision rule plus an information operator from start to finish. We show that procedures based on these known rules in search are linear procedures and that such rules are not H tractable given the number of alternatives the consumer faces in the marketplace.

We introduce a new psychological decision rule based on a set information operator, and show that it leads to a sublinear procedure. Next, we perform an experiment to show that humans have the ability to employ such a rule effectively, and finally we show that markets in both physical space and cyberspace are organized to facilitate the use of such set rules by consumers. In cyberspace, decision rules can be encoded as decision aids, which can be considered to have an H tractable constant complexity from the perspective of the user.

Chapter 5: Repeated Price Search

In this chapter we consider repeated price search. Consumers check few sites in online purchases. We perform repeated price search experiments that are dynamic Bayesian optimization problems for which the subjects could not calculate the optimal strategy. Instead, they used heuristics whose performance is better than random and less than optimal. To investigate online price search performance we surveyed students on their online textbook purchases. Students achieve good performance because they start with a good strategy and because of the online market organization of marketplace and meta-search sites. An important factor is that algorithms at sites searched perform calculations that reduce the computational complexity of the search.

We argue that economic price search theory is flawed because computing the reservation price is H intractable and in repeated price searches consumers learn relative prices of sellers not the distribution of prices of the current search. Finally, new decision aids on the internet and on smart phones that effectively reduce the computational complexity of a price search to an H tractable constant complexity are changing price search strategies.

1.4   Item Search and Budgeting

In the next three chapters we present our theory of how consumers solve the economic consumer problem. We relax the assumption that tastes are given and assume that preferences are learned. If pressed, very few economists would assert that consumers acquire a complete preference ordering neatly encoded in their genome at conception. When cardinal utility was formulated in the 19th century, consumers had few choices and the rate of technological advance was slow. Under these conditions it was a reasonable assumption to assume that a consumer had learned his preferences by the time he became an adult consumer. Today consumers face a very large number of alternatives and frequently encounter products that have new features or are completely new. Under such conditions they learn their preferences as part of the item search. The important question is to what extent is it efficient for consumers to learn their preferences.

Chapter 6: Repeated Item Search: Forecasting

Consumers in considering their alternatives need to forecast the future performance of an alternative in its intended use. When consumers have developed stable preferences over specific alternatives, this forecast is encapsulated in the utility function.

For frequently purchased goods such as food, consumers can forecast the future performance and learn their preferences by a sequential trial and error (STE) strategy that is a strategy in which consumers sequentially try different alternatives until preferences are formed. We investigate how students use this strategy to choose which restaurants to frequent for lunch.

The longer the time period between purchases and the greater the rate of technological change, the less useful a STE strategy becomes for forecasting and the less the value of prior consumption. With the rapid rate of technological change and the proliferation of goods and services in the marketplace, consumers must develop strategies for forecasting the performance of alternatives with which they may have had little experience.

As consumers have limited ability to test most products, consumers must gather data from others including media ads, data supplied by the sellers and manufacturers, product reviews by current users and experts. We review the development of data sources first in newspapers, magazines and now the Internet. How much data should a consumer acquire to forecast? It is not "perfect information" because this concept is not easily definable in that the potential limit of data a consumer could acquire and process is determined by the Heisenberg uncertainty principle. Given that acquiring and processing data has real costs, it is readily apparent that consumers acquire and process a truly minuscule fraction of the data that could be provided to them. The information value of data is a function of its processing cost, reliability and capacity to discriminate among alternatives.

In forecasting beyond consumption experience, consumers use a wide variety of procedures that we demonstrate using digital cameras as an example.

Chapter 7: Repeated Item Search: Choice

A typical consumer item search has the following steps:
1. Goal and start set
2. Several set decision steps
3. Evaluation of specific alternatives in the final set
4. Selection of preferred item or items.

With repeated searching the number of alternatives in the start set decreases and in some case it can decrease to one in which case an item search has been reduced to a replacement operation. The amount of System 2 effort involved in making the various steps decreases over time and steps are combined.

Over time a consumer develops a variety of types of item searches for different types of goods that vary greatly depending on the frequency of purchase, the cost, the type of goods, and the rate of technological change. There is also tremendous variation in item search for the same type of product among consumers.

Consumers achieve search efficiency through repeated searches by acquiring a great volume of consumer knowledge about market organization and goods and services. The acquisition of this knowledge starts in early childhood and while prosaic, is extensive. In repeated searches there is no point in remembering preferences over specific alternatives that will be replaced by new products by the time of the next search for that good. An important factor in consumer search efficiency is that consumers learn decision rules and preferences over sets and attributes that will be useful in future shopping. We demonstrate this factor with a study of students' search for jeans.

Chapter 8: Budgeting

An optimal solution of budgeting considering every possible bundle is H intractable. Even allocating money into alternative accounts is a quadratic process. For example, there are 5050 possible allocations in the case of allocating $100 into three accounts in $1 increments. How do consumers obtain H tractable heuristics to solve the budgeting problem?

In order to understand budgeting we conducted several surveys of students who lived in apartments. At our university most students live in a dorm the first year and move into apartments the second year, a move that requires them to allocate money into several accounts. What we observe is that students use an incremental adjustment process. They monitor the flow of funds and make adjustments. What makes this type of budgeting difficult is not the amount of calculation, but rather controlling the flow.

Some students are feast or famine budgeters in that when they receive funds they initially feast and then starve towards the end of their budget period. Other students have good control over the flow of funds and some are soft budgeters in that they can ask their parents for more money if needed. Another area where student budgeters differ greatly is in the amount of budget planning they perform. Only a few use spreadsheets to budget or budgeting software such as Intuit's Quicken. The latest trend is budget applications on cell phones. Budgeting is not a computational intensive process, but rather a intuitive adjustment process.

We compare our results with the previous results of [Thaler (1991)] on budgeting.

1.5   How Close to Optimal and Better Performance

In the next two chapters we ask how close to optimal is consumer performance and what potential innovations could be created to improve consumer performance.

Chapter 9: How Close to Optimal?

Given the difficulty of the consumer optimization problem relative to what is tractable for an unaided human processor, the question to ask is how close to optimal is human consumer performance. This question presents a very difficult measurement problem given the ordinal nature of utility theory.

We define the attributes of the reference model we will use to measure performance. We consider a one period model with savings as the variable that connects the periods. We consider both anticipated or decision utility and realized or experienced utility. We review the various measures that have been created to identify mistakes and evaluate performance relative to both anticipated and realized utility.

We then consider two experiments that are good approximations to our reference model. These two important studies involving a small number of periods and no long term decisions such as retirement are data obtained from an experiment in a psychiatric ward, [Battalio *et al.* (1973)] and [Cox (1997)] and the animal experiments, [Kagel *et al.* (1995)]. In these studies the subjects were presented with few options and quickly learned their preferences. Also, for comparative statics purposes, the consumption decisions were repeated each period. The results demonstrate behavior consistent with the theory.

In this book we have discussed simplifications that consumers use to solve their consumer optimization problem. We review numerous articles concerning the identification of mistakes and performance evaluation in each of these simplifications. We first consider psychological limitations to achieving optimal performance. Then we consider the performance implications of shifting from bundles to item-by-item searches. Finally, we consider decisions involving a subset of consumer purchases in the marketplace.

We assess the current status of research on consumer performance. It is currently impossible to quantitatively determine how close to optimal is the typical consumer.

Chapter 10: Improving Consumer Performance

Given the increasing value of consumers' time and the increasing difficulty of solving the consumer problem, consumers have need of improved data, strategies, and decision aids in order to improve their performance. In this Chapter we consider the role of government, business, and research to achieve this goal.

We review the role of government in reducing fraud, setting standards, promoting safety, and providing data in the marketplace. Because of the need to reduce budget deficits and conservatives opposition to regulation, government is not likely to play a major role in improving consumer performance in the near future.

We consider five current developments concerning the interaction between business and consumers. The first is the creation of wellness programs and the second more effective savings programs for employees. The third is the creation of social media, which is improving the communication between business and consumers. Next we consider consumers as inventors and innovators, a role improved by better communications. Finally, we consider consumer tracking by firms. The first four developments are positive and the last negative.

In the near future, firms will create technology for better measurements. One example, are scanners that measure body sizes in order to select clothes that fit without having to try them on. Another problem that must be addressed to improve consumer performance is fake review optimization.

However, the major improvement in consumer performance will come from improved decision aids by third party Internet review sites. Because humans process a small fraction of the available data in consumption decisions, the question to ask is how should the data be framed to improve consumer performance. This differs fundamentally from marketing which focuses on framing the data to sell the product. We present our research on creating software for digital camera selection that we demonstrate with a field experiment provides better advice than the advice of sales people.

In the long term, households will have integrated computer-communications systems that reflect all aspects of household activities. This development will create a framework for much better decision aids. Finally, we discuss the type of research needed to promote bounded-rational procedural economics.

Chapter 2

Computational Complexity

2.1 Introduction

Computational complexity is a statistic devised by computer scientists to measure the difficulty in solving a problem, which in our case is the consumer optimization problem. The statistic is an asymptotic statistic which measures how the cost function (or time function) grows with respect to a growth parameter of the problem, which in our case will frequently be the number of alternatives from which the consumer must choose a preferred item. Recall in Chapter 1, the number of alternatives, especially in the number of bundles, that a consumer faces has grown steadily since the beginning of the 19th century. This growth justifies applying computational complexity methodology to the consumer problem.

In the next section, we start by describing how algorithms will be represented in this book. Then we provide a set of definitions that define the concept of computational complexity. In order to make the methodology intuitive to readers not familiar with computational complexity, we provide several examples of increasing computational complexity.

In applying computational complexity to human algorithms we shall consider System 2 (conscious) processes. To illustrate this approach we provide an example of using a binary comparison to find a preferred pen in Section 3. We then analyze the computational complexity of solving a discrete version of the microeconomic consumer optimization problem using a binary comparison operator. For this problem, we show that the computational complexity of optimal budgeting is the maximum of an exponential in the number of alternatives and a quadratic in the number of budget increments. We discuss recent research that shows in general the consumer problem is a NP-hard problem, but if we restrict our attention to utility functions that explain the data, the problem is polynomial.

But, is reducing the computational complexity to polynomial enough to make the problem tractable for an unaided human consumer? In Section 4, we introduce the concept of tractability as it is used in computer science. Implicit in this concept is the processing speed of the relevant processor. Given the slow speed of System 2 operations we argue that for unaided humans a tractable process is sublinear and this provides a computational complexity definition of Simon's concept of bounded rationality.

One approach to solving intractable problems is simplification. We assert that consumers simplify the consumer problem by:

- Searching for the goods in their market basket one-by-one
- Using set operators in the early stages of in item search
- Solving their budgeting problem using a learned feedback control mechanism.

Finally, a clearly specified algorithm can be analyzed using mathematic logic, but many human algorithms must be inferred from human behavior.

2.2   Computational Complexity

To study procedures the decision process is modeled as a computer algorithm, which could be defined in various ways. Traub, Wasilkowski and Wozniakowski (1988) abstractly define an algorithm as a function from the problem element to the solution range. A common practice is to define algorithms with respect to a particular language, such as a quasi-Algol, Aho, Hopcroft and Ullman (1974), or a particular computer model such as a Turing machine. Algorithms can also be described formally in computer languages using the Backus-Naur Form specification, [Pagan (1981)]. In this paper we shall follow the example of [Knuth (1973)] and describe in English the algorithms that will be sequences of information operators and decision operators. This should help make the simple algorithms presented in this book transparent to the reader.

In the next subsection we provide definitions of computational complexity and in the following subsection we provide several examples to illustrate the concept.

2.2.1 *Computational Complexity Definitions*

Computer scientists compare computer algorithms based on the time required for execution, the cost involved, or the required memory. To make such comparisons, the time, cost, or memory are usually parameterized with respect to an important attribute of the problem, such as n, the number of items to be ordered. We can make these comparisons with a fixed finite n, or make the comparisons as n increases. Computer scientists find the latter method advantageous because, asymptotically, only the dominant factor in an algorithm matters.

We now present the framework for the computational complexity analysis, which is standard combinatorial complexity with the addition of information operators. Let $\psi_i \in \Psi$ be an algorithm in the finite set of I algorithms that solves each problem element $s_l \in S$, the finite problem set of L elements, using the finite set of information and computational operators $\Upsilon = \{v_1, v_2, \ldots v_m\}$. Let c_j and t_j be the unit cost and unit time, respectively, of executing a given v_j. Also let $N_{\psi_i[s_l]}(v_j)$ be the number of times ψ_i executes v_j in solving s_l. The cost and time functions for algorithm ψ_i to solve s_l are the number of operations times its unit cost or time:

$$\text{Cost: } C(\psi_i[s_l]) = \sum_j c_j \cdot N_{\psi_i[s_l]}(v_j) \tag{2.1}$$

$$\text{Time: } T(\psi_i[s_l]) = \sum_j t_j \cdot N_{\psi_i[s_l]}(v_j) \tag{2.2}$$

We now define the worst case and expected case. We define the worst case for each algorithm $\psi_i \in \Psi$ in solving all $s_l \in S$ as:

$$\text{Cost: } C_{W[S]}(\psi_i) = \max_{s_l \in S} C(\psi_i[s_l]) \tag{2.3}$$

$$\text{Time: } T_{W[S]}(\psi_i) = \max_{s_l \in S} T(\psi_i[s_l]) \tag{2.4}$$

Assuming each $s_l \in S$ is equally likely, we define the expected case for each algorithm $\psi_i \in \Psi$ in solving all $s_l \in S$ as:

$$\text{Cost: } C_{E[S]}(\psi_i) = \sum_{s_l \in S} C(\psi_i[s_l])/L \tag{2.5}$$

$$\text{Time: } T_{E[S]}(\psi_i) = \sum_{s_l \in S} T(\psi_i[s_l])/L \tag{2.6}$$

In both the worst case and expected case we choose the efficient algorithm in the set of algorithms for the respective definition:

$$\text{Worst case Cost: } C^*_{W[S]} = \min_i C_{W[S]}(\psi_i) \qquad (2.7)$$

$$\text{Worst case Time: } T^*_{W[S]} = \min_i T_{W[S]}(\psi_i) \qquad (2.8)$$

$$\text{Expected case Cost: } C^*_{E[S]} = \min_i C_{E[S]}(\psi_i) \qquad (2.9)$$

$$\text{Expected case Time: } T^*_{E[S]} = \min_i T_{E[S]}(\psi_i) \qquad (2.10)$$

Expected case analysis is generally much harder to perform than worst case analysis. Because cost and time analysis have the same format above, we shall focus solely on cost analysis, which can include the value of time. The goal is establishing *how the worst case or expected case cost for* Ψ, *which solves* S, *grows with respect to a growth parameter* n. To define the worst case computational complexity of S given Ψ let $Y = Y(n)$ be a nonnegative function that we wish to compare with the worst case cost function of ψ_i, $C_W(i, n) = C_{W[S[n]]}(\psi_i)$. Frequently Y is n, n^2 etc, and since the definitions for the worst case and expected case are the same we shall leave off the worse case or expected case subscript on the cost function.

Consider the following definitions:

D1. $C(i, n)$ is $O(Y)$ if there exist $j, l > 0$ such that $C(i, n) \leq jY(n)$ for all $n > l$.

D2. $C(i, n)$ is $\Omega(Y)$ if there exist $j, l > 0$ such that $C(i, n) \geq jY(n)$ for all $n > l$.

D3. Given Ψ, S has computational complexity Y if there exists an algorithm $\psi_i \in \Psi$ such that $C(i, n)$ is $O(Y)$ and for all algorithms $\psi_j \in \Phi$, $C(j, n)$ is $\Omega(Y)$.

Let us now consider how one determines the computational complexity of a particular S. First, one creates an algorithm that solves S and determines $O(Y_{upper})$ for this algorithm. This establishes an upper bound, Y_{upper}, on the computational complexity of solving S. Then one examines the elements s_i of S to find a property that limits the cost of all algorithms in Ψ to at least $\Omega(Y_{lower})$. This establishes a lower bound, Y_{lower} on the computational complexity of solving S. If $Y_{lower} = Y_{upper}$, the computational complexity has been established. Generally, establishing a lower bound is more difficult than establishing an upper bound.

The concept of computational complexity divides problems into equivalence classes. With these definitions, problems can be identified as "easy", (for example, members of the n equivalence class) or "hard", (for example, members of the exponential equivalence class). If the computational complexity of executing an algorithm has a computational complexity of n, we shall call the process a n order process. For example, if n is 1, we shall call the process a linear process.

2.2.2 Examples

To give the reader unacquainted with algorithms and computational complexity an intuitive grasp of the difficulty of algorithms we shall consider some examples:

A constant problem

A linear problem and a sublinear problem

Polynomial problems

An exponential problem and a NP-hard problem

A transfinite problem

2.2.2.1 A constant problem

A constant complexity problem is one in which the cost function is a fixed constant. This means the cost of processing 10 alternatives is the same as processing 10,000. When a consumer clicks on a search algorithm on the Internet, this is approximately true from the perspective of the consumer because given the speed of the server processor the user would not notice the time difference.

2.2.2.2 A linear problem and a sublinear problem

Given a set of arbitrarily arranged integers $N = i_1, i_2, \ldots, i_n$, let us first construct an algorithm to find the largest integer in the set focusing on the use of the greater-than operator $>$

Largest element algorithm, LE

Step 1: Set $i_{max} = i_1$ and set $k = 2$
Step 2: if $i_k > i_{max}$, then set $i_{max} = i_k$
Step 3: Increment k by 1
Step 4: Perform Steps 2 and 3 until $k = n$
END

Consider the set 4, 3, 5, 2, 8, 9, 7, 9. As the algorithm proceeds the sequence of i_{max} values is 4, 5, 8, 9. Note that in the case of a tie, the algorithm picks the first tied element. If we had used the $\geq$ operator instead of $>$, the algorithm would pick the last tied element.

The degree of difficulty in performing an algorithm is specified by its associated cost function, which can be measured in terms of cost, time or space required to perform the algorithm. In this section let us focus on cost. The cost function associated with performing algorithm LE on a set of n elements is:

$$C_{LE}(n) = c_1 + c_{(2 \ \& \ 3)}(n - 1) \tag{2.11}$$

where c_1 is the cost of executing step 1 and $c_{(2 \ \& \ 3)}$ is the cost of executing steps 2 and 3. The difficulty of performing an algorithm is determined by the critical operation (or operations) that must be performed the greatest number of times to solve the problem. In our algorithm the $>$ operation is critical. To find the largest element, the algorithm performs $n - 1 >$ operations. Now let us consider what happens when n increases; that is, how does the number of required $>$ operations grow with respect to the growth parameter n? For this algorithm the number of required $>$ is a linear function of n.

Now consider the impact of the fact that the elements of N can be ordered in $n!$ different ways. Let s_i be a particular arrangement and S the set consisting of the $n!$ elements s_i. An assumption of the problem is that there is no knowledge about how the elements of s are ordered; consequently the algorithm must perform $n - 1 >$ operations for each element s of S.

Establishing the worst case computational complexity of performing this algorithm requires finding the element $s_i \in S$ that requires the most $>$ operations. Because each element s_i of S requires $n - 1 >$ operations, the worst case is also $n - 1$. Now let us consider the expected computational complexity. For simplicity we assume the discrete probability of occurrence of s_i is $1/n!$, that is, equally likely. In this case the expected computational complexity of performing an algorithm is the average number of $>$ operations for solving each element s_i of S. Again because the number of $>$ operations does not vary, the expected number of $>$ operations is also $n-1$. Our LE algorithm demonstrates $n - 1 >$ operations is an upper bound to the difficulty of solving the problem. For discrete optimization problems, where an algorithm must consider every possible case, the expected cost and the worst case cost will be the same. For many types of problems, such as linear programming, the expected cost is less than the worst case cost.

To determine a lower bound to the difficulty of solving the problem, we ask whether there exists another more efficient algorithm based on the $>$ operator to solve each element $s_i \in S$. It is easy to show by induction that $n - 1 >$ are required for any algorithm based on the $>$ operator. This demonstrates the $n - 1$ operations is a lower bound to solving the problem. Since the upper bound equals the lower bound, we can assert that solving S is a linear process for efficient algorithms using the $>$ operator. One method of establishing the computational complexity of a problem is to first construct an algorithm and determine its cost and to then show that this algorithm is efficient.

Finding a preferred item in a set of using a binary comparison operator $\succ$ is also a linear process because in the algorithm above the $>$ operator is replaced with the $\succ$ operator. In order to achieve a sublinear search algorithm, the consumer needs a more powerful operator than the $\succ$ operator. If a consumer can select a subset of a set in one operation, then the consumer can achieve a sublinear algorithm. This means that the consumer does not process the members of the set individually. Even identifying the members of a set would lead to a linear process. We shall discuss such algorithms in much greater detail in Chapter 4.

2.2.2.3 *Polynomial problems*

A polynomial problem is one for which an efficient algorithm, P, has a cost function of the form:

$$C_P(n) = c_c n^j \tag{2.12}$$

where j is the degree of the polynomial. Equation (2.2) could also have terms of lower degree, but since they do not affect the definitions of computational complexity, they are left out. Only the term with the largest degree matters. An example of a polynomial algorithm is standard matrix multiplication of two $n \times n$ matrices, where each element in the resulting matrix is the product of a row multiplied by a column. The degree j is 3 as there are n^2 elements in the product and each element requires n multiplications. However, standard matrix multiplication is not an efficient algorithm for matrix multiplication. Polynomial processes are important because they are considered tractable for a digital computer. That is, a digital computer can compute problems with relatively large values of the growth parameter in a time considered reasonable.

Let us now consider a condition that creates a lower bound. As was pointed out, one approach to determine the computational complexity of a process is to construct an efficient algorithm. Showing an algorithm is efficient can be challenging. For this purpose one can show that a problem has a characteristic that creates a lower bound on the efficiency of an algorithm. Let us consider one such lower bound: how the consideration of a history precludes more efficient than quadratic algorithms. The reader is probably most familiar with the concept of a history with respect to repeated games, but in this book we shall consider the concept with respect to repeated searches. We assert that consumers, because of the opportunity cost of time, have an incentive to improve the efficiency of their search procedures. Let us label the history of searches, $s_1, s_2, s_3, \ldots, s_n$. Now consider an algorithm to improve the search that before each new search processes one operation over each element of the history. Prior to the $n + 1$ search the total number of operations that the algorithm has executed is $1 + 2 + 3 + \cdots + n - 1$ which equals $n(n + 1)/2$. Any algorithm that processes each element in a history before the new decision cannot be more efficient than quadratic.

2.2.2.4 *An exponential and a NP-hard problem*

In Chapter 1 we provided an example of an exponential process in the grocery store example where the consumer must search through 30^{10} shopping carts to find the preferred bundle. The general case is m^n where m is the number of items and n is the number of alternatives to each item. If we consider n as fixed and m as the growth parameter, the increase in the number of bundles is polynomial. But, if we consider n as the growth parameter, the number of bundles grows at an exponential rate. The growth of exponential problems is so explosive they are not considered tractable for current digital computers.

Now let use consider another type of problem considered intractable for digital computers. Given consumer incentives for efficiency, an important problem in a search involving many stores in physical space is how to minimize the travel time in transiting among the n stores to search for a preferred item; a variation of the well known traveling salesman problem. Consider the graph on the next page of given transit times among 4 stores-1,2,3, and 4 -and home - H.

A simple algorithm for this problem is to enumerate all possible paths and to then use the $<$ operator to find the minimum. There are 12 possibilities that are shown above. The fastest path is H2134H with a time of 49. Suppose we add another store to the graph; the number of possible paths increases from from 12 to 60. The number of possible paths for n nodes is $n!/2$. The factor of $1/2$ exists because it makes no difference which direction the consumer travels the path. This indeed is a difficult problem known as a NP-hard problem. We will discuss how a consumer avoids having to consider the traveling salesman problem in Chapter 5 and 7.

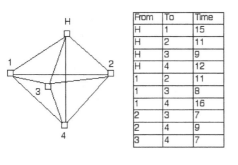

Path	Total Time
H1234H	52
H1243H	51
H1432H	56
H1423H	56
H1324H	51
H1342H	50
H2314H	54
H2413H	53
H2134H	49
H2143H	54
H3124H	49
H3142H	53
H3214H	55

From	To	Time
H	1	15
H	2	11
H	3	9
H	4	12
1	2	11
1	3	8
1	4	16
2	3	7
2	4	9
3	4	7

Fig 2.1: An NP-hard Problem

2.2.2.5 *A transfinite problem*

Let us consider the standard microeconomic utility function model of a consumer with a utility function

$$\max_{x_1,\ldots,x_n} U(x_1, x_2, \ldots, x_n) \qquad (2.13)$$

$$\text{subject to } p_{x_1}x_1 + p_{x_2}x_2 + \cdots + p_{x_n}x_n = I \qquad (2.14)$$

where $x_i \in \mathbb{R}^+$ is a good, $p_{x_i} \in \mathbb{R}^+$ is its price, and $I \in \mathbb{R}^+$ is the income.

If the consumer problem has an analytic solution, it would be computable; but, in the general case the problem does not have an analytic solution. For now, let us consider the implications of using numerical analysis procedures to solve this problem. Numerical analysts traditionally find algorithms that asymptotically converge and rank these algorithms by their respective rates of asymptotic convergence. An alternative approach is to consider the complexity of obtaining an ϵ approximation, for example see Traub, Wasilkowski and Wozniakowski (1988). One possible algorithm to solve this problem would be to substitute the constraint into the objective function to reduce the dimensions of the problem by one and use a conjugate gradient algorithm. Obtaining an exact solution in a finite number of steps with such an algorithm is generally impossible and the problem is labeled transfinite. Therefore, in the general case the traditional consumer problem is not computable.

2.3   Discrete Consumer Problem

To describe a human algorithm we must describe the algorithm in terms of operators that humans use in decision making. Currently a developing theory in psychology is the dual processing theory of the brain, for an overview see [Evans (2008)]. The basic idea is that there is a distinction between decision processes that are fast and automatic based on parallel processing and those that are slow and deliberate based on sequential processing. [Evans (2008)] uses neutral terms to define the former as System 1 and the later as System 2. The reader unfamiliar with dual processing is likely to know System 1 as unconscious and System 2 as conscious. Psychologists avoid these terms to clearly separate current thinking from past usages. For a readable discussion of System 1 and System 2 the reader might read Part 1 of [Kahneman (2011)].

From the perspective of this book, the reader needs to know that System 1 is online at all times and provides an overview of the current state. System 2 is expensive to operate and comes online when needed to address a problem that System 1 can not solve. For example, System 2 is required to execute psychological decision rules of the type discussed in Chapter 4. System 1 makes numerous types of intuitive judgements. In some cases System 2 makes adjustments to System 1 judgements.

Consider a binary comparison, a System 2 operation. [Norman *et al.* (2003)] determined that on average subjects took 3.2 seconds to perform a binary comparison between two pens. It needs to be pointed out that making a binary comparison can take much longer, such as a comparison between two cars based on a consumer making a test drive of both. Our objective is given the time to process a System 2 operation, solving the consumer problem is H intractable.

2.3.1   *Discrete Two-Stage Budgeting Model*

We now consider the [Norman *et al.* (2001)] computational complexity analysis of a discrete two-stage consumer model. Two-stage budgeting dates back to the creation of the separable utility model, [Strotz (1957)]. To see a summary of the literature on separability and budgeting see Deaton and Muellbauer (1980) or Gorman's collected papers edited by Blackkorby and Shorrocks (1995).

We shall characterize the computational complexity of optimal budgeting for the discrete problem, which has the two stage budget property described below. The material in this section is from [Norman *et al.* (2001)].

Given the discrete nature of modern packaging, consumers mostly make discrete purchases of one or more items from a category of close substitutes. There are n categories and X^i, where $1 \le i \le n$, might represent a finite set of different types of fruit, boxes of cereal or types of toothpaste. Those few items that consumers buy in continuous amounts are discretized by rounding off to the nearest cent, and X^k might present different brands and types of gasoline. For simplicity the number of alternatives in each set X^i is equal to q_A times the maximum number of units that can be selected is q_μ. Thus, the number of choices associated with X^i is $q = q_A \times q_\mu$. A discrete choice model can be considered realistic. The consumer is selecting $(x)_i$ where:

$$(x)_i = (x_{i_1}^1, x_{i_2}^2, \ldots, x_{i_n}^n)$$
$$x_{i_1}^1 \in X^1 = \{x_1^1, x_2^1, \ldots, x_q^1\}$$
$$x_{i_2}^2 \in X^2 = \{x_1^2, x_2^2, \ldots, x_q^2\}$$

$$\vdots$$

$$x_{i_n}^n \in X^n = \{x_1^n, x_2^n, \ldots, x_q^n\} \tag{2.15}$$

Now let us construct a separable utility function defined over a discrete number of argument values. The function $\mu(x_j^i)$ is the number of units of x_j^i selected or, in the case of a good like gasoline, the discrete amount selected. The n categories are divided into l subsets where $\beta(j)$ is the index of the first category of the jth subset and $\gamma(j)$ is the index of the last category.

$$U(\mu((x)_i)) = U_1([\mu(x_i), 1]) + U_2([\mu(x_i), 2]) + \ldots + U_l([\mu(x_i), l]) \tag{2.16}$$

where

$$[\mu(x_i), j] = (\mu(x_{i_{\beta(j)}}^{\beta(j)}), \mu(x_{i_{\beta(j)+1}}^{\beta(j)+1}), \ldots, \mu(x_{i_{\gamma(j)}}^{\gamma(j)})) \tag{2.17}$$

and

$$(x_{i_{\beta(j)}}^{\beta(j)}, x_{i_{\beta(j)+1}}^{\beta(j)+1}, \ldots, x_{i_{\gamma(j)}}^{\gamma(j)}) \in \{X, j\} = X^{\beta(j)} \times \cdots \times X^{\gamma(j)} \tag{2.18}$$

We shall assume n is divided into l equal subsets so that the computational complexity of each subproblem is the same; otherwise the computational complexity is dominated by the computational complexity of the largest subgroup. We shall consider values of the growth parameter n such that n/l is an integer. Also we shall divide I into m equal integer quantities, $a_i = I/m, i = 1, 2, \ldots, m$ and $I/m \ge 1$ cent. For example, I/m could equal 1 cent, 1 dollar, or 100 dollars. These m quantities are to be optimally allocated among the elements of $(I)_l$ in the following discrete consumer problem:

$$\max_{(I)_l} \sum_{j=1}^{l} (\max_{[x_i,j]} U([\mu(x_i),j])) \tag{2.19}$$

$$\text{subject to for all } j \sum_{k=\beta(j)}^{\gamma(j)} p_{i_k}^k \mu(x_{i_k}^k) \leq I_j \text{ and } \sum_{j=1}^{l} I_j = I \tag{2.20}$$

where $p_{i_k}^k > 0$, $I > 0$, and $I_j \geq 0$. We assume that this problem is defined for a single budget time period such as a month if the consumer receives her income monthly. We define it this way because we shall focus on repeated budgeting and search procedures.

Now let us consider the relationship between this problem and the two stage budgeting problem for the continuous weakly separable utility function. For the latter problem, Strotz (1957) asked under what condition can we optimally allocate I into $(I)_l^* = I_1^*, I_2^*, \ldots, I_l^*$ where $\sum I_j^* = I$ and solve l smaller optimization problems instead of one large optimization problem. Gorman resolved this issue with a set of Slutsky conditions, see Chapter 2 of Blackorby and Shorrocks (1995).

For the discrete case above, the second stage problem is

$$\max_{[x_i,j]} U([\mu(x_i),j]) \tag{2.21}$$

$$\text{subject to } \sum_{k=\beta(j)}^{\gamma(j)} p_{i_k}^k \mu(x_{i_k}^k) \leq I_j^* \text{ for } j = 1, 2, \ldots, l \tag{2.22}$$

where the I_j^*s are determined by (2.19-2.20) above. It is straightforward to demonstrate by contradiction that the discrete model has the two-stage budget property, which is that an optimal solution to (2.19-2.20) is an optimal solution to (2.21-2.22) and an optimal solution to (2.21-2.22) is an optimal solution to (2.19-2.20).

We make the following assumptions:

1. **Binary Comparison**: We will consider the set of algorithms that solve (2.20-2.21) by comparing two bundles, $[\mu(x_i),j]$ and $[\mu(x_k),j]$ using a binary ranking operator, $B([\mu(x_i),j],[\mu(x_k),j])$ where $\rightarrow [\mu(x_i),j] \succeq [\mu(x_k),j]$ if $U_j([\mu(x_i),j]) \geq U_j([\mu(x_k),j])$ else $[\mu(x_i),j] \prec [\mu(x_k),j]$. We treat this binary comparison operator as a computational primitive.

2. **Interactions Affects**: There are interaction affects among the goods in each subgroup so that in order to determine the utility of a subgroup bundle, $[x_i,j]$ an algorithm must evaluate $U_j([x_i,j])$. This eliminates additive

utility functions, which would greatly simplify the computational problem.
3. **Bundle Organization**: In order to create an algorithm we have to specify how the bundles that the consumer is comparing are organized. For now, we shall assume that the bundles in each category are arranged by ascending cost with index $k = 1, 2, \ldots, q^{n/l}$. In the introductory chapter we used an explicit example of this organization with the bundles grocery store where consumers searched through a long line of shopping carts to find the preferred bundle. The cost of the kth bundle is represented by $c(k)$ and the preferred bundle in separable group s for the rth level of income is represented by $([\mu(x_*), s], rI/m)$. The rows for the various subgroups are adjacent to each other.

Given these assumptions the computational complexity of the two-stage discrete budgeting problem is:

Theorem 2.1. *The worst case and expected computational complexity of the optimal budgeting is* $\max(lq^{n/l}, lm^2)$.

The proof is presented in Appendix A, at the end of the book. Given the number of goods in the marketplace $lq^{n/l}$ dwarfs lm^2. Nevertheless, allocating money into categories is a quadratic process that we shall argue is not tractable for unaided humans.

2.3.2 *Recent Advances*

We now mention recent computational complexity results showing that the discrete consumer problem is NP-hard and that if we restrict our attention to utility functions that explain observed data, it can be solved in polynomial time. Two recent advances in research into the computational complexity of the consumer problem are Gilboa, Postlewaite and Schmeidler (2010) and Echenique, Golovin and Wierman (2011a).

In Gilboa, Postlewaite and Schmeidler (2010), the authors formulate the consumer problem as a discrete combinatorial decision problem and show that this problem is a member of the NP complete class. From complexity theory, this implies that the corresponding optimization problem is NP hard, which means that solving the optimization problem is at least as hard as solving the traveling salesman problem.

In Echenique, Golovin and Wierman (2011a), the authors have an ambitious agenda. They ask if the computational complexity of the consumer problem can be reduced if we restrict our attention to utility functions that explain the observed data. The answer is yes. The computational complexity of solving the consumer optimization problem is reduced to a polynomial for utility functions that explain the data. Readers interested in pursuing formal computational complexity arguments in economic theory should read this paper carefully.

Reducing the computational complexity of the consumer problem to a polynomial means that it would be considered tractable to a digital computer. The question we ask in the next section is does that mean it is tractable to an unaided human processor?

2.4   Bounded-Rational Human Procedures

After determining the computational complexity of a problem, the next question to ask is whether the problem is tractable for the computational agent without simplifications. We argue that for an unaided human computational agent sublinear is tractable which implies the human agent must make simplifications to solve the consumer problem. We then discuss the three simplifications humans make to solve the consumer problem. In the last subsection we discuss various approaches to applying computational complexity analysis to economic agents.

2.4.1   *Tractable*

Computer scientists consider polynomial or P algorithms tractable and not polynomial or NP algorithms intractable. Tractability is actually an economic concept. What it means is that the speed of a digital computer is sufficient that it can solve large polynomial problems quickly enough so that the time or resource cost is less than the benefit. But, with NP problems the number of operations increases so quickly that this is not the case.

Tractability depends on the speed of the processor. Let us compare a generic computer processor that can perform 1 billion operations a second with a generic System 2 human processor that can perform 1 elementary operation a second in performing a linear and a quadratic process. Based on our research presented in Chapter 3, 1 second is a conservative estimate for decision rules requiring acquiring and processing data. We constructed Table 1.1 shown below.

Let us consider a set of alternatives that a consumer must process to find a preferred item. The growth parameter in this case is the number of alternatives to process. Even if we consider each alternative in the set a

Table 2.1 Time to perform.

No. Alternatives	Comp: Lin	Comp: Quad	Human: Lin	Human: Quad
Number	Seconds	Seconds	Hours	Hours
1000	1×10^{-6}	0.001	0.28	277.8
10000	1×10^{-5}	0.1	2.8	27777.8
90000	9×10^{-5}	8.1	25	2250000
250000	2.5×10^{-4}	62.5	69.4	17361111
1,000,000	0.001	1000	277.8	2777777778

single item and not a bundle then there are a large number of alternatives in the marketplace. Amazon.com has more than a million books listed, a modern book store before the shift to eBooks could have had 250,000 books in stock, and an early record store could have had 90,000 records on hand for sale. If we consider each alternative as a bundle of goods, the numbers are very large, indeed.

Given the slowness of the human processor, even a linear algorithm is not tractable for the number of alternatives found in the marketplace. Our assertion is that for an unaided human processor using System 2 procedures, **sublinear is tractable and this defines Simon's (1956) bounded rationality in terms of computational complexity.**

In this book we shall frequently discuss judgment and decision heuristics. [Kahneman (2011)] defines a heuristic as "a simple procedure that helps find adequate, though often imperfect answers to difficult questions." We define 'simple' as H tractable.

2.4.2 *Simplifications*

From [Norman *et al.* (2001)] and [Norman *et al.* (2004)] we will argue that consumers use three main simplifications to achieve H tractable procedures to solve their consumer problem:

1. item-by-item search
2. set decision rules
3. budgeting by incremental adjustment

Consumers search for goods and services item-by-item and very seldom buy goods in bundles. One example of a bundle might be renting a car with the purchase of a airplane ticket. But even in this case the two choices are made sequentially. As our example in Chapter 1 about the grocery store makes clear, the number of bundles exponentially explodes with the number of items in a category. In reference to the two-stage budgeting problem, (2.21-2.22) consumers are assumed to divide the n categories of goods into l groups determined by the separable utility function. To simplify the problem consumers divide the n categories into n groups, each of which has one category.

This simplification is well known in the literature. In an early computational complexity analysis of the consumer problem, [Velupillai (2000)] provides an analysis of Leijonhufvud's Marshallian Consumer which makes sequential choices. The decision process terminates in a finite number of iterations if the constraints are assumed to be linear.

The fact that consumers select their goods item-by-item does not mean that they simplify their utility function to an additive utility function. When a consumer selects an item, she has previous selections in memory and can anticipate future selections. For example, in buying new furniture a consumer knows which color and fabric combinations would blend well with the color scheme of her residence and existing furniture. In deciding between a Mac and a PC a consumer can forecast the availability of software for the selected operating system.

As will be discussed in Chapter 4, consumers use set selection rules when faced with a large number of alternatives. This is shown by demonstrating the psychological decision rules discussed by decision psychologists leading to linear algorithms inconsistent with our human sublinear processing assumption. Human System 2 processes may be slow, but they have powerful operators in being able to decide on sets in one operation. We perform an experiment to demonstrate that humans use set operators. Markets are organized to facilitate set rules and we demonstrate with an experiment that humans are adept at using set rules.

Consider allocating \$100 into three categories in \$1 increments, (0, 0, 100), (0, 1, 99), (0, 2, 98), and so on. There are 5050 possible allocations. Considering every possible allocation is a quadratic process. We will argue in Chapter 8 that humans simplify the budgeting process by using an incremental adjustment procedure in which monitoring the flow of funds plays an important role.

Now given the simplifications consumers make to simplify their consumer problem we need to reformulate the problem. Consumers make repeated searches for goods and services all their lives. Consumers have incentives such as performance and opportunity costs to improve search efficiency. We need to ask how they learn to improve efficiency. Since we are starting with birth, we can assume that one aspect of these searches is learning their preferences. To what extent is it efficient to learn their preferences? Since these searches are made at different frequencies, we should expect variation among the types of searches made by consumers.

2.4.3 *Inferring Human Procedures*

Analyzing human algorithms requires a very different approach than analyzing computer algorithms. Computer algorithms are specified so that they can be mathematically analyzed. Human algorithms must be inferred from human behavior. The fact that computational complexity definitions are based on a fixed cost of elementary operations does not create a problem in analyzing human procedures. With learning, the cost of performing an elementary operation is likely to decline. This does not affect the computational complexity definitions as long as there is a lower bound representing the learning limit. The definitions strip constants in determining to which equivalence class an algorithm belongs.

To determine the difficultly in solving a problem with a computer algorithm the researcher constructs an algorithm and shows that a more efficient algorithm does not exist, thus establishing the computational complexity of the problem. The approach is to use mathematical analysis of the specified algorithm, for example [Norman and Jung (1977)]. A traditional computational complexity approach can be used to study economic theory, such as providing an explanation for money, [Norman (1987)] and a Bayesian explanation of F. Knight's uncertainty versus risk, [Norman and Shimer (1994)]. For a discussion of the relationship between computability, complexity and economics see [Velupillai (2010)] and [Velupillai (2005)].

In studying procedures used by humans the procedure must be inferred from the subjects' behavior. Analysis of human procedures can be done by watching the hand motions of subjects handling the test objects or which buttons the subjects click on a computer screen. Also, asking the subjects what they are doing can be illuminating. Algorithms that are members of different equivalence classes can be identified using statistical techniques such as regression analysis. We use these approaches in determining what procedures humans use in ordering alternatives in Chapter 3.

Chapter 3

Ordering

3.1 Introduction

The usefulness of ordering to humans depends on the cost of ordering. In this Chapter we will show that humans have a very efficient procedure for ordering, and in the rest of the book we discuss numerous examples where humans use ordering to increase their efficiency in item searching and budgeting.

We experimentally examine the procedures that individuals use to order sets of objects. Our focus is not the static properties of the ordered objects, but rather the properties of the procedures that humans use to make the ordering. By comparing human procedures with known computer ordering algorithms, we can determine their properties. We use complexity theory to measure cost and to formulate hypotheses to test among alternative human procedures.

If humans were limited to a binary ranking operator in ordering a set of n items, the most efficient ordering procedures humans could employ would be nonlinear, with a computational complexity of $n \log_2 n$ in both the worst and expected cases. But, if consumers were able to assign an ordinal utility value to each item in the set, they could employ a conceptually simple linear ordering procedure called a bucket sort. We discuss several computer sorting algorithms in the next section.

Then, we present the experimental design for ordering sets of pens, notebooks and Hot Wheels$^{®}$ cars, describe the problem of incentives, and present the observations of the subjects' behavior. The observations and regression results show that subjects are using the linear modified bucket sort to order the selected objects. Our ordering data also indicate that humans are not consistent in their orderings of pens.

The material in this Chapter is a minor revision of [Norman *et al.* (2003)], which is a major expansion of [Norman *et al.* (1997)].

3.2 Computer Ordering

In this section, we examine ordering algorithms, commonly referred to as sorting algorithms, Aho, Hopcroft and Ullman (1974), [Knuth (1973)] and [Mehlhorn (1984)]. In this paper we asymptotically compare algorithms by the time taken to sort as the number of items, n, increases.

In order to discuss sorting algorithms consider a set $B_n = \{b_1, b_2, \ldots, b_n\}$ of close substitutes. First, we characterize algorithms based on two operators: (1) an information operation to determine the attributes of each good and (2) a binary comparison operator. We define the information operator $D(b_i) = a_i$. Like Myer and Alper (1968), we assume the subjects employ an information operator that determines only those attributes necessary to make comparisons.

Subjects use the information operator in order to execute a ranking operator, $R(a_i, a_j) \Rightarrow b_i \succeq b_j$ or $b_j \succeq b_i$ that determines the preferences between two items, b_i and b_j. We do not assume transitivity in this paper because of the increasing empirical evidence of intransitive preferences, starting with [Tversky (1969)]. Intransitivity will not affect the complexity of the algorithms, just the extent to which the orderings have desirable properties.

We assume each type operator, $D(b_i)$ and $R(a_i, a_j)$, incurs a cost c_D and c_R respectively considered constant during the ordering process. We also assume that each type operator $D(b_i)$ and $R(a_i, a_j)$ is performed during the ordering process in a fixed time t_D and t_R, respectively. Thus we are assuming an equivalence between cost and time complexity, a standard assumption in complexity analysis.

In discussing sorting algorithms we assume that humans will employ the most efficient algorithm they are capable of implementing. As computer scientists have spent several decades developing sorting algorithms, it is unlikely that humans intuitively use an algorithm not mentioned in this section.

We therefore might expect humans to use a variation of a bubble sort to order a set of pens. A possible algorithm to order the pens in a complete preference ordering from left to right is as follows:

A Bubble sort algorithm

Step 1: Write with the first pen, $D(P_1) = a_1$, and place on the table.

Step 2: Write with the second pen, $D(P_2) = a_2$. If $R(a_1, a_2) \Rightarrow P_2 \succeq P_1$, place P_2 to the left of P_1, else place P_2 to the right of P_1.

Step 3: Now consider the placement of the mth pen after the $m-1$ pens have been ordered. Starting with the pen furthest to the right, compare P_m with each pen moving to the left until the following condition is satisfied: $P_m \succeq P_i$ and $P_{i+1} \succeq P_m$. Place P_m between P_i and P_{i+1}. If $P_m \succeq P_{m-1}$ place P_m to the left of P_{m-1}.

Step 4: Repeat Step [3] until all pens are ordered.

END

Because this algorithm requires $1 + 2 + 3 + \ldots n - 1$ $(=n(n-1)/2)$ binary comparisons in the worst case and half that number in the expected case, it is $O(n^2)$ both in the worst and expected cases. The absolute - but not the asymptotic - cost of this algorithm can be reduced by starting the comparison of each new pen with the existing ordering in the middle and proceeding up or down depending on the pairwise comparisons. If the sorter started in the middle, on average he would only have to compare the new pen with $1/4$ of the pens in the existing ordering.

Efficient algorithms exist for ordering which are only $O(n \log_2 n)$ in the worst and expected value cases, Mehlhorn (1984). Let us consider one of the algorithms efficient in the worst case (and expected case), Mergesort. A human might employ this algorithm to order 16 pens in the following manner:

A Mergesort algorithm

Step 1: Write with all sixteen pens.

Step 2: Lay the pens in a row.

Step 3: Merge the first with the second, the third with the fourth, ..., the fifteenth with the sixteenth. Merging the first with the second requires comparing the first with the second and ordering them in a column with the preferred item first. This results in 8 columns of two members each.

Step 4: Merge the first column with the second, the third with the fourth, ..., the seventh with the eighth. This step results in four columns of 4 members each.

Step 5: In a similar fashion, merge the four columns merged into two columns of 8 members each.

Step 6: Merge the two columns into one ordered column.

END

Another ordering algorithm, efficient in the worst case, is the Heapsort algorithm; yet another ordering algorithm, efficient in the expected value case, is the Quicksort algorithm. Because each of these algorithms takes considerable time to understand, they are not likely to be used intuitively. Nevertheless, use of one of these algorithms would be observable from the way the subjects organized the objects and from their hand motions.

But, if humans can assign ordinal utility values to items in a set, they can use a more efficient algorithm. This is because we are dealing with a discrete, finite model and not the problem of the existence of the utility function in the case of the continuum. Also, intransitivity is not a problem here. Consider the bucket ordering algorithm used to sort n integers contained in the interval (k, l), where k and l are integers. This sorting process uses the following algorithm for $(l - k - 1)$ integers on the interval:

A Bucket sort algorithm

Step 1: Create $(l - k - 1)$ buckets.

Step 2: Pick an integer and determine its value.

Step 3: Place it in the bucket with the corresponding value.

Step 4: Repeat Steps [2] and [3] until all numbers are assigned to buckets.

END

The integers are now sorted. Thus, a human wishing to efficiently sort a set of integers could use a bucket sort. This idea, however, is not limited to sorting integers. Consider a human ordering n items in a set B. If a human can use an information operator $G(b_i)$ to assign an ordinal utility value to each item, then the human could use a placement operator $P(b_i)$ to place each b_i in the correct bucket. The number of G and P operations is $O(n)$ for this bucket sort; consequently, the computational complexity is n in time and cost, assuming each operation has fixed unit cost and time during the ordering process. Defects in assigning ordinal utility values would affect the consistency of the outcome, but not the efficiency of the algorithm. A bucket sort is the only known linear algorithm for sorting.

In determining what algorithm subjects use we shall:

1. Observe subjects' object organization and their hand motions.

2. Analyze the regression results.

3. Ask the subjects questions.

3.3 Experimental Ordering Design

Groups and Subgroups: To determine how humans actually establish a complete preference ordering, we selected 320 undergraduates at the University of Texas at Austin and divided then into ten groups of 32 that we divided further into subgroups of 8 subjects. Each subject was given a practice set of three objects to sort to ensure that they were following the instructions. Then each subject ordered three sets of objects as shown in Table 3.1 below. Thus, each of the 8 members of group 9, subgroup 3 or-

Table 3.1 Groups, subgroups and the size of the 3 sets to order.

Groups↓ Subgroup→	1	2	3	4
Groups 1-6	(3, 6, 17)	(3, 7, 16)	(3, 8, 15)	(3, 9, 14)
Groups 7-10	(3, 5, 9)	(3, 6, 10)	(4, 7, 11)	(4, 8, 12)

ders sets of 4, 7, and then 11 objects. The numbers were chosen to provide variation over many numbers for the regression analysis.

Objects: We chose pens, notebooks, and Hot Wheels® toy cars of cast metal for objects that student experimenters thought the student subjects would be familiar. We made a concerted effort to ensure that the objects were distinctive. We included pens with various types of points, ink, colors, size, style and cost. Similarly, we selected notebooks on which the students might take their class notes, including notebooks of different sizes from 3×5" to $81/2 \times 11$", color of paper, binding, and writing pads such as legal pads (we even included a clipboard and a three-ring binder). From a very large selection of Hot Wheels® cars, we selected sports cars, station wagons, pickups, a garbage truck, and even a tank. In selecting subsets of pens, notebooks, or Hot Wheels® cars to order, we made an effort to make these subsets representative of the various types of objects in the respective set.

Subjects performed strong and weak orderings on the listed objects as shown in Table 3.2 on the next page where in the first row Ord, S, and W are Ordering, Strong, and Weak respectively. In the second row Obj, P, NB, and HW respectively stand for Object, Pens, Notebooks, and Hot Wheels® cars respectively.

Table 3.2   Objects for experiment.

Group	1	2	3	4	5	6	7	8	9	10
Ord	S	W	S	S	S	S	S	S	S	S
Obj	P	P	P	P	P	P	P	NB	HW	HW

Evaluation: There are two processes in this experiment: the evaluation of objects and the ordering, or placement, of objects. Since our focus is on ordering, we want the subject to evaluate each object in an experiment in approximately the same amount of time. In an earlier version of the experiment, subjects initially started writing their signatures with each pen and then gradually reduced the amount they wrote to a short wiggle. To correct for this and ensure that subjects evaluated each object in a uniform amount of time subjects were asked to write 'ABC' with each pen, write 'ABC' in each notebook with a given pen, and roll each Hot Wheels® car down a runway.

Incentives: The fundamental issue in this experiment is the choice of algorithm; how well the subjects execute the selected algorithm is secondary. Since our paper tests the choice of algorithm and not the choice of objects, by the logic of choice mechanisms, we should ideally give the subjects algorithms to take home. But, as this would not be a reward to most students, our approach to incentives was to show that the results are robust to variations in the incentives.

The design and incentives must consider the fact that ordering is tedious. In reviewing a previous version of the experiment for which the subjects had to order 5, 10, 15, 20, and then 25 pens, we observed that some subjects had a very large number of inconsistencies. In this experiment, the number of sets of objects the subjects had to order was reduced to three, and the largest of these sets had no more than 20 objects. When asked, subjects indicated that they were more than adequately compensated for the task as the total time involved was less than 15 minutes for which subjects were paid over $5 in cash and goods. All of our incentive systems included a flat fee component to ensure that subjects were easy to recruit and felt adequately compensated. In the table below a flat fee of $4 is indicated by F4.

We considered two incentives to increase the consistency of the orderings. If the subjects were completely consistent, they would order the objects with consistent preferences. For groups 3 and 6-7, subjects were paid $0.25 for consistency, indicated by 25↑, in each binary comparison and for group 4 subjects were deducted $0.25 for each inconsistency, indicated by 25↓. A colleague suggested that we make the experiment incentive compatible with the secondary objective by randomly choosing two objects in the ordering and giving the subjects the object with the higher position in the ordering. We employed this incentive for the 2nd and 3rd orderings in all groups with the letters 'Ra' in the incentive table below.

Both incentives have positive and negative features. Because both emphasize binary choice, they may not be neutral among the class of possible algorithms. The random award of an object from the ordering is incentive compatible with the secondary objective, but may not be very salient. Specific payment for consistency is probably more salient, but might induce the subjects to modify their preferences.

For the pen orderings we tried seven variations in the design to test how the variation affected the ordering result. For the notebooks we tried one incentive system. For the Hot Wheels® cars some subjects prior to the experiment were given 10 Hot Wheels® cars not in the experiment and asked to develop evaluation criteria. A table of the incentive systems for the various groups is presented in Table 10.3 below.

Table 3.3   Incentives for each group.

Group	Incentive	25↑	25↓	Ra
1	F4			
2	F4			
3	F2	+		
4	F5		+	
5	F4			+
6	F4	+		+
7	F4	+		+
8	F4			+
9	F5			+
10	F5			+

Evaluate and Place: In the previous version of the experiment about 90% of the subjects wrote with a new pen and placed it in the partial ordering before writing with a new pen. However, in the early rounds there were about three subjects who wrote a list of ABCs with all the pens before ordering any of them. There were two subjects who switched to the dominant algorithm after the first set because processing the list became progressively tedious. The one subject who wrote a list with all the pens for each of the three sets before trying to order them became increasingly frustrated with trying to remember which pens he had pulled from the list. Since processing the list is possibly a quadratic process and this algorithm is less efficient, we organized the instructions so that all the subjects would shift to the dominant "evaluate and place" algorithm in the practice round. Subjects could have used the list processing algorithm, but it was more natural to shift immediately to the "evaluate and place" algorithm.

Additional Measurements: Many subjects order pens quickly. Using the "evaluate and place" algorithm some subjects can order 16 pens in less than a minute. We performed additional consistency tests to check how consistently the subjects were ordering the objects.

For each subgroup some pens from the second ordering were included in the set of pens given to the subject for the third ordering. This helped verify consistency in ordering between the second and third orderings. The position of ordered objects passed without the subjects' knowledge from the completed ordering 2 to the 3 set to be ordered are displayed below in Table 3.4 where for Group 8, subgroup 2, objects in positions 2,4, and 5 of the second ordering are passed to the third set to be ordered. A higher number is preferred over a lower number.

Table 3.4   Rank position of objects passed from ordering 2 to 3rd set to be ordered again.

Groups(col) Subgroup(row)	1	2	3	4
1-6: Objects in 2 $\Rightarrow$ 3	1,2,3,4,5,6	2,3,4,5,6	2,4,6,8	3,6,9
7-10: Objects in 2 $\Rightarrow$ 3	2,4,5	2,4,5	3,5,6	3,5,6

Groups 3 through 10 were asked to make a binary comparison with selected pairs after completing the third ordering. Subjects did not see us select the objects, could not see the previous ordering, and had to make each decision with only the information gained from writing the two ABC's

Table 3.5   Rank position of objects for binary comparison.

Group	Subgroup	Binary Comparisons
3 - 4	1	(12,16), (3,7), (11,14), (5,8), (13,15), (4,6), and (9,10)
3 - 4	2	(11,15), (2,6), (10,13), (4,7), (12,14), (3,5), and (8,9)
3 - 4	3	(10,14), (1,5), (9,12), (3,6), (11,13), (2,4), and (7,8)
3 - 4	4	(10,14), (1,5), (9,12), (3,6), (11,13), (2,4), and (7,8)
4 - 6	1	(9,12), (8,10), (6,7)
4 - 6	2 - 4	(8,11), (7,9), (5,6)
7 - 10	1	(5,8), (4,6), (2,3)
7 - 10	2 - 3	(6,9), (5,7), (3,4)
7 - 10	4	(7,10), (6,8), (4,5)

or rolling the two Hot Wheels® cars down the track and their previous experience. The selected pairs are shown in Table 3.5 above.

Bubble Sort: We also trained 16 subjects in subgroups of 4 to perform a bubble sort using Group 10 specifications. Prior to the experiment they examined Hot Wheels® cars that were not used in the experiment and wrote a paragraph giving their evaluation criteria. Subjects were taught the bubble sort procedure during the practice round and then used this algorithm to order three additional sets. To keep the bubble sort as simple as possible, we had each subject start with the worst Hot Wheels® car and make binary comparisons up the ordering until he or she found the proper position for the Hot Wheels® car to be inserted into the order.

3.4   Observations

Basic Algorithm: Given the instructions, all subjects used some variation of the "evaluate and place" algorithm. They ranked the sets of objects in a sequential manner creating a partial ordering of the first $1, 2, 3, \ldots, k$ objects until finished. With the exception of Group 9, almost all subjects appeared to evaluate pens and notebooks at a constant rate: they wrote ABC with pens on paper, wrote ABC in notebooks, or rolled the Hot Wheels® car down the runway and immediately proceeded to the placement phase. With few exceptions, subjects thought for a few seconds after evaluating each new object before placing the object into the partial ordering.

Variations: In each group there were usually one or more outliers whose behavior deviated from the other participants. These deviations were mostly in how they evaluated the objects and were less often in the way they placed the object. Rather than try to create criteria for eliminating outliers, we made the groups large enough so that the results are robust to outliers.

An important variation in ordering pens is how many times the subjects wrote with each pen. Of the 128 subjects in groups 1-4, 41 wrote ABC once with each pen, 83 subjects made less than 6 rewrites, and 3 subjects made more than 32 rewrites. Most subjects occasionally rewrote with pens when they needed to refresh their memory about a particular pen. One subject tentatively placed each new pen in the partial pen ordering and rewrote with the pen on both sides, resulting in 57 rewrites. The subject who made 87 rewrites wrote ABC with each pen several times and subjectively weighed each pen in his hand. Another subject post-processed the ordering according to visual characteristics alone without rewriting with any of the pens. These subjects expended a much greater effort in evaluating each pen, but their actions certainly are not *a priori* a nonlinear algorithm.

Most subjects processed the pens in the order that the pens were placed in front of the subjects. A minority processed pens in subgroups by observable characteristics. One subject created columns for the pens of each color. For example, all the ABCs' for the red pens were written in one column. This procedure facilitated consistency in ordering the pens.

Evaluation Problems: In Group 9 many subjects ordering Hot Wheels® cars took less time making the larger third ordering than they did making the smaller second ordering. It appeared that subjects needed extra time to create evaluation criteria in rounds 1 and 2. For example, one subject in Group 9 rolled each Hot Wheels® car at least three times down the track during the first two orderings. Then she appeared to have made up her mind and only rolled each Hot Wheels® car down the track once during the third ordering. She finished the third ordering in less time than the second, though the second ordering had about half as many Hot Wheels® cars. We modified the Hot Wheels® cars experiment for Group 10 so that the subjects were given ten Hot Wheels® cars not in the experiment and asked to write a paragraph on their evaluation criterion. With prior criteria creation, subjects appeared to evaluate the Hot Wheels® cars in the experiment at a constant rate.

From observing the subjects' object organization and hand motions we can exclude the efficient binary sort algorithms. Subjects trained to perform a bubble sort generally held the Hot Wheels® car to be placed in the partial ordering above the Hot Wheels® car in the partial ordering with which they were making a binary comparison. They proceeded up the partial ordering until they placed the new addition. Because in Groups 1-10 the final placement of an object in partial ordering was almost always within one object of the initial placement we can exclude the use of a bubble sort because the time to perform a binary comparison is clearly observable. **Our maintained hypothesis is that the subjects were using a modified bucket sort.**

When asked to describe the algorithm they used, subjects described the criterion they used rather than how they placed the objects. The one subject who participated in the original experiment and was later one of the new subjects who was trained to perform a bubble sort was emphatic that she initially used a bucket sort.

The major difference in the human bucket sort and a computer bucket sort is how the buckets are created. In a computer bucket sort, the buckets are created before the sort is initiated. However, in the human bucket sort for a small number of objects, the subjects create buckets in a **single** motion as needed. If the subject decides that a pen should be placed between the current fourth and fifth pens the subject simply creates a new bucket between the fourth and fifth pens in one motion and the old fifth pen becomes the new sixth pen. If, when writing with a pen, the subject decides that the pen is much better than the currently ordered pens, the subject places the pen some distance to the right of the existing order.

Some insight into how the subjects placed the pens was obtained by the response of the first two groups to the following question:

> In placing a new pen into the ordering, I did it by
>
> a. Assigning the pen a number as in the numerical ordering experiment and comparing with numbers of pens already ordered.
>
> b. Assigning the pen a verbal descriptor such as "very good" and comparing the pen to the verbal descriptors of the pens already ordered.
>
> c. Intuitively, without assigning numbers or verbal descriptors.

Of the 64 subjects asked this question, 3 responded with **a**, 13 responded with **b**, and the remaining 48 responded with **c**. Thus, they were acting as if they were assigning utility values.

3.5   Analysis of Algorithms

This section follows the format of the corresponding section of [Norman *et al.* (2003)]. The difference is that we test for homoscedasticity and normality. We switch from regular to robust regressions and consider an additional data set of combined observations.

Before considering the regressions, it is desirable to discuss the relationship between asymptotic complexity theory and identifying algorithms using regressions based on small samples. Because the subjects write with each pen and the number of writes plus rewrites appears linear in n, the regressions should have a linear factor. Complexity theory tells us that if the subjects were using a binary comparison algorithm, we should find a higher power term to be significant in the regression. The size of the sample required to demonstrate this depends on the time required to perform a binary comparison. We determined that the average time needed to perform a binary comparison is 3.2 seconds and we are 90% confident that it is greater than 1.5 seconds. We demonstrate that the number of objects is adequate.

Let us examine the three hypotheses and the regression results concerning the relationship between time T, and the number of pens, X, where we assume ϵ_i to be distributed $N(0, \sigma_\epsilon^2)$. Let us start with the maintained hypothesis: a bucket sort for which $T_i = \beta n_i + \epsilon_i$. We tested the hypothesis of normal errors for each group with the Shapiro-Wilf W, Shapiro-Francia W, and the Skewness/Kutosis tests. For each group all three reject the hypothesis of normal errors with a significance level of 1%. For each group we tested the hypothesis of homoscedasticity with the Breusch and Pagan (1979)/ Cook-Weisberg test and rejected this hypothesis in all cases with a significance level of 1%. The results using [White (1980)] robust regression that corrects for heteroskedasticity for the maintained hypothesis, a bucket sort, are shown in Table 3.6 on the top of the next page. We know that the function intersects the origin because each subject began working immediately and, thus, displayed no fixed cost. To test this, we estimated the equation (1) including an intercept term α. We failed to reject the hypothesis that $\alpha = 0$ at the .05 significance level. Based on this, we concluded that excluding the constant term is reasonable.

Now let us consider the first alternative hypothesis: a bubble sort, for which $T_i = \beta n_i + \gamma n_i^2 + \epsilon_i$, where the constant term is for the evaluation process and the quadratic term is for the number of binary comparisons. We tested the hypothesis of normal errors for each group with the

Table 3.6   Maintained hypothesis: Bucket sort ($T_i = \beta n_i + \epsilon_i$).

Gr	1	2	3	4	5	6	7	6+7	8	9	10
Obs	96	96	96	96	96	96	96	192	96	96	96
β	7.33	8.62	9.17	8.23	8.58	8.59	9.04	8.75	10.43	8.69	10.1
σ_β	0.29	0.66	0.41	0.46	0.57	0.48	0.59	0.37	0.42	0.34	0.43
t_β	25.1	13.1	22.1	17.7	15.0	18.0	15.33	23.6	24.7	25.59	23.5

Shapiro-Wilf W, Shapiro-Francia W, and the Skewness/Kutosis tests. For each group all three reject the hypothesis of normal errors with a significance level of 1%. For each group we tested the hypothesis of homoscedasticity with the Breusch and Pagan (1979)/ Cook-Weisberg test and rejected this hypothesis in all cases with a significance level of 1%. The results using [White (1980)] robust regression that corrects for heteroskedasticity are shown in Table 3.7 below.

Table 3.7   First alternative: Bubble sort ($T_i = \beta n_i + \gamma n_i^2 + \epsilon_i$).

Gr	Obs	β	σ_β	t_β	γ	σ_γ	t_γ	Power
1	96	7.33	0.72	10.1	-0.00068	0.060	-0.01	>0.95(95)
2	96	7.72	1.29	6.0	0.066	0.11	0.60	>0.95(85)
3	96	8.25	1.03	8.0	0.067	0.09	0.75	>0.95(90)
4	96	7.49	0.79	9.5	0.053	0.08	0.67	>0.95(95)
5	96	7.32	1.30	5.7	0.091	0.12	0.75	>0.95(75)
6	96	6.43	0.75	8.6	0.156	0.070	2.24	>0.95(<75)
7	96	7.35	1.61	4.6	0.18	0.212	0.8	>0.75(<75)
6+7	192	7.7	.0.84	9.2	.084	0.06	1.29	>0.95(95)
8	96	9.81	1.32	7.5	0.068	0.157	0.43	>0.95(75)
9	96	10.94	1.12	9.74	-0.244	0.121	-2.02	na
10	96	9.78	1.21	8.1	0.036	0.15	0.25	>0.95(80)

Groups 1-8 and 10: Because we failed to reject the hypothesis that $\gamma = 0$ at the .05 significance level for all groups except 9 (significant negative), we consider it reasonable to assume that $\gamma = 0$ in these cases.

Group 9: The negative γ coefficient is significant, indicating that the subjects increased their speed in the third round. Assuming that the subjects had trouble establishing criteria to evaluate the Hot Wheels® cars but increased their speed once they had decided how to evaluate them, we modified the Hot Wheels® cars experiment. Before starting the experiment, the Group 10 subjects were asked to run 10 Hot Wheels® cars, which were not in the sets to be ordered, down the track and write a paragraph describing the criteria they would use to order the sets of Hot Wheels® cars. With prior evaluation the results for Group 10 show no significant increased speed and we can assume $\gamma = 0$.

Group 6: The one group that is nearly significant is Group 6, for which the γ coefficient would be significant at <0.05. As there was no observable change in the algorithm used by the subjects, we decided to obtain more observations to see if γ would not be significant at 0.05. Combining the observations of Groups 6 with 7 results in a γ coefficient would not be significant for any $\alpha < 0.10$.

Power: To determine the power of our test that the subjects were using a modified bucket sort and not a modified bubble sort or an efficient binary sort we tested the following hypotheses shown in Table 3.8 below. H_O is

Table 3.8   Power of the test.

Bubble vs Bucket γ for X^2	Efficient Binary vs Bucket γ for $X \log_2 X$
$H_O : \gamma = 0$	$H_O : \gamma = 0$
$H_A : \gamma = b/8$	$H_A : \gamma = b$

the hypothesis that the subjects were using a modified bucket sort and H_A is the hypothesis that the subjects were using a modified bubble sort or an efficient binary sort. On average for the bubble sort, assuming the pens are in random order, each subject will start at the center and will have to make $m/4$ binary comparisons to place the new pen in the m pens that already have been ordered. Using the Gauss formula for summing $1 + 2 + 3 \ldots + m = m(m+1)/2$ the coefficient of the quadratic term X^2 should be $b/8$, where b is the time to make a binary comparison that is 3.2 seconds and 1.5 seconds in the worst case scenario.

For all results other than those of Groups 7 and 9 the power of the test is >0.95. For Group 6 combined with Group 7, the power of the test is >0.95. The results for the worst case scenario of b = 1.5 seconds are in Table 3.7 in the Power column in (). Even in this case the power of the test is greater than 0.75 in all but three cases.

Actual bubble sort: We trained subjects to perform a bubble sort, for which $T_i = \beta n_i + \gamma n_i^2 + \epsilon_i$. Subjects used the bubble sort to order Hot Wheels® with a pre-evaluation described for Group 10. We tested for homoscedasticity and normality using the test described above. Because the data failed both tests with an α of <0.05, the results for a robust regression are shown in Table 3.9 below. It is important to note that for subjects

Table 3.9   Actual Bubble sort $(T_i = \beta n_i + \gamma n_i^2 + \epsilon_i)$.

Gr	Obs	β	σ_β	t_β	γ	σ_γ	t_γ
Bub	48	7.95	2.78	2.86	0.58	0.37	1.57

performing a bubble sort the linear evaluation process is reflected in a significant linear coefficient and the quadratic number of binary comparisons is reflected in a quadratic coefficient significant for an α of 0.06. Also, the value of the coefficient is close to the forecasted value of 0.4. Therefore, for all groups we can reject the hypothesis that the subjects were using a modified bubble sort.

The prospect for a simple unknown efficient binary comparison with the hand motions exhibited by the subjects is extremely remote. Nevertheless, let us consider the second alternative, an Efficient Binary Sort, for which $T_i = \beta n_i + \gamma n_i \log_2 n_i$. We tested the hypothesis of normal errors for each group with the Shapiro-Wilf W, Shapiro-Francia W, and the Skewness/Kutosis tests. For each group all three reject the hypothesis of normal errors with a significance level of 1%. For each group we tested the hypothesis of homoscedasticity with the Breusch and Pagan (1979)/ Cook-Weisberg test and rejected this hypothesis in all cases with a significance level of 1%.The results using [White (1980)] robust regression that corrects for heteroskedasticity are shown in Table 3.10 at the top of the next page. Because for the Efficient Binary Sort we failed to reject the hypothesis that $\gamma = 0$ at the .05 significance level for any of the Groups except Group 8 (which is significant and negative), we consider it reasonable to assume that $\gamma = 0$ in all these cases. Nevertheless, for completeness sake, we performed the statistical analysis to show that the subjects were not using some unknown efficient binary comparison sort. The power of the tests in the worst case scenario are greater than 0.75 in all relevant cases. Therefore, for all groups we can reject the hypothesis that the subjects were using an efficient binary comparison algorithm.

Table 3.10 Second alternative: Efficient binary sort ($T_i = \beta n_i + \gamma n_i \log_2 n_i$).

Gr	Obs	β	σ_β	t_β	γ	σ_γ	$t_{\gamma)}$	Power
1	96	6.9	1.2	5.8	0.10	0.36	0.28	>95(95)
2	96	6.3	2.1	3.1	0.63	0.65	0.96	>95(85)
3	96	7.7	1.7	4.6	0.40	0.51	0.78	>95(90)
4	96	6.9	1.5	4.72	0.36	0.49	0.74	>95(95)
5	96	6.6	2.26	3.1	0.53	0.691	0.77	>95(75)
6	96	5.1	1.4	3.8	0.94	0.45	2.09	>95(<75)
7	96	6.4	2.5	2.6	0.83	0.93	0.89	>95(<75)
6+7	192	6.8	1.3	5.4	0.55	0.42	1.32	>95(95)
8	96	9.7	2.1	4.6	0.25	0.73	0.34	>95(75)
9	96	12.6	1.76	7.1	-1.24	0.57	-2.2	na
10	96	9.52	2.0	4.9	0.19	0.68	0.28	>95(80)

3.6 Additional Analysis

In revising the results for the book, we decided to combine all the data
from the seven pen groups and perform robust regressions for the bucket,
bubble, and efficient binary sort hypotheses. The results are shown below
shown in Tables 3.11 and 3.12 at the bottom of this page and Table 3.13
at the top of the next page. The coefficient for the n_i^2 term in the bubble

Table 3.11 Bucket sort regression
($T_i = \beta n_i + \epsilon_i$).

Gr	Obs	β	σ_β	t_β
1-7	672	8.47	0.19	43.8

Table 3.12 Bubble sort ($T_i = \beta n_i + \gamma n_i^2 + \epsilon_i$).

Gr	Obs	β	σ_β	t_β	γ	σ_γ	t_γ
1-7	672	7.75	0.41	19.01	0.054	0.037	1.45

Table 3.13   Efficient Binary Sort $(T_i = \beta n_i + \gamma n_i \log_2 n_i)$.

Gr	Obs	β	σ_β	$t_{\beta)}$	γ	σ_γ	t_γ
1-7	672	7.03	0.69	10.27	0.39	0.21	1.80

sort is significant for an α of 0.10 and the coefficient for the $n_i \log_2 n_i$ term in the efficient binary sort is significant for an α of 0.05. With a large number of observations the subjects' ordering algorithm definitely appears to have a nonlinear factor. Rather than accept either of the two alternative hypotheses as correct, we will now present evidence establishing that the bucket sort has a nonlinear factor.

Subjects wrote ABC with each pen before placing the pen. If they desired, they could write ABC again as many time as they wanted in order to evaluate the pen. The greater the number of pens in a partial ordering, the greater the probability that two pens will have close utility values that would require greater effort on the part of the subject to place a pen between or adjacent to pens with nearly equal utility values. For each subject and each round we recorded the number of rewrites. We analyzed the number of rewrites by dividing the number of rewrites by the number of pens in the ordering. The results are shown in Table 3.14 below. The data is the

Table 3.14   Average number of rewrites/number for ordering items.

Gr	Obs	Ordering 1	Ordering 2	Ordering 3
1-6	192	0.18	0.25	0.31
6	32	0.17	0.24	0.47

average of the number of rewrites in the indicated ordering divided by the number of pens in the ordering. For groups 1-6 the average for ordering 3 is 0.31 and the average for ordering 1 is 0.18. The average for ordering 3 is significantly greater for a difference in means test for an α of 0.02. Group 6 alone the average for ordering 3 is significantly greater than the average for group 1 with an α of 0.06. This explains why the results for Group 6 deviated from the results of the other groups. The coefficient value of the quadratic term is 1/10 the value of the corresponding coefficient of the actual bubble sort. In watching a large number of subjects perform the sorting it was not readily apparent that they were slowing down in placing the pens with larger numbers of pens. This is consistent with a small value on the nonlinear term.

Redoing the regression using robust regression instead of regular regression made very minor differences in the results. One change was that the α value at which the quadratic coefficient was significant in the actual bubble sort increased from 0.04 to 0.06. We decided for the sake of completeness to train subjects to perform a bubble sort using pens. In trying to set up the experiment with the current members of the research group we determined that such an experiment would fail because the subjects would not restrict themselves to only using binary comparison.

An example demonstrates the problem. The subjects were supposed to start each time at the worst end and make binary comparisons up the ordering to find the correct position. One member, after ordering 9 pens, picked up the 10 and wrote ABC. Then she picked up the best pen and rewrote with it. Next, she quickly moved up the ordering and placed the pen before the previous best. Once she wrote with the 10th pen, she knew approximately where the pen was going to be placed and could not restrict herself to just gaining binary comparison data.

In retrospect, we now believe that the bubble sort with Hot Wheels® worked because the subjects had very little or no recent experience with these objects. The need to run a pre-evaluation step with Group 10 in order to make the bucket sort work is consistent with this hypothesis.

Now let us summarize our arguments that the dominant "evaluate and place" algorithm is a modified bucket sort.

(1) Given the hand motions of subjects we can eliminate all algorithms based on a binary comparison except the bubble sort.

(2) Subjects and members of the research group who performed the evaluate and place algorithms were emphatic that the "evaluate and place" algorithm was not a bubble sort.

(3) Subjects displayed numerous examples of knowing the approximate utility of a pen once they wrote with it. In placing the first pen in an ordering they tended to place it near the best marker if it was a good pen, in the middle if it was a fair pen, and near the worst marker it was a poor pen. They used their utility estimate to implement a more efficient algorithm than a bubble sort.

(4) The value of the quadratic coefficient in the robust bubble sort regression in Table 3.12 is $1/10$ the value of the corresponding coefficient in the actual bubble sort. We can explain this small nonlinear factor in the evidence that as the number of pens in an ordering increased it became more difficult to place a pen as shown by the number of rewrites. The

fact that the average number of rewrites/(number of elements in the ordering) for ordering 3 is significantly greater the the corresponding average for ordering 1 also supports this theory.

The author has now been writing code for 50 years and initially assumed that a human processor, like digital processors, executes operations at a fixed speed. In revising the paper it become obvious that the time humans take to execute an operation can vary. This makes discriminating among human algorithms very difficult. Researchers should not assume that humans execute an operation at a fixed speed and should consider what factors might affect the speed of an operation.

3.7   Concluding Remarks

Would the human ordering algorithm remain linear for a large samples of say 1000 pens? This may not be testable as subjects appear to be near their limits to meaningful discrimination among the number of pens considered in this experiment. Humans might linearly sort a large number of pens into equivalence classes, but the inconsistencies of the current experiment suggest that the boundaries of these equivalence classes might be fuzzy.

The experiments with Hot Wheels® cars suggests that humans can order, sort, or prioritize a wide variety of alternative sets given they can create ordering criteria. Also, the consistency of such orderings is directly related to the effort put into creating the criteria for ordering. In subsequent chapters we will emphasize that item searches proceed from the general, such as brands or stores, to specific alternatives defined by their attributes. We claim that humans can order stores, brands, or categories of goods such as large SUVs, minivans, and station wagons. They can also order attributes such as color combinations.

In Chapter 7 we shall discuss how consumers' ability to order a small number of alternatives greatly improves their efficiency in repeated item searches.

Chapter 4

Computational Complexity: Decision Rules

4.1 Introduction

In this chapter we construct algorithms using known psychological decision rules to analyze the computational complexity of an item search. Using these rules, we show that performing an item search is a linear process. Given the slow speed at which a consumer processes these rules, we postulate that consumers must have more powerful rules.

We show that the [Tversky (1972)] linear elimination-by-aspects (EBA) rule can be modified to create a set-selection-by-aspects (SSBA) rule. Performing an item search with this rule is a sublinear process. We perform an experiment that demonstrates that subjects are approximately efficient in switching from an SSBA rule to a EBA rule when finding an apartment with certain characteristics. We also provide numerous examples showing that markets in both physical space and cyberspace are organized so that consumers can apply the SSBA rule.

The material in this chapter is [Norman *et al.* (2004)] with some minor editing.

4.2 Linear Item Search

Decision psychologists divide decision rules, which could also be called decision heuristics, into two categories: compensatory and non-compensatory. A compensatory decision rule involves at least one tradeoff in which the consumer weighs the values of two or more attributes of the alternatives. In such tradeoffs a high value of one attribute can compensate for a lower value of another attribute. Non-compensatory rules, such as the EBA rule mentioned above, lack any possibility of such compensation. For a list of psychological decision rules see [Hogarth (1987)].

We construct an algorithm for each decision rule and its associated information operator and assume that each algorithm terminates in a preferred item. We show that performing an item search with any of these rules is linear process in all but one case. The exception is the EBA rule, which can be a quadratic process in the worst case. Let us motivate this exercise. We will show that an algorithm based on any of these rules, or for that matter any combination of these rules, is not tractable for an unaided human. Then we ask what consumers do to achieve a tractable algorithm given the number of alternatives they face in the marketplace.

4.2.1 *Compensatory Decision Rules*

We first examine an item search to find a preferred item in a set using a binary comparison operator. Consider a simple model of a consumer obtaining a preferred item from a finite set of close substitutes $X = \{x_1, x_2, \ldots, x_n\}$. The number of alternatives is n and each item has m attributes. For example, if X were a set of houschold vehicles, one attribute would be body type – 2-door, 4-door, SUV, small SUV, full sized pickup, small pickup, or sports car. Other attributes would be 2- or 4- wheel drive, the body color, automatic locks and so on. The consumer determines the values of the attributes of x_i using the information operator, $In(x_i) = \{a_{i1}, a_{i2}, \ldots, a_{im}\}$ that has the property of completeness over the set under consideration. A is an $n \times m$ matrix of attributes with row i obtained using $In(x_i)$.

In order to determine preference between two items, x_i and x_j, a consumer executes a binary ranking operator, $R(a_i, a_j) \to x_i \succeq x_j$ or $x_i \prec x_j$, that has the properties of completeness and reflexivity over the set under consideration. We will discuss the impact of the possibility of intransitivity after considering the efficiency of the algorithm. We make explicit that the execution of R compares the respective attribute values of rows a_i and a_j. We also consider the compensatory decision rules proposed by psychologists that are linearized variations of a utility function. These rules can be formulated as variations of the binary comparison operator.

One alternative is the additive linear compensatory model:

$$V(x_i) = \sum_j w_j \times U(A_{i,j}) \tag{4.1}$$

This equation gives the value of x_i as the sum of the products of the weight w_j for each attribute times the utility or scale value of that attribute $U(A_{i,j})$.

Two other variations of the linear model are the additive difference model and the ideal point model. The additive difference model can be specified as:

$$V_\triangle(x_i, x_k) = \sum_j w_j \times U_j(A_{i,j} - A_{k,j}) \tag{4.2}$$

The terms in the summation could be either positive or negative depending on whether the utility of the difference in the jth option between x_i and x_k is positive or negative. The ideal point model is also a variation of the linear compensatory model:

$$V_I(x_i) = \sum_j w_j \times U_j(I_j - (A_{i,j})) \tag{4.3}$$

In this value function the utility or scale function measures the utility of the difference between the ideal I_j and the actual alternative.

The following binary comparison operator can be constructed from these linear value functions:

$$\left. \begin{matrix} R_v(x_i, x_j) \\ R_\triangle(x_i, x_j) \\ R_I(x_i, x_j) \end{matrix} \right\} \rightarrow x_i \succeq x_j \text{ if } \left\{ \begin{matrix} V(x_i) \geq V(x_j) \\ V_\triangle(x_i, x_j) \geq 0 \\ V_I(x_i) \geq V_I(x_j) \end{matrix} \right\} \text{, else } x_i \prec x_j \tag{4.4}$$

The goal is to find a preferred item that is defined as follows: $x_i^* \in X$ such that $x_i^* \succeq x_j$ for all $x_j \in X$. Finding a preferred item with a ranking operator is analogous to finding the largest number in a set of numbers. Compare the first item with the second, then compare the better with the third, and so on. For a statement of this algorithm below, let $B(a_i, a_j) \in \{R, R_v, R_\triangle, R_I\}$. An item search algorithm to find a preferred item is:

The PREF Algorithm

Step 1: $max = 1$ $i = 1$ Perform $In(x_{max})$
Step 2: As long as $i < n$, repeat Step 3.
Step 3: Let i increase by one. Perform $In(x_i)$. If $B(a_{max}, a_i) \neq x_{max} \succeq x_i$
  then $max = i$.
END

The PREF algorithm terminates with max equal to the index of a preferred item.

Let us now consider the cost of finding a preferred item with respect to the growth parameter n, the number of alternatives, and a fixed m, the number of attributes for each alternative. For this algorithm performed on s, which is an element of the set of problems S consisting of the $n!$ combinations of the n items in the set, the cost function is:

$$C(Pref[s]) = C(In) \times L(In) + C(B) \times L(B) \qquad (4.5)$$

where $C(\cdot)$ is the cost of executing the argument and $L(\cdot)$ counts the number of times the argument has been executed.

Now let us consider the cost of executing In and B. For simplicity, they are modeled as constant over the entire set of items. An inexperienced consumer might gradually lower his or her information costs to some fixed value as the consumer develops an efficient procedure, and in the case of such learning the costs are bounded between the initial costs and the efficient costs. The case of learning has no effect on the subsequent results, provided there is a fixed lower bound. In the marketplace there would be considerable variation in executing these operators even after learning. The fixed cost can be considered the average cost after learning.

We will model In and B as elementary operations with costs c_{In} and c_B, respectively. As m is taken as a fixed constant, the cost of executing In is constant. B's execution cost is also fixed for each of the four possibilities: $R, R_v, R_\triangle$, and R_I. The first, R, requires one nonlinear function evaluation over $2m$ arguments, and the other three, $R_v, R_\triangle$, and R_I, require $2m$ function evaluations over 1 argument and up to $2m$ arithmetic operations. We assume that all the functions are tractable for humans.

For this algorithm the worst case and expected computational complexity are the same because the algorithm must process every item and the cost does not depend on which combination is being processed. We prove this formally below.

Theorem 4.1. *The worst case and expected computational complexity of finding a preferred item using In and B is n*

Proof. Any algorithm based on In and B must perform the R operation at least $n - 1$ times in order to test all the items. Therefore the problem is bounded from below by $\Omega(n)$ (Definition D2, Chapter 2).

The number of R operations and In operations that the PREF algorithm requires is $n - 1$ and n, respectively ; therefore, this algorithm is $O(n)$. By definitions D1-D3 in Chapter 2 the computational complexity of this problem is n. $\qquad \square$

Comment: Since [Tversky (1969)] experimental evidence has been accumulating that humans are not always transitive. This does not change the computational complexity properties of the procedure, only the possibility that the outcome might be inconsistent. For example, it is easy to show that with intransitivity the preferred item selected by the algorithm depends on the order the alternatives are processed.

Up to now, we have not assumed any organization of the set of items from which the consumer will choose the preferred item. Without a specified organization, the consumer has no criteria to create a reasonable stopping rule for satisficing performance. We now ask whether non-compensatory decision rules lead to item search procedures more efficient than linear computational complexity.

4.2.2 *Noncompensatory Decision Rules*

We now consider several decision rules: the elimination-by-aspects, lexicographic, conjunctive and disjunctive decision rules. These rules are considered non-compensatory because a high value of one attribute does not necessarily compensate for a lower value of another attribute.

Elimination by Aspects Rule

In this section we shall examine the elimination-by-aspects rule in order to determine in what sense it is more efficient than the compensatory rules considered in the previous section. [Tversky (1972)] defines the choice function underlying the elimination-by-aspects rule formally. Surprisingly, he defines the actual elimination-by-aspects rule intuitively. The decision maker chooses an aspect then eliminates all items which do not possess the aspect and then repeats the process until only one item remains. What is ambiguous about the description of the EBA algorithm is the information operation required to implement the algorithm. We shall assume that he meant one observation is required for each element of the set under consideration to see if it possesses the aspect.

To compare the EBA rule with the previously considered compensatory rules, we shall first define an aspect. An *aspect* describes whether the item in question manifests some value or values for one or more of its attributes. For example, if the aspect is a small SUV, then each of the items in X, a set of household vehicles, either has or does not have the aspect. For example, a vehicle aspect might be "small SUV plus 4-wheel drive" or it could be a range of values such as digital cameras with 5-8 megapixels.

EBA Algorithm

Step 1: i = 1. Nomenclature: $X^0 = X$

Step 2: Define a new aspect γ_i over the m attributes.

Step 3: Sequentially examine each item in X^{i-1} and eliminate all those that do not possess aspect γ_i to obtain X^i.

Step 4: Increment i by 1 and repeat steps 2–4 until X^i has one element.

END

In order to compare the EBA rule with the previously considered compensatory rules we make four assumptions: (1) a consumer must make one information operation per item to determine whether the item possesses the aspect, (2) m aspects $\Gamma = \{\gamma_1, \gamma_2, \ldots, \gamma_m\}$ are required to reduce the set X to X^m that contains only one item, (3) in the worst case only one item is removed by each cycle of Steps 2 and 3 until the mth cycle when $n - m$ items are removed leaving X^m with one item, and (4) in the expected case each cycle removes a fraction $(n-1)/m$ where as n increases we consider values such that $(n-1)/m$ is an integer .

To consider the cost of executing EBA we must define the costs of the individual operations. Let D_{γ_i} and c_{γ_i} represent the operation and the cost of defining aspect γ_i respectively, and let D_{obs} and c_{obs} represent the operation and the cost of determining whether an item possesses γ_i and eliminating the item if it does not possess the aspect. The cost function for the EBA algorithm is:

$$C(\omega[s]) = c_{\gamma_i} \times L(D_\gamma) + c_{obs} \times L(D_{obs}) \tag{4.6}$$

where, as before, $L(\cdot)$ counts the number of times the argument has been executed.

Theorem 4.2. *The worst case and expected computational complexity of finding a preferred item using the EBA algorithm based on D_{γ_i} and D_{obs} is n.*

Proof. The number of D_γ operations that the algorithm requires is m. The number of D_{obs} operations is less than or equal to n for each of the m cycles in the worst and expected cases, with the total D_{obs} operations less than mn. Thus the EBA algorithm is $O(n)$ in both the worst and expected cases.

The number of D_{obs} operations required for the first cycle is n. Thus $\Omega(n)$ operations are needed. As these results do not depend on the order of the items being processed, the worst case and expected computational complexity are both n by definitions D1-D3 in Chapter 2. $\qquad\square$

If we also make m a growth parameter the analysis becomes more complicated. In the worst case the process is quadratic. In marketplace use of the EBA rule, one would expect the consumer to order the applications of the EBA so that the first cycle removed the most items, the second cycle the second most and so on. If on average $1/2$ of the remaining items were removed each cycle the expected EBA process would be linear.

Lexicographic

Lexicographic preferences are frequently used in economic analysis, for example [Encarnacion (1987)]. The options for lexicographic rules are quantified with more being better than less, option by option as specified below:

$$x_i \succ x_j \text{ if } \begin{cases} a_{i1} > a_{j1} \text{ or} \\ a_{ik} = a_{jk} \text{ for } k = 1, 2, \ldots, v < m \quad a_{i,v+1} > a_{j,v+1} \end{cases} \tag{4.7}$$

The attributes of x_l are $(a_{l1}, a_{l2}, \ldots, a_{lm})$ where $l = i$ or j and the attributes are measured as a numerical measure . To illustrate the lexicographic procedure let us represent each option as $Z_{ij} = a_{ij}/a_{max,j}$ where $a_{max,j}$ is the maximum of the jth column of A. Consider the following Z matrix:

$$\begin{pmatrix} 1 & 1 & 1 & 1 & 1 & 1 & 1 \\ 1 & 1 & 1 & 1 & 1 & 1 & .9 \\ 1 & 1 & 1 & 1 & 1 & .3 & .8 \\ 1 & 1 & 1 & 1 & .6 & .3 & .7 \\ 1 & 1 & 1 & .3 & .5 & .6 & .6 \\ 1 & .1 & .4 & .6 & .4 & .7 & .5 \\ 1 & .6 & .1 & .6 & .2 & .1 & .4 \\ .6 & .5 & .2 & .5 & .1 & 0 & .3 \end{pmatrix}$$

The lexicographic rule can be viewed as a variation of the elimination-by-aspects rule where the order in which the columns will be processed is given, but processing each column requires an extra step, the determination of $a_{max,j}$. If we assume that determining the maximum must be performed by binary comparisons, then the determination of the maximum of a sequence of numbers is a minor variation of the PREF algorithm where $a_{ij} \succeq a_{ik}$ if $a_{ij} \geq a_{ik}$. Processing an entire column has complexity n. It is easy to show that since m is taken as fixed, the worst case and expected complexity of the lexicographic algorithm is n.

Conjunctive and Disjunctive

Now let us consider conjunctive and disjunctive decision rules. In a *conjunctive* rule, the decision maker sets certain cutoffs on values of the attributes.

Any alternative which has a value of an attribute below a designated cutoff is eliminated. Recall that the consumer determines the values of the attributes of x_i using the information operator, $In(x_i) = \{a_{i1}, a_{i2}, \ldots, a_{im}\}$. Assume the number of attributes upon which a cutoff has been established is $k \leq m$ and assume that the attributes are ordered such that the first k have a cutoff. Let the cutoffs be $\{f_i : i = 1, 2, \ldots, k\}$. The conjunctive rule is x^* is kept if $a_{*,i} \geq f_i$ for $i = 1, 2, \ldots, k$.

In the *disjunctive* model a decision maker might permit a low score on a dimension provided there is a very high score on one of the other dimensions. Consider the same cutoffs defined for the conjunctive model above. There are several ways in which this psychological decision rule could be defined. Let us define it as x^* is kept if $a_{*,1} \geq f_1$ or $a_{*,2} \geq f_2$ or ... or $a_{*,k} \geq f_k$. Defined this way the conjunctive rule is an "AND" rule in terms of Boolean logic and the disjunctive rule is an "OR" rule. For comparison purposes with the elimination-by-aspects rule we shall assume that only one item meets all the criteria for both the conjunctive and disjunctive rules. In addition, the decision maker is not aware of this fact. The execution of an algorithm using either rule would require a single pass to process each of the n items and it is easy to show that the worst and expected case computational complexity for both is n.

All of the rules considered so far have been linear rules, which immediately implies that an algorithm based on any combination of these rules is also linear. To execute any of these rules we need at least one observation per alternative. We shall consider a more efficient rule based on set information operators.

4.3   A Sublinear Item Search

While the decision rules discussed in the previous section are linear, the absolute cost of exercising one of these rules can be very high when n is large. If a human is aided by a computer, then linearly processing 2.5 million alternatives, such as the list of books at Amazon.com, is a tractable problem because even an inexpensive personal computer can execute a several hundred million operations per second. In contrast, a human may take seconds to execute one operation, and even at one second per item, a human would take almost 700 hours to linearly process the Amazon.com book list. Within the range of human capability, linear algorithms are not H tractable.

Also, an item search algorithm that is constructed from a combination of the decision rules discussed in the previous section will not lead to a more efficient than linear algorithm because each of these rules requires one observation per alternative. This raises the question whether humans execute more powerful rules in item searches.

4.3.1 *The SSBA Rule*

One approach to creating a more powerful decision rule is to introduce an information operator that only requires one observation to determine the subset of items in X that possess the aspect. Whether this is possible or not depends on how X is organized. For example, if all the items are heaped into a big pile, then the consumer would have to examine each item individually to observe the aspect under consideration. As we shall discuss in greater detail in a subsequent section, goods for sale are frequently organized by attributes. For example, a new car dealer organizes the models on the lot by make and model. Thus, a consumer in the phone directory can select the Honda dealers in one information operation and upon arriving at the lot can select the display of Civics in one information operation.

Let us now consider the efficiency of the EBA rule with a more powerful information operator, $Q(\gamma_i, X^{i-1}) = X^i$. We shall call this the set-selection-by-aspects (SSBA) rule, where the information operator Q means that given X^{i-1} and γ_i the consumer can determine X^i in a single information operation with cost c_Q. In a mens' clothing store, a consumer examining a circular rack of mens' pants selects in one operation all pants that have a particular waist band by observing the labels on the rack.

For the SSBA rule the order in which the γ_i are executed is crucial. If a consumer in a metropolitan area started an item search procedure for a new car by selecting that the car must have a CD player, the consumer would have to go to every car dealer, examine every car and create a giant list. Market organization dictates that a consumer can only apply the set information operator effectively for a small number of the possible sequences of aspects.

The SSBA is a refinement of the [Earl (1986)] characteristic filtering rule, a clarification of the EBA rule, in which he pointed out that the sequence of EBA steps is not arbitrary, but ordered. In his examples, it is clear that the economic agents must sometimes be using set information operators and sometimes item information operators.

Also, market organization usually requires the consumer to switch to a linear rule before selecting the preferred item. Yet, in this subsection, we shall assume that the items to be processed are organized so that the consumer can use the SSBA rule throughout the entire process in order to characterize its efficiency. We also assume that for a given sequence of Γ, X could be organized so that the SSBA rule could be applied.

SSBA Algorithm

Step 1: i = 1. Nomenclature: $X^0 = X$
Step 2: Define aspect γ_i over the m attributes.
Step 3: Execute $Q(\gamma_i, X^{i-1})$ to obtain X^i.
Step 4: Increment i by 1 and repeat steps 2–4 until X^i contains one item.
END

In order to compare the SSBA rule with the previously considered EBA rules we make four assumptions: (1) a consumer must make one information operation per set to determine whether the subset that possesses the aspect, (2) m aspects $\Gamma = \{\gamma_1, \gamma_2, \ldots, \gamma_m\}$ are required to reduce the set X to X^m that contains only one item, (3) in the worst case only one item is removed by each cycle of Steps 2 and 3 until the mth cycle when $n - m$ items are removed leaving X^m with one item, and (4) in the expected case each cycle removes a fraction (n-1)/m where as n increases we consider values such that $(n - 1)/m$ is an integer.

The cost function for the SSBA algorithm performed on problem set element s is:

$$C(SSBA[s]) = c_{\gamma_i} \times L(D_\gamma) + c_Q \times L(Q). \tag{4.8}$$

where $L(\cdot)$ counts the number of times the argument has been executed.

Theorem 4.3. *The expected and worst case computational complexity of the SSBA algorithm is 1 (constant).*

Proof. The SSBA algorithm requires no more than m D_γ or m Q operations; hence it is $O(1)$. Given the data structure, the SSBA algorithm requires at least m D_γ operations and at least m Q operations; hence the SSBA algorithm is $\Omega(1)$. The number of operations does not depend on the order of the items; hence by definitions D1-D3 the expected and worst case computational complexity of the SSBA algorithm is constant. $\qquad\square$

To clearly understand the relationship between the EBA and SSBA rule one needs to assume that there are r values for each attributes and that

$n = r^m$. Then, the SSBA rule constitutes a logarithmic reduction in cost from the EBA rule.

The SSBA rule is a powerful rule that offers consumers the possibility of better performance in finding a preferred item. We need to consider two questions related to this rule.

1. Are humans approximately efficient in its use?
2. Are markets organized to facilitate its use?

4.3.2 *Design of SSBA Experiment*

We are going to use a UT student searching for apartment to test whether a subject is efficient in the use of decision rule involving a set information operator. The experiment investigates how many times subjects use a SSBA rule before switching to a linear rule when hunting for a specified apartment. By varying the time delay on the sublinear and linear rules we can control when it is efficient to shift from the sublinear rule to the linear rule and see if subjects vary their shift points optimally with respect to the changing time delays. The shift point is determined by the relative time delays and the number of alternatives.

Subjects were given incentives to find an apartment with specified traits shown in Table 4.1 below as fast as possible. To find the specified apart-

Table 4.1 Specified apartment traits.

No. Bedrooms	Location	Price
1	Riverside	$200-300
2	West Campus	$300-400
3	Hyde Park	$400-500
4	Far West	$500-600

ment, the subject may click on either trait buttons or object buttons. The trait buttons select those apartments with the specified trait and eliminate the rest. The object buttons represent randomly ordered apartments; clicking an object button tests that item individually to see if it has the desired attributes. The decision process that is three levels deep is shown in Figure 4.1 on the next page. Initially there are 8 possible apartments in experiments 1 and 4, 27 possible apartments in experiments 2 and 5, and 64 apartments in experiments 3 and 6. If the subject clicks on the correct trait

Decision Tree

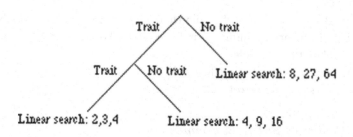

Fig 4.1: Decision tree.

button, the number of possible apartments is reduced to 4, 9 or 16 respectively. If the subject clicks again on the correct trait button, the number is further reduced to 2, 3 or 4.

The subject might click on the trait buttons twice to reduce the options to 2, 3 or 4 individual buttons. They also could click on the trait button only once and then switch to a linear hunt over the 4, 9, or 16 remaining object buttons. Alternatively, they can simply start with a linear hunt by clicking on up to 8, 27, or 64 object buttons without using trait selection at all.

Whether it is efficient to click on a trait button, reducing the number of object buttons over which a linear hunt must be conducted, depends on two factors. One is the longer delay incorporated into the trait buttons versus the 1 second delay incorporated into the object buttons. In experiments 1-3 the trait delay is 7 seconds and in experiments 4-6 the trait delay is 3 seconds. The other factor is how many alternatives of each trait are included in the experiment. The data are shown in Table 4.2 on the next page. To illustrate the decision process facing each subject, we display side by side the initial interfaces for experiments 1 and 3 in Figure 4.2 on the top of the page 62.

First, the subjects see the trait buttons for the number of bedrooms on top and the individual buttons for all the apartments on the bottom. Suppose in the first screen the subject clicks on button for 2 bedrooms in experiment 3. The program eliminates all apartments that do not have 2 bedrooms and redraws the frame. In the second screen, the subject has the choice of 4 location trait buttons on top and a row of 16 individual apartment buttons on the bottom that all have 2 bedrooms. Now suppose the subject clicks on the Riverside trait button. The program redraws the

Table 4.2   Experimental factors.

Exp	Trait Delay	No. of Traits	No. of Buttons	Apartment to Find
1	7 sec	$2 \times 2 \times 2$	8,4,2	2 bed-Riverside-$200-300
2	7 sec	$3 \times 3 \times 3$	27, 9, 3	1 bed-Hyde Park-$300-400
3	7 sec	$4 \times 4 \times 4$	64, 16, 4	4 bed-Riverside-$300-400
4	3 sec	$2 \times 2 \times 2$	8,4,2	1 bed-West Campus-$200-300
5	3 sec	$3 \times 3 \times 3$	27, 9, 3	3 bed-Riverside-$300-400
6	3 sec	$4 \times 4 \times 4$	64, 16, 4	3 bed-Far West-$300-400

frame with no trait buttons and a row of individual buttons on the bottom that all have the traits of 2 bedrooms and the Riverside location. The subject clicks on the individual apartment buttons in succession until he or she finds the specified apartment, in this case the one priced $300-400.

Alternatively, the subject could simply click on the individual object buttons on the bottom and never click on any of the trait buttons. Instead of narrowing his hunt, the subject would look at all the possible apartments until the correct one is found. Subjects must decide whether clicking on the trait buttons or clicking only on the object buttons is faster.

The text areas at the top of the interfaces provide the subjects with useful information. The text area on the right displays "Go" to inform the subject that the buttons will respond to a click. The text area on the left displays messages such as "wrong button" or "FANTASTIC, YOU FOUND THE RIGHT ONE. Start the next round when the frame is redrawn."

In the experiment, each of the 25 undergraduate subjects was paid a flat $7 for participating and could win $10, 5, 3, or 2 if they performed the hunt in respectively the fastest, second fastest, third fastest, or fourth fastest times. These incentives encouraged subjects to click on the buttons as quickly as possible. There were three identical rounds in each experiment. At the end of three rounds the total time for the experiment was shown in the left frame and the winners were paid. Prior to starting the paid experiments the subjects performed 6 practice rounds. They differed from the paid rounds in two respects: (1) the numbers of alternatives in each round were 2×2, 3×3, and finally 4×4 and (2) in the first round the subject had to use the trait buttons, in the second round the subject had to use only object buttons, and in the third the subject could use

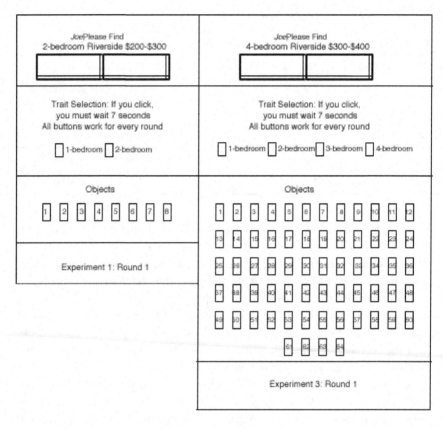

Fig 4.2:   Initial interfaces for Experiments 1 and 3.

either. The purpose of the practice rounds was to ensure that the subjects had an intuitive grasp of the speeds at which the alternative decisions
executed.

4.3.3 Experimental Results

Since the object buttons are in random order, a subject would on average have to click on half of them to find the specified apartment. The expected delay time in a linear rule is compared with the delay time for a SSBA rule in Table 4.3 below.

Table 4.3 Expected time delays for SSBA versus a linear rule.

Exp ↓	1st Trait		2nd Trait		3rd Trait
Rule →	SSBA	Linear	SSBA	Linear	Linear
1	7	4	7	2	1
2	7	13.5	7	4.5	1.5
3	7	32	7	8	2
4	3	4	3	2	1
5	3	13.5	3	4.5	1.5
6	3	32	3	8	2

The mean number of times the trait and object buttons were clicked are displayed in Table 4.4 below. As expected, the subjects increased their use

Table 4.4 Number of times buttons clicked.

	Trait Buttons			Object Buttons	
Exp	Forecast	Mean	SD	Mean	SD
1	0	0.35	0.55	3.70	2.44
2	1	0.77	0.60	7.49	6.65
3	2	1.39	0.53	7.21	6.85
4	1	0.72	0.70	2.94	1.90
5	1 or 2	1.32	0.54	4.71	4.87
6	2	1.79	0.41	3.96	3.98
SIG		.0001		.0001	

of the trait buttons when the total number of alternatives increased and when the trait execution delay decreased.

But, are these differences significant? The experimental design is a 3 × 2 balanced factor design with the dependent variable, *level*: 0, 1, or 2 levels of trait buttons clicked. The first factor is *size*, the number of alternatives: 2 × 2 × 2, 3 × 3 × 3, or 4 × 4 × 4; and the second factor is *delay*: 7 or 3 second delay on the execution of the trait buttons. The results are significant, as is shown in Table 4.5 below.

Table 4.5   Analysis of variance procedure. Dependent variable: *level*; Independent variables: *size* and *delay*.

Source	DF	Sum of Squares	Mean Square	F Value	Pr > F
Model	5	80.12	16.02	50.88	0.0001
Error	336	105.82	0.31		
Corrected Total	341	185.94			

The Duncan test indicates that the effects of the two delays were significantly different and the effects of the three sizes were also significantly different. Before starting the experiment with cash incentives we would like the subjects to perform enough practice rounds so that they develop a trait/object button strategy. Another important consideration is whether the 6 practice experiments were sufficient for the subjects to do this. To test this using ANOVA *trait* is the dependent variable and *round*, that is round 1, 2, or 3, is the independent variable. If the subjects were changing their strategy in the experiments with prizes, the means will be significantly different. The fact that there is no change in performance is shown in Table 4.6 below.

Table 4.6   Analysis of variance procedure. Dependent variable: *level*; Independent variables: *round*.

Source	DF	Sum of Squares	Mean Square	F Value	Pr > F
Model	2	1.27	0.63	1.16	0.31
Error	339	184.68	0.54		
Corrected Total	341	185.94			

With the exception of experiment 1, subjects on average used slightly fewer trait buttons than forecasted. A much larger sample would be required to demonstrate that this shift is significant. If we consider the winners' use of the trait buttons, they generally used the trait buttons more often as the number of alternatives increased and the delay time on the trait button decreased, but they too used the trait button slightly less often than one would expect from the table of expected delays. For example, the winner of experiment 5 used the trait button once each round instead of twice, although the difference in time is slight. But, in experiment 4, the winner did not use the trait button, and in experiment 6 the winner used it twice each round.

The experiment indicates that the subjects in general and the winners in particular were approximately efficient in their use of the trait and object buttons.

4.4 Market Organization

Books on retail design, such as [Riewoldt (2000)], Barr and Broudy (1986), and Barr and Field (1997), emphasize the visual display of goods and the creation of an appropriate ambiance for prospective customers. They do not, however, emphasize that competition among sellers provides incentives for those sellers to organize their merchandise in a fashion that reduces the item search costs of the consumer. Consider two stores that offer over 10,000 items for sale with the same selection and prices. The first store simply places the merchandise in a big heap without any sort of organization, forcing the consumer to hunt through the heap in order to find a preferred item. The second store organizes the merchandise into display cases by attributes. Most consumers would prefer the organized store because the average item search costs will be lower if they can perform several SSBA steps before switching to linear rules. Such reasoning is implicit in store design and becomes explicit when there is a problem. For example, Red Jacket redesigned its Virgin megastores to help customers locate departments and travel between them, [Staff (2001)].

What enables consumers to apply SSBA steps in their item searches is not that stores specifically organize goods in sets defined by the consumer's aspects. Rather, when stores organize goods in a nested structure by attributes, they make SSBA steps feasible. For example, clothing stores organize women's and men's clothes in different areas of the store. Within the men's clothing area, goods are further organized into sports clothes, suits, underclothes and so on. Automobile dealers organize their new car lots by make and model. This organization enables buyers to use many selection-by-aspect steps on aspects defined over the attributes because sellers provide customers with labels to recognize sets, organize goods in patterned displays which customers learn to recognize, organize goods in catalogues hierarchically through indices, and on web sites, provide acquire item algorithms that return the set with the specified characteristics.

To perform several SSBA steps, the consumer must define a sequence of aspects consistent with the goods' organization so that he can execute several SSBA steps in the item search procedure. For example, if a consumer started the search for a new car by insisting that the car had a CD player, the consumer would have to process every new car lot item-by-item to determine the set of new cars with CD players. To use an SSBA rule in the initial steps of an item search, the consumer must start with aspects that can be determined in a single operation such as the make and model of a car.

Organizing goods in a nested structure by attributes simplifies the administration of a store and makes acquiring items by potential customers more efficient. The profit motive of the store overlaps with the desire for an efficient procedure for a consumer, but the two are not identical. Organization of goods in stores also has a marketing aspect which attempts to attract customers to goods that are the most profitable.

We will now consider the organization of markets in physical space and cyberspace in more detail.

4.4.1 *Physical Space*

Consider the organization of a department store, apartment listings, and automobile dealers' displays. Sellers in physical space have an incentive to enable consumers to perform one or more SSBA steps in order to reduce their search costs, which are part of the total cost of the purchase.

Tower Records in Austin was a CD department store that carried roughly 93,000 CDs. To increase the efficiency of consumers' procedures Tower Records was organized by attributes such as musical styles and further organized into musical groups/composers that are organized alphabetically, and then by album as is shown in Figure 4.3 on the next page.

As can be seen there are two basic attributes: *music* and another to *non-music*. *Music* then splits into two branches, upstairs and downstairs. Both of these have almost identical structures, however upstairs also contains the choice of *composer*, along with *artist*, thus *upstairs* and *downstairs* cannot

Tower Records

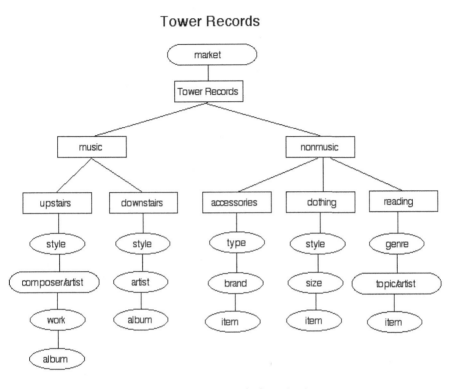

Fig 4.3: Tower Records Organization

be combined. If a consumer wanted a recording of a Phillip Glass work, the consumer would execute SSBA steps to move upstairs, select a style, the artist Phillip Glass, and then would look for specific works. If all the CDs were in a heap, consumer would need about 26 hours to select a particular recording using a linear rule if they could observe one CD per second on average. The organization of Tower Records is typical of a department store where the customer can perform several SSBA steps before switching to linear rules.

Now let us consider a student at the University of Texas at Austin hunting for an apartment in physical space using: (1) the classified section of the *Austin-American Statesman*, (2) an apartment guide, or (3) an apartment locator service. Because there are about 1000 possible rentals typically listed in the Austin newspaper, a linear rule to find an apartment might take as many as 110 hours assuming the student made an appointment and drove to personally evaluate each rental. Each of these alternative processes is organized to allow students to use SSBA steps in their hunt.

The classified advertisements for rentals are first organized by type as (1) unfurnished apartments, (2) condos/town houses, (3) unfurnished duplexes, or (4) unfurnished houses. Then each type is further organized by location in the Austin Standard Metropolitan Statistical Area (SMSA). The *Greater Austin Apartment Guide* provides data on over 250 apartment complexes divided into 5 sets by location. If the student knew the desired Austin location and rental type, the student could use a SSBA step over this combined aspect before switching to a linear procedure. An apartment locator asks the student for the student's preference over price, location and number of bedrooms. In a single SSBA operation (from the perspective of the student) the locator shows most students no more than four apartments to be evaluated by linear rules.

Now let us consider the organization of automobile displays at car dealerships. In the market for automobiles tens of thousands of items exist, a number that makes it impossible to operate a hunt using an item-by-item rule. At any given time there are approximately 300 brand new cars in any given lot. If a buyer were to test-drive each car at just one dealership for 20 minutes it would take the buyer over four days of non-stop driving.

The organization of automobile data and auto displays at dealerships enables the consumer to execute several SSBA steps in a hunt for a preferred vehicle. Austin's Capital Chevrolet Dealership divides its lot into cars, trucks, sport utility vehicles, and vans. The main areas are then further classified by style. Thus a potential customer, for example, could execute SSBA rules to examine alternative colors and options on an SUV. The Buick dealership has a slightly different approach. Buick has five different models. In the showroom they display two of each model, one custom version and one limited model. The customer walks around the showroom and decides which model they would like to purchase, rather than walking around in a parking lot. The salespeople at Buick cater to the more focused buyers and ask the consumers questions to determine the desired aspects. This requires an SSBA rule because the customer is deciding exactly what he wants in a car. On the outside, the Buick dealership is divided into five sections, similar to the Chevrolet divisions, and the salespeople can then select the set of cars that fits the given description.

4.4.2   *Cyberspace*

In cyberspace the sequence of decision rules is frequently presented to the consumer as a decision aid. Let us start with a student hunting for an apartment in cyberspace. One such site is ApartmentGuide.com. On the first page the student would select the state and city. On the second page the student would select the areas of town in which the student desires to live; the site provides maps for those who want them. The third page asks the student to indicate a price range, the preferred number of bedrooms and any desired amenities. The program presents the student with a list of all apartments matching the specified qualities. The various apartment complexes provide the prospective renter with the details concerning the apartment and apartment complex.

The new car decision guide at AutoTrader.com is one example of a decision aid for selecting an automobile. The consumer starts by selecting new or used, the body type, such as sedan or SUV. Next, the consumer selects the maximum price. Third, the consumer ranks a number of options, such as air-conditioning, from no opinion to must-have. Then the consumer ranks a number of safety options. Next, the consumer specifies the gas mileage range, the number of cylinders, and the type of brakes. Then the consumer indicates a preference over the number of passengers the vehicle can carry, the number of doors and the amount of room per passenger. The consumer is asked to accept or reject various manufacturers and finally ranks the criteria to order the list of final selections.

Another site that has decision aids for a variety of products is Active-BuyersGuide.com. These decision rules are compensatory and the consumer is asked questions to determine the weights among the various attributes of the product. Decision guides provide the consumer with quick, low cost tools to run scenarios that help assess the importance of various criteria. In addition many sites enable a consumer to create a table of alternative products with the attributes listed side by side. This is much more efficient than obtaining the same information from brochures for the various products. For most consumers, a necessary step in selecting an apartment is viewing the apartment, just as a key step in selecting an automobile is test-driving the vehicle.

Internet sites can provide consumers with an efficient method of narrowing the hunt to final candidates that would then require direct sensory evaluation. To execute an online search the user clicks on a button after determining a small number of parameters. From the perspective of the user the search is effectively of constant complexity given the speed of the server processor.

4.5   Conclusions

In this chapter we have presented a powerful set decision rule that leads to an item search being a sublinear process. In Chapter 7 we will introduce other set decision rules and discuss how consumers determine their decision rules in repeated item searches.

Chapter 5

Repeated Price Search

5.1 Introduction

In their study of the online searching of over 10,000 households, Johnson, Moe, Fader, Bellman and Lohse (2004a) find that on average consumers search less than 2 sites each for books, CDs, and air travel services. In the standard one-period price search theory, for example see Kohn and Shavell (1974) or McMillan and Rothschild (1994), consumers are assumed to perform a price search as a random drawing with a fixed cost. They continue drawing as long as the price found is greater than the reservation price that they calculate knowing the distribution of prices. Given that the fixed cost of searching an online site is low, this theory implies consumers would search numerous online sites. The experiments of [Kogut (1990)] and [Sonnemans (1998)] show subjects draw too few times. The experimenters argue that subjects are considering the sunk costs and are not calculating a marginal cost decision based on the reservation price.

This standard one-period price search theory assumption of a random drawing ignores the fact that consumers are really performing repeated price searches, learning and incorporating the relative prices of sellers into their searches. We investigate in several experiments how many times subjects check prices at both stores to learn the relative prices of two sellers in one, two, and four period problems. We compare the performance of two groups, one that completed a statistics course, and one that had not. In the one period problem the performance of both groups was statistically significantly better than random choice and worse than optimal. The performance of the statistics course group was statistically superior to that of the non-statistics course group. Using regression analysis we determine a heuristic explaining the performance of both groups. In the two-period Bayesian optimization problem, many subjects in both groups demonstrated a lack of knowledge of Bayes theorem. We also studied the behavior of 25 subjects in 2-period and 4-period problems. In all of the problems the subjects checked prices at both stores less than an optimal number of times and in three out of the four cases this difference was statistically significant. Can consumers achieve good price search performance by checking a small number of sites and making suboptimal calculations?

To answer this question, we investigated student textbook buying behavior at the University of Texas at Austin, (UT), using surveys. Students buying textbooks online also only check a small number of sites. Student price search performance is a function of market organization and how students establish and update their price search strategy. Because online marketplace sites can list several hundred sellers of popular first-year textbooks, a student only has to check a few sites to achieve good performance for different risk levels. Marketplace and meta-search sites improve consumer performance by providing decision aid algorithms that perform calculations to reduce the computational complexity of search. Most students start searching online with good prior information by first seeking the advice of students with experience buying textbooks online. In repeated searches they update the list of sites to search.

We conclude with a brief discussion of the latest in decision aid algorithms improving consumer performance. This chapter is [Norman *et al.* (2012)] with minor editing.

5.2   Experiments

We performed a series of experiments designed to test subjects' performances in solving problems associated with repeated price search. In the book we shall present an overview of the experiments. If you are interested in the details of the experiments, you can perform them at http:www.eco.utexas.edu/Homepages/Faculty/Norman/00Julia/. We recommend that you use a Firefox browser.

5.2.1   *Design*

These experiments included Bayesian multiperiod optimization experiments to test whether students are capable of devising a strategy to optimally learn which store has the lowest relative prices. As these optimization problems are often intractable, Norman and Shimer (1994), we obtained a computationally tractable experiment by using discrete distributions and only three alternatives. The subject needs to buy a textbook each semester and has three choices each period:

1. Travel to store A and buy from store A
2. Travel to store B and buy from store B
3. Travel to both stores A and B, and buy from the cheaper store

The Bayesian question is how many times should the subject check prices at both stores in order to learn which store is cheaper and improve future performance. In the first four experiments the choice is simplified to "Check prices at both stores: Yes or No".

In the four one period experiments, subjects were presented with travel cost and relative price information to solve the problems presented in Table 5.1 below.

Table 5.1   Anticipated price differences.

Stores	Anticipated Price Difference	Check prices at both stores	
A and B	$5	Yes ◯	No ◯
C and D	$10	Yes ◯	No ◯
E and F	$15	Yes ◯	No ◯
G and H	$20	Yes ◯	No ◯
I and J	$25	Yes ◯	No ◯

In the four one period problems, Anticipated Price Difference, APD, means by how many dollars you anticipate that one store will be cheaper than the other. What varies in the four problems is the information provided to the subjects about the travel costs and how much they know about the relative prices of the two stores. The subject is informed the cost, $C1$, to check the price at one store and buy from that store and the expected cost, $C2$, to check prices at both stores and buy from the cheaper. In the first two problems, to be labeled 1PnoI 1 and 2, the subject has no information concerning which store is cheaper. In problems three and four, to be labeled as 1PperI 1 and 2, the subject is given a prior probability, expressed as a relative frequency, that the store on the left is cheaper. In the four experiments the anticipated price differences are listed above and the variation in travel cost and knowledge about relatives prices are summarized in

Table 5.2   One-period problem summary.

Problem	(C1:Cost - Check one)	(C2: Cost - Check both)	(Probability left store cheaper)
1PnoI 1	$3	$7	No Info
1PnoI 2	$5	$12	No Info
1PperI 1	$3	$7	0.60
1PperI 2	$3	$7	0.77

Table 5.2 below. After completing 1PnoI 1 and 2 subjects were shown the decisions they made and asked to write a description of their problem solving strategy for these two experiments. The same is the case after 1PperI 1 and 2.

Next, subjects solved four 2 period Bayesian optimizations problems labeled 2P 1-4. The subjects were informed about the travel costs, relative prices of the two stores, and were presented the problem to solve in the following display:

Anticipated Price Difference $= y_i$

	Semester 1	
Check just one store ◯		Check both stores ◯
	Semester 2	
(blank textbox 1) ◯	(blank textbox 2) ◯	(blank textbox 3) ◯

Semester 1 choice defines the blank HTML textboxes in Semester 2:

Blank textbox is replaced depending on which ◯ is checked in Semester 1

Blank	Semester 1 check one	Semester 1 check both
1	Check just one store	Buy from cheaper store semester 1
2	Check both stores	Buy from more expensive store semester 1
3	DO NOT USE	Check both stores

The one variable that varies in the two-period problems is APD, the value of y_i listed above. The values for the four problems are listed in Table 5.3 below. The variables that are the same for the four problems are

Table 5.3   Two-period problem: Values of y_i in display above.

Problem	2P 1	2P 2	2P 3	2P 4
APD	$5	$15	$45	$65

the travel costs and the information provided about the relative prices of the two stores. The travel cost, $C1$, to check prices at one store and buy from that store is \$6 and the expected travel cost, $C2$, to check prices at both stores and buy from the cheapest is \$14. The subjects are informed that the probability that one store is cheaper is 0.9 (expressed as a relative frequency); but, you have NO information as to which store is cheaper prior to your first semester decision. If you check prices at both stores the first semester, then you will have one observation which store is cheaper for your second semester decision. After completing 2P 1-4 subjects were shown the decisions they made and asked to write a description of their problem solving strategy for these four experiments.

There were two 49 member subject groups, EcoStat and NoStat where:

1. EcoStat: Economic majors who had completed the undergraduate economic statistics course, which included a section on Bayes theorem.

2. NoStat: Students majoring in Liberal Arts (except Economics), Communications, Fine Arts, or Education who had not taken any university course in statistics. They also must not have taken more than 3 hours of economics or 6 hours of mathematics.

Subjects gave us permission to verify these requirements and we did. We provided each subject in both groups with a calculator and a sheet of scratch paper to eliminate as many arithmetic errors as possible .

The incentives for the experiment were:

> Assume you are being paid to advise 100 freshmen about buying a certain textbook. If your recommendations are better in the sense of lower costs on average, you earn more money. The maximum possible earnings is \$21
> 1. You will receive a flat fee of \$6 for coming to the experiment.
> 2. There are 34 questions. You will receive (your score)/(perfect score) × \$15.

To see the details of the experiments, use Firefox to go to http://www.eco.utexas.edu/Homepages/Faculty/Norman/00Julia/ to perform the experiments.

5.2.2 *Results*

First let us compare the mean performance of the two groups. m_{NS} and m_{ES} denotes the mean performance of the 49 NoStat subjects and 49 EcoStat subjects, respectively. Ran is the expected performance based on random selection. Opt is the performance based on optimal selection in

Table 5.4   Mean performance.

Ran	m_{NS}	m_{ES}	Op
76	91.99	95.69	100

Table 5.5   *t* Tests of differences in mean performance.

Test	Ran< m_{NS}	Ran< m_{ES}	$m_{NS} < m_{ES}$	m_{NS} <Opt	m_{ES} <Opt
Sig	<0.001	<0.001	<0.001	<0.001	<0.001

price savings. The data and one tail t tests of the means are presented in Tables 5.4 and 5.5 above. The $m_{NS} < m_{ES}$ test was performed assuming unequal variances.

We have three groups of problems, 1PnoI 1&2, 1PperI 1&2, and 2P 1-4. If we consider the performance on each of the groups separately, we get the same relative performance results with a significance of less than 0.025. In all cases, mean subject performance is closer to optimal performance than random performance.

Now let us consider the performance of the strategies of the two groups in the one period problems. Because all subjects had a calculator and scratch paper, arithmetic errors were not considered an important factor. All these problems were designed with a shift point, such that for all anticipated price differences less than the shift point, the correct choice was to only check prices at one store, and for all anticipated price differences greater or equal to the shift point, the correct choice was to check prices at both stores. The shift points for the one period problems, each of which had anticipated price differences of \$5, \$10, ... ,\$25, are shown in Table 5.6 below.

Table 5.6   Shift points for one period problems.

Page	1PnoI 1	1PnoI 2	1PperI 1	1PperI 2
Shift Point	\$10	\$15	\$15	\$20

The subjects wrote a description of their strategy to solve the one-period problems. Very few subjects gave a succinct formula for their strategy. In many cases they described the strategy verbally or used an example. The correct rule for the first two problems, 1PnoI 1&2 is:

if $1/2APD > C2 - C1$, check both buy cheaper, **else** check one and buy there.

Where APD is the anticipated price difference, $C2$ is the expected cost of checking prices at both stores and buying from the cheaper, and $C1$ is the cost of checking the price at one store and buying there. Two members of the EcoStat group and one member of the NoStat group wrote this rule and executed it correctly. The most common strategy of the two groups was:

if $APD > C2$, check both buy cheaper, **else** check one and buy there.

Twenty members of the EcoStat group and ten members of the NoStat group wrote this rule and executed it correctly. This rule gives the correct response for the anticipated price differences used in the first two problems.

The correct rule for the second two problems, 1PperI 1&2 is:

if $(1 - P)APD > C2 - C1$ check both buy cheaper, **else** check one and buy there.

where P is the probability that the first store is cheaper. Nine members of the EcoStat group and one member of the NoStat group wrote this strategy and correctly executed it. Twenty members of the EcoStat group and thirty three members of the NoStat group wrote that they used an intuitive approach to solve the second set of two problems and correctly executed it.

The greater the absolute difference between the anticipated price difference and the shift point, the greater the absolute difference in value between checking one store and checking both stores. We hypothesize that the greater the absolute difference between these two choices, the greater the likelihood subject's strategies would select the correct choice as postulated in the following regression:

$$c_n = \alpha + \beta D_n + \delta \Delta_n + \epsilon_n \qquad (5.1)$$

where c_n is the number correct, α, β , and δ are constants, D_n is a dummy variable which $= 0$ for the EcoStat group and 1 for the NoStat group, Δ_n is the difference in performance, and ϵ_n is the error term that is assumed to be independent and distributed $N(0, \sigma_n^2)$. We tested the hypothesis of normal errors with the Shapiro-Wilf W, Shapiro-Francia W, and the Skewness/Kutosis tests. All three do not reject the hypothesis of normal errors with a significance level of 5%. We tested the hypothesis of homoskedasticity with the Breusch and Pagan (1979)/ Cook-Weisberg test and rejected this hypothesis with a significance level of 5%.

The results using [White (1980)] robust regression that corrects for heteroskedasticity are shown in Table 5.7 on the next page.

Table 5.7 Regression 2. Number correct: Number of obs = 40, F(2,37) = 18.39, and Prob > F < 0.0001.

Var	Coef	Std Err	t val	P > |t|
δ	1.96	0.33	5.90	<0.001
β	-4.5	1.51	-2.98	.005
α	36.23	1.31	27.59	<0.001

As can be seen, all three coefficients are significant. The larger the gap in performance between the two choices, the better the performance of the subjects' formula and intuitive heuristics. On average, the EcoStat group has 4.5 more correct responses than the NoStat group.

Now let us consider the 2 semester problems for which 3 members of the EcoStat group and 2 members of the NoStat group got all four pages correct.. The rule for the first semester is:

if $1/2APD + ([(.9)(.9) + (.1)(.1)]APD - 1/2APD) = 0.82APD > C2 - C1$ check both buy cheaper, else check one and buy there.

The shift point for this rule is 9.76 and if both stores are checked in the first semester, the rule for the second semester is:

if $0.18APD > C2 - C1$, check both, buy cheaper, else check one and buy there.

The shift point for this rule is 44.44. No subject wrote the correct rule for either problem.

The decision that is revealing is the second semester decision for a price difference of $45 and $65. Let us consider the behavior of the 46 EcoStat subjects and 40 NoStat subject that correctly choose to check prices at both stores in the first period. The breakdown of their behavior in the second period is shown in Table 5.8 below.

Table 5.8 Second semester decision for APD of $45 and $65.

Group	1 and 1	2 and 1	1 and 2	2 and 2
EcoStat	25	1	4	16
NoStat	20	1	1	18

where for 1 and 1, ..., and 2 and 2 the first number is the number of stores checked in the $45 case and the second number is the number of stores checked in the $65 case.

The behavior of the various groups is reflected in their written strategies. The 25 EcoStat subjects and the 20 NoStat subjects that chose 1 and 1, either explicitly in their responses or implicitly in their actions, assumed that if they checked prices at both stores in the first period, the store that they had found with the cheaper price would have the cheaper price in the second period with a 90% probability. One EcoStat subject even calculated that the APD would have to be $80 to warrant checking both prices in the second period.

Of the 16 EcoStat and 18 NoStat subjects that chose 2 and 2, the most common strategy of these subjects was the heuristic that the greater the APD relative to $C2$, the greater the incentive to check both. One example is, "As the price difference increases, the risk of losing money increases, yet a 90% probability makes it more difficult to decide whether to check both stores. But as the difference goes farther and farther away from $14 dollars, it becomes more and more convenient to check both stores". Only two EcoStat subjects and one NoStat subject clearly indicated that with only one observation, it was not possible to know with certainly which store was the cheaper 90% of the time.

In conclusion, on average subjects performed statistically better than random selection and statistically worse than optimal selection. The subjects with economic statistics had better performance, but many of this group did not understand Bayes theorem, a topic in their statistics course. The subjects in this experiment were less Bayesian than those of Mahnoud and Grether (1995).

We include some results from one of our prior experiments that had 4 periods. For this experiment the subjects were 25 students from an author's freshman economics class. We offered a flat fee of $10 for participating and as much as $25 more for answering questions correctly. In this experiment we were interested in whether subjects could devise an optimal strategy and paid them if they could.

The parameters and the results for the earlier experiment are shown in Table 5.9 at the top of the next page. If interested, use Firefox to view and perform the experiment at: http://www.eco.utexas.edu/Homepages/ Faculty/Norman/00Ashley/. This experiment has two important results. For all three problems the average number of checks of prices at both stores was less than the optimal number of checks and this difference is significant

Table 5.9   Parameters and results.

	Problem 1	Problem 2	Problem 3	Problem 4
Periods	2	4	4	4
Information	NoP=80	NoP=80	NoP=80	NoP=80
Travel Costs	(5,10)	(5,10)	(5,10)	(5,10)
Anticipated Price Difference	$30	$10	$20	$15
Optimal # to check both	2	1	3	2.32
No. Subjects Correct	6	10	3	2
Avg Checks	1.4	0.88	1.52	1.48
No. Skips	1	7	4	5

for an α of 0.05 for Problems 1, 3 and 4. Also, a subject should check prices at both stores at the beginning with no skips. The row labeled No. Skips indicates the number of times subjects skipped before checking prices at both stores.

From our experiments we conclude that consumers lack the knowledge to compute an optimal strategy in repeated price searches. Can consumers achieve good performance with heuristic computations?

5.3   Buying Textbooks Online

To determine repeated price search performance using heuristics, we investigated student behavior in buying textbooks online. The data for this section comes from three student surveys of online textbook buying behavior and from checking the prices of economics textbooks online. We had 107 students fill in a four-page questionnaire and 51 students fill in a later one-page questionnaire; 34 students filled in both surveys. These students were either attending a meeting of the Texas Economics Association or were enrolled in an upper division economics class. Students were paid $1 per page for their time taking the survey. We also recorded online prices for 23 economics textbooks for 19 days between 28 Dec 07 and 19 Jan 08, collecting 437 data points to determine the lowest prices in the market.

Students at UT buy textbooks each semester. The professor usually defines exactly which books are needed for the class, and students can purchase them from the UT Co-op Bookstore online or at UT Co-op stores near campus. They have the choice of buying a new U.S. edition at the specified price or a used U.S. edition at 75% of the list price regardless of the condition of the used book. Since many students add or drop classes, the UT Co-op Bookstore offers a 12th class day return policy. If students keep the book past the 12th class day, they can sell it back to the Co-op at the end of the semester for half of its current price, regardless of whether the copy was purchased new or used and assuming a professor has requested the book for the next semester. Students buying textbooks at the UT Co-op Bookstore pay 8.25% sales tax, but at the end of the academic year, they have the opportunity to receive a 10% rebate towards future Co-op purchases.

Students can save substantially by buying books online. U.S. editions are frequently cheaper online and for popular textbooks there are less expensive soft-cover foreign editions printed in color on quality paper, and much less expensive soft-cover foreign editions printed in black and white on newspaper quality paper. Also, the price of used textbooks is determined by supply and demand considerations based on the quality of the used book. But, students buying online face a risk that the book will be delivered late, not delivered, or delivered in a condition different than listed.

As was the case of consumers buying books, CDs, or airline travel services, students buying textbooks online checked few sites. In the one-page survey, online textbook buyers were asked: "How many sites did you check before you made your final textbook purchases last semester?" The average of the 51 economic majors was 3.2 sites. To determine what performance they can achieve in checking few sites we must consider market organization, and how students generate and update their search strategy.

5.3.1 *Market Organization*

Most of the online sites that students use to purchase textbooks are what we call "marketplace websites" that list third-party sellers, who describe their offering and set a price. These third party sellers can be students, bookstores, or even other marketplace websites. Unfortunately, there is a risk that the third-party seller will not ship the book on time or will fail to accurately describe the product. To combat this problem, marketplaces provide a rating system of sellers based on comments from previous buyers, but these rating systems vary among marketplace sites and are frequently not comparable. Amazon.com Marketplace, Half.com, Book-Byte.com, and AbeBooks.com are examples of this genre. Meta-search sites such as PriceGrabber.com, CampusBooks.com, Bigwords.com, and Froogle.com search a variety of mid to large sized sellers to provide a list of vendors ordered by price. Meta-search sites specializing in textbooks, such as CampusBooks.com, search much smaller sellers than general meta-search sites, such as PriceGrabber.com.

Now let us consider the prices of economics textbooks online. We recorded the lowest online market prices for 23 of the undergraduate economics course textbooks for 19 days between between 28 December 2007 and 19 January 2008. We considered three editions: U.S., international color, and international black and white. We also considered two levels of risk: cheapest price with no concern for the reliability rating of the seller and cheapest price from a seller with a 95+ rating with at least 30 transactions. For those sites that used a different rating system, we used as close an approximation as possible. For the U.S. books, we also recorded three quality levels of textbooks: (1) new U.S. edition; (2) good quality U.S. edition with no missing pages, highlighting, or writing; and (3) acceptable used book. For the international editions, only prices for new textbooks were recorded.

In order to determine what sites to check, we started with the meta-search sites. Of these, we found CampusBooks.com and Directtextbook.com to be the most useful. From these search engines, we determined which sites would be most useful to check on a daily basis. We checked A1.com, Abebooks.com, Alibris.com, Amazon.com, BN.com, Biblio.com, eBay.com, Express.eBay.com, Half.com, Textbooks.com, Textbooksnow.com, TextbooksRus.com, TextbooksX.com, and Valorebooks.com. We consider the search comprehensive because smaller sellers, who have their own websites, frequently list textbooks at the large marketplaces such as Amazon.com and Half.com.

In Table 5.10 on the top of the next page, we show the frequency at which sellers had the lowest price in each of the three categories and the two risk levels for U.S. published textbooks. Sellers who had the lowest price in less than 5% of the surveys were combined into the "Other" category. If students buying economics textbooks only checked prices at Half.com and Amazon.com and then bought from the cheaper, they would find the lowest price at least 49% of the time. However, the real issue is how close students are to the optimal strategy; if they miss the cheapest book half the time but only pay a cent extra, the difference is negligible. We can estimate how good a strategy is by comparing the students' performances with checking all sites, just Half.com, just Amazon.com, or both Amazon.com and Half.com for the lowest prices. This is shown in Table 5.11 at the top of the next

Table 5.10   Cheapest sites in price survey: % of 437 data points.

Site	New	New R95	Good	Good R95	Fair	Fair R95
Half.com	28	48	30	49	28	49
Amazon.com	35	31	34	30	21	23
AbeBooks.com	5	5	9	7	12	12
Textbooksnow.com	4	5	2	0	9	8
Valore.com	6	0	6	7	6	1
Other	22	11	19	7	24	7

Table 5.11   Performance of Amazon.com and Half.com strategies.

Strategy	New	New 95	Good	Good 95	Fair	Fair 95
Both	1.05	1.03	1.06	1.02	1.08	1.02
Amazon.com	1.12	1.14	1.13	1.12	1.14	1.12
Half.com	1.12	1.06	1.12	1.06	1.13	1.05

page, where performance is measured relative to the cheapest price set to 1. Assuming the students are searching for "Fair" quality textbooks, the table shows that checking both Amazon.com and Half.com would result in a strategy that is at most 8% higher than the lowest price we found. In the cases where students are searching for new textbooks and use a 95+ rating to reduce risk, the increase is no greater than 3%. We then compared these prices with the listed UT Co-op Bookstore prices. In an earlier version of the paper we showed that there is a slight upward trend in price data. Therefore, we show this comparison for three different days in Table 5.12 below. We assume that students buying online would start

Table 5.12   Cheapest prices relative to UT Co-op Bookstore (Percent).

Day	New	New 95	Good	Good 95	Fair	Fair 95
28 Dec	58	64	66	69	65	68
6 Jan	61	66	68	77	66	72
19 Jan	60	67	73	83	72	78

their search by checking the ISBN numbers of their course textbooks and recording the listed prices. These prices would be lower than the online prices 1%, 2%, and 6% of the time in the cases of "New 95," "Fair," and "Fair 95" respectively. However, the buyer could not tell whether the UT Co-op Bookstore actually had the textbook in stock without a phone call or actually visiting the store, an additional labor cost. By the time the semester has started, the UT Co-op Bookstore frequently has run out of some textbooks.

We also checked prices for new international black and white and new international color at two risk levels each. The low cost sites are shown in Table 5.13 below. Again, a strategy just to check prices at Abe.com and

Table 5.13   Cheapest sites for new international editions (Percent).

Site	NIB	(NIB R95)	NIC	(NIC R95)
Abe.com	53	84	28	33
eBay .com	16	14	30	42
TextbooksRUS.com	9	1	21	7
a1.com	22	0	7	0
Valore.com	0	0	4	13
Other	0	0	9	4

eBay.com results in the lowest price 69%, 98%, 58% and 75% of the time for the four categories. In the case of international editions, we did not collect data in order to determine how close the top two would be to optimal.

Given the organization of the online textbook market, students only have to check prices at a small number of sites in order to achieve good performance. Marketplace sites such as Amazon can list several hundred third party sellers of popular textbooks. Amazon encourages competition among these sellers by providing the buyer with a list ordered from lowest to highest price. This list also reduces the computational complexity of finding the lowest price from linear to constant: Instead of making $n-1$ comparisons to find the lowest price in a list of n items, the buyer selects the first item. Buyers frequently want to make a price decision in which they consider the tradeoff between higher seller risk and lower price. With a list ordered by increasing price implementing such a heuristic is straightforward, but not so with an unordered list. As was shown in Chapter 3, humans are capable of implementing a linear algorithm for sorting a small number of items, but the number of alternatives and price data would make the implementation of such an algorithm difficult.

Using a meta-search site a consumer does not have to consider solving the Bayesian optimization problem for the sites searched by the meta-search site. Because these sites do not search continuously, a student can go to a site only to find the low cost book displayed by the meta-search site is no longer available. Nevertheless, they do provide useful data as to which sites are worth checking.

5.3.2 *Search Strategy*

Now we can discuss how students obtain knowledge about their alternatives for purchasing textbooks. Of the 107 students who filled in the four-page questionnaire, we excluded 11 for indicating a major other than economics and 4 for too much missing data. When asked for their information sources, the students responded as shown in Table 5.14 below. In our survey, when

Table 5.14 Data sources for students using many sellers (n=92).

Source	Number	%
Friends/Relatives	73	78
Professors	17	18
Search Engines	54	58
Advertisements	23	24
Other	4	4

asked "From how many people did you obtain advice?" the average response of those that sought advice was 3.5 people. Is this enough to obtain good advice?

Let us consider the sites students would recommend. On page three of the survey participants were given a list of sites and asked which sites (1) they would recommend freshmen check textbook prices, (2) they had checked prices, (3) they had bought textbooks, and (4) they were previously unaware. Their responses are displayed in Tables 5.15, 5.16, and 5.17 on the top of the next page.

Table 5.15　Questions about sites (n=92) meta-search sites.

Source	Recommended this site	Checked this site	Bought from site	Unaware of site
PriceGrabber.com	5	25	1	57
Froogle.com	7	21	1	62
BigWords.com	2	8	3	78
CampusBooks.com	14	36	10	48

Table 5.16　Questions about sites (n=92) marketplace sites.

Source	Recommended	Checked	Bought	Unaware
1: AbeBooks.com	28	40	26	48
2: Alibris.com	7	19	10	66
3: Amazon.com	76	85	75	0
4: B & N Online	15	67	12	8
5: BookByte.com	5	15	7	63
6: eBay.com	46	74	43	1
7: Half.com	62	72	63	8
8: Texbooks.com	8	34	10	44

Table 5.17　Questions about sites (n=92) UT Co-op and campus stores.

Source	Recommended	Checked	Bought	Unaware
1: UT Co-op Online	10	73	32	8
2: Half-Price Books	22	57	28	13
3: UT Co-op Bookstore	13	76	58	0

As can be seen from these tables, students most frequently recommend and buy from Amazon.com. Half.com is second in these two categories. All but one of the students recommended at least one of these two sites, and 63 out of the 92 recommended both. Also, 68% of the 58 students who bought international edition textbooks recommend at least one of the top sites for these textbooks. Therefore, students do not have to talk to many previous buyers to obtain good information concerning relative prices, and this limits their need to search a large number of sites. Also, 57% of these students used at least one of the meta-search sites, which eliminates the need to check prices at listed sites without low prices.

It is important to question how students modified their buying strategy to see if they improve their performance over time. The data shows students have searched for textbooks online from multiple sources an average of 5.01 times with a range from 1 to 12 times. Let us investigate using regression analysis how their behavior changed with the number of times they search for textbooks online. We postulated the following regressions with the assumption that β_2, β_4, and β_5 would be positive and that β_3 would be negative, where sem_n is the number of semesters and summer sessions the

$$ch_n = \alpha_2 + \beta_2 sem_n + \epsilon_{2n} \qquad (5.2)$$

$$unk_n = \alpha_3 + \beta_3 sem_n + \epsilon_{3n} \qquad (5.3)$$

$$buy_n = \alpha_4 + \beta_4 sem_n + \epsilon_{4n} \qquad (5.4)$$

$$rec_n = \alpha_5 + \beta_5 sem_n + \epsilon_{5n} \qquad (5.5)$$

student bought textbooks online, ch_n is the number of sites the students checked over all searches, buy_n is the number of sites from which the student bought over all searches, rec_n is the number of sites the student recommended from the searches, and unk_n is the number of unknown sites after completing the searches. We tested the hypothesis of normal errors for these four regressions with the Shapiro-Wilf W, Shapiro-Francia W, and the Skewness/Kutosis tests. All three test rejected the hypothesis of normal errors with a significance level of 5% for the fourth regression above, but all three tests did not reject the normal hypothesis for any of the other regressions. We tested all four regressions for the hypothesis of homoskedasticity with the Breusch-Pagan/Cook-Weisberg test. The hypothesis of homoskedasticity was not rejected with a significance level of 5%. The F test for the regressions was significant at < 0.01 for regressions (2) - (4) and significant at < 0.103 for the regression (5). The results for the β coefficients are displayed in Table 5.18 on top of the next page.

The signs of β_2, β_4, and β_5 are positive with decreasing significance. These coefficients have small values indicating that these variables change slowly with an increasing number of searches. The sign of β_3 is significantly negative and larger in absolute value than the coefficient β_2. The fact that $\beta_2 - \beta_5$ have small values demonstrates the fact that students start with a good search strategy and make small adjustments with subsequent searches.

Table 5.18   Regression 2: Number checked.

Equation	Coef	Value	Std Err	t val	P > |t|
(2) Number Checked	β_2	0.30	0.10	2.87	.005
(3) Unknown	β_3	-0.42	0.11	-3.8	<0.001
(4) Number Bought	β_4	0.16	0.07	2.38	.02
(5) Number Recommended	β_5	0.13	0.08	1.65	0.102

Students add sites, but they also drop sites. The forty students who filled in both the one-page and four-page questionnaires on average checked prices at 6.6 sites during all their searches and 3.3 sites the last time they checked prices. One student checked the same number in both measures and the rest checked more sites during all their searches. The difference is significant for a significance level of $1.0 \times 10^{-8}\%$. From our questionnaires we found that students would drop sites from future consideration if they had no success at a site. Another reason students drop sites is to reduce future risk of late delivery or of no delivery at all. Of the 92 students, 54 had a book delivered late, and 2 had a book that was never delivered. Of these students, 12 dropped the seller from future consideration. In addition, students limit their search to reduce risk. When asked, 47% of the one-page survey students checked "I prefer to check prices at sites with a large number of buyers and sellers such as Amazon.com or Half.com because they have a well-defined rating system that I use to reduce risk". Also, 47% of these students indicated that they were not looking for new sites because it was not worth the effort or risk.

On page two of the survey, subjects were asked, "For those years you bought books at sites other than the UT Co-op or UT Co-op Online, please estimate to the nearest 10% how much you saved relative to the UT Co-op price (new or used as appropriate)?" Subjects were asked to fill in their percent savings in boxes for "First year", "Second year", "Third year", and "Fourth year". The mean of the 77 observations for students who had bought textbooks online for at least two years was 29.9% for the first year and 34.5% for the second year. The difference is statistically significant for a one-tail test with a significance level of 0.1%, indicating that students believe their performance improves with experience.

Now let us consider how student strategies achieve performance without much calculation. In obtaining advice from experienced online textbook buyers, the knowledge of which sites to search is passed from one generation of textbook buyers to the next. There is no need to be able to compute Bayesian optimization strategies and this is amplified by meta-search sites.

5.4   Conclusion

The Internet market organization has marketplace sites like Amazon.com and meta-search sites like PriceGrabber.com for many products so consumers are able to obtain good performance in a price search for many different types of products checking just a few sites. The marketplace on the Internet is undergoing continual change. Business to consumer sales are growing, and the use of the Internet to do background research about prices and products is growing even faster. The growth of price searching online is indicated by the fact that Experian bought PriceGrabber.com in 2005 for $485 million, see top news December 15, 2005 at Socialtech.com.

Price search is in flux because of new technology such as price search applications such as ShopSavvy and RedLaser on the iPhone and other smart cell phones. The consumer takes a picture of a barcode on a product in a store and the app gives the consumer prices from competing sellers, both online and in local stores. On the Friday after Thanksgiving 612,488 consumers used ShopSavvy to find the best price, see "ShopSavvy iPhone App Black Friday Numbers" posted December 2, 2008 at Geardiary.com. In addition to the efficiencies of an ordered list discussed at the end of section 4.1, these apps can be initiated any time a consumer encounters a product of interest in a store.

In Chapter 2 we stated our proposed research agenda for procedural economists. If a problem is not H tractable, then researchers should ask how do economic agents actually solve the problem and what level of performance do they achieve. In the [Sonnemans (1998)] model, he presented subjects with a drawing from 100 elements. The calculation of a discrete expected value with 100 points is tedious and not something that most unaided humans are capable of doing. In the one period search theory the number of alternatives in the drawing is left unspecified. With a large number the computations are not H tractable.

But, a more basic problems exists. In the experiments in this Chapter the number of calculations was very small. Most subjects made mistakes because they did not how to correctly specify the problem to be solved. We expand our list of problems for which procedural economist should ask how humans actually solve the problem to include any problem involving an expected value.

Measuring performance is not easy because the criteria is frequently subjective. In a price search for textbooks many students are concerned about the risk and make a tradeoff between price and perceived risk. This subjective element of the criteria makes a quantitative measure of performance difficult. We are left with only being able to make a qualitative statement that they achieve "good performance".

Chapter 6

Repeated Item Search: Forecasting

6.1 Introduction

We shall focus on repeated item searches in this and the next chapter. Consumers perform item searches to find various preferred items all their lives. Let us start with a brief overview of an item search, which varies widely, but generally has the following steps:

(1) Start set based on a goal: The subset of all marketplace alternatives chosen to initiate the search

(2) Sets then subsets: A consumer uses set rules to reduce the size of the set

(3) Final set: A consumer evaluates the specific alternatives in this set one by one in order to obtain the preferred item

Each step in the item search is the result of executing one of the rules of the type discussed in Chapter 4. In this chapter we shall focus on consumer forecasting in order to execute a decision rule.

In Section 2 we consider the topics of knowledge, forecasts, and judgments. Then in Section 3 we show how consumers can forecast from personal experience using a sequential trial and error strategy. The less frequent the search or the greater the rate of technological change, the less the value of personal experience in forecasting. In Section 4 we consider such cases where a consumer must collect data from others in order to forecast. We define the information value of data and evaluate Internet data using this concept. Then in Section 5 we show that there is tremendous variation in how consumers forecast in search of a similar product. Finally, we conclude in Section 6.

6.2   Forecasts, Judgments, Knowledge, and Data

Let us now consider an example of buying ripe fruit that illustrates the relationship among preferences, judgments and knowledge. We have asserted several times in this book that preferences are learned. Through past experience in consuming fruit, consumers develop their preferences regarding fruit. But these preferences are for an ideal fruit such as a ripe peach versus a ripe pear. Suppose in the display of fruit in a grocery store, the consumer wants a ripe peach. The consumer would employ a heuristic based on color, softness, and smell to judge the ripeness of the fruit displayed in order to choose. The heuristic is acquired knowledge developed through experience and the advice of others.

The longer a consumer takes to execute a rule in an item search the greater the probability the consumer is making some type of forecast in order to execute the rule. This can happen with frequently purchased goods of variable quality such as fruit. Also, the less frequent the purchase and the greater the rate of technological change the greater the likelihood of forecasts. While consumers can obtain test results of products from consumer union and other organizations that are conducted with good scientific methodology, most of the time they use intuitive heuristics to make forecasts. Decision psychologists call forecasts made using heuristics "judgments".

A consumer makes both objective and subjective forecasts. Let us now consider some examples of objective forecasts. In the early stages of an item search, a consumer must judge what attributes of a product are necessary to accomplish the goal. Let use consider the type of flash to buy on a digital camera. This depends on the intended use of the camera. The internal flash on digital cameras will not illuminate a large room. If the intended use is to take pictures of large dimly lit rooms, the consumer must consider a digital camera with an external flash integrated to the camera with a hot shoe. A less desirable option in terms of performance would be to buy non-integrated slave flash that fires in response to the internal flash. In general, the less consumers know about alternatives they face, the more knowledge they must acquire to make a judgment about the usefulness of the various alternative attributes.

Later in an item search, a consumer performs judgments about the short and long term performance of alternatives. For example, in comparing two cars a consumer might make a judgment about their gas mileage and drivability. For the longer term, a consumer might want to judge their durability and resale value.

A subjective forecast might be a judgment about whether a particular item of clothing being considered for purchase will make a fashion statement with friends and relatives or will coordinate with the wardrobe in the closet at home. Another example here is whether a new piece of furniture will mesh with the current furniture.

There are two basic ways a consumer acquires knowledge and data in order to make judgment forecasts. One is through direct personal experience from prior acts of consumption and testing. From childhood on, a consumer gains knowledge about goods and services. In finding a preferred item a consumer must first make a judgment about what attribute values of a product are essential, desirable, or unimportant. While this consumer knowledge may seem very prosaic, it increases search efficiency. However, under rapid technological change, or first time purchases, a consumer must use data prepared by others. Let us now consider the first of these approaches.

6.3 Sequential Trial and Error, STE Strategy

One approach to judge the short term performance of a product is to test it. In the marketplace, consumers can test some products before purchase. In buying clothes, such as jeans, a consumer can try on a pair to see if it fits. Another example is test driving a car. Frequently a consumer can listen to a music selection prior to purchase. Before buying a personal computer, a consumer can interact with a display model. Modern packaging limits a consumer's ability to test many products. For example, for most consumers how smoothly a pen writes is an important aspect in judging its utility. Encasing pens in plastic containers makes test writing with a pen impossible.

For frequent, low cost purchases, a simple strategy to judge the short term performance of an alternative is through sequential trial and error testing, a STE strategy. With repeat purchases consumers try new alternatives until they have determined a set with the desired performance. In this section we will use students choosing a restaurant for lunch as an example. Here the student wants to find a set of restaurants that serve meals the student likes, at an affordable price and at a reasonable distance from the student's lunchtime location on campus. A consumer will generally have some information to make a prior estimate about the alternatives so only a subset need be tested. Second, the earlier the STE testing takes place the longer the period the consumer can use the knowledge gained. Consumers can use such a strategy for food and many household products bought weekly or monthly. A STE strategy can be used for more than developing preferences over specific final alternatives, it can also be used to develop preferences over intermediate steps in an item search such as stores. The more frequent the purchase, the greater the probability the consumer uses such a strategy.

Let us consider a student STE strategy to find a restaurant. We could formulate this problem as a Bayesian optimization problem, but as students solve such problems with heuristics we shall focus on an empirical study of student behavior. At our university, students usually live in a dorm with a meal plan the first year, and move to rented apartments or houses with no meal plan after the first year. We performed two surveys of undergraduate students shown in Table 6.1 below. In the first survey we included 79

Table 6.1   Lunch surveys.

Date	No. Subjects(Good data)	Financial Reward	No. Restaurants
Jan 07	51(48)	$5	79
Feb 11	43(40)	$7	100

restaurants near campus and in the second survey we updated the list and expanded it to 100 by including restaurants a bit further from campus.

To investigate their STE strategy for selecting on and near campus restaurants we asked the following question:

4. **For Table Below:** Fill in the table below for lunch (not snacks) according to the following instructions.

a. **Regular:** Consider a typical period of 2 workweeks (2 Mon Fri) = 10 days. For restaurants you eat at frequently, write the number of days that you eat at the given restaurant per those 10 days. If you eat there once a workweek, write 2. If less than once every two workweeks, use the Occasional column. **The sum in the Regular column should equal 2 times the number in the last row of Question 2.**

b. **Occasional:** Write an X if you go to that restaurant at least once every other month.

c. **Tried:** For restaurants **that you do not currently go to for lunch,** write the number of times you have tried that restaurant. If zero, leave blank. If you've been many times but can't remember the exact number, write Many. If the restaurant is a chain, then include times you've eaten at another franchise of the same chain.

d. **Aware**: Write an X if you are aware of the restaurant; leave blank if you've never heard of it before.

We display the first four of the 79 restaurants in the questionnaire in Figure 6.1 below.

Restaurants on or near Campus	Regular	Occasional	Tried	Aware
I. Dobie Mall				
The Cream Aisle				
Gyro King				
Oma's Kitchen				
Nikki Pizza and Pasta				

Fig 6.1:   First four restaurants.

The first two questions for the two surveys were:

1. How many semesters have you obtained your lunch without a meal plan?
2. How many times *during the workweek (Monday through Friday)* do you eat the following types of lunch? On campus: Restaurant

The results are displayed in Table 6.2 below. We solicited students who

Table 6.2   Lunch survey response to questions 1 and 2.

Date	No. Subjects(Good data)	Question 1	Question 2
Jan 07	51(48)	2.71	3.43
Feb 11	43(40)	3.43	2.78

were not on a meal plan and dropped a couple of questionnaires from subjects who did not purchase at least one meal a week at an On Campus restaurant. Nevertheless, they were paid.

Their responses are organized by the number of semesters without a meal plan and displayed in Table 6.3 at the top of the next page, where Yr Survey is date of the survey, Sem is the range of semesters without a meal plan, Num is the number of students in the Sem category, Res/wk is the times during the workweek that they eat at a restaurant, and Regular, Occasional, Tried, and Aware are the number of different restaurants satisfying the definitions above. For Regular, Occasional, and Tried the number in the () is the number of restaurants that are local and not part of a chain.

Table 6.3   Restaurant choice: Spring 07 survey: 48 subjects, 79 restaurants (44 local); Spring 11 survey: 40 subjects, 100 restaurants (48 local).

Yr Survey	Sem	Num	Res/wk	Regular	Occasional	Tried	Aware
S07	1 & 2	23	3.5	3.5(0.9)	9.5(2.3)	25.0(7.9)	47.3
S07	3-8	25	3.4	3.4(0.6)	5.9(1.5)	21.9(7.9)	41.2
S11	1-3	18	2.7	3.7(1.1)	10.1(3.0)	26.6(9.9)	53.5
S11	4-9	22	2.8	4.1(0.8)	9.7(2.7)	32.3(11.6)	60.1

One statistic for which the two surveys are identical is that in both the subjects have tried, on average 29% of the listed restaurants.

Let us consider some factors that influence students deciding to try a restaurant. We queried the students in our survey concerning the reasons for first time choice of a restaurant with the following question:

In choosing a restaurant for **lunch during the workweek (M-F)**, what criteria are important to you in trying a restaurant for the first time? They were presented with the following criteria:

(1) Friend's recommendation
(2) Critic's praise (e.g. in a magazine or online)
(3) Busyness/crowdedness when passing by
(4) Menu and ambiance
(5) Group consensus (when passing by)
(6) A past positive experience at another franchise
(7) Proximity to where you are or need to be after you finish eating
(8) Parking availability (if you have a car)

For each criterion they were asked "Yes/No" and "How much so?" (1 for not important, 2 if it matters a bit, 3 if it's very important). The responses are shown in Table 6.4 at the top of the next page. The four most important factors in trying a restaurant are:

(1) Proximity to where you are or need to be after you finish eating
(2) A past positive experience at another franchise
(3) Friend's recommendation
(4) Menu and ambiance

The distance between restaurants near campus can be greater than a mile and most students do not have a car on campus. These four factors explain

Table 6.4 Criteria for trying a restaurant (n = 91).

Criterion	Yes/No		How much so?		
	Yes	No	1	2	3
1. Friend	81	10	15	41	35
2. Critic	31	59	64	18	9
3. Busy	62	29	38	30	23
4. Menu	76	15	19	37	35
5. Group	74	17	23	35	33
6. Positive	79	12	21	29	41
7. Proximity	83	8	11	24	56
8. Parking	62	27	37	30	24

why on average they test less than 30% of the restaurants to find preferred restaurants. The number of restaurants tried varies by a factor greater than 5 among the subjects, from less than 10 to over 50. Two factors that might explain the range are the fact that students have differential amounts of information concerning on or near campus restaurants and that they have differential demands for variety. We did not collect data to investigate the range.

We have asserted that it pays to try alternative restaurants early in order to gain from the acquired knowledge. From this criterion we would not expect to have a significant upward trend in the number of restaurants tried as a function of the semesters without a meal plan. We tested this hypothesis with the following regression:

$$T_n = \alpha + \beta D_n + \delta N_n + \epsilon_n \qquad (6.1)$$

where T_n is the number of restaurants tried, α, β , and δ are constants, D_n is a dummy variable which $= 0$ for the 07 group and $= 1$ for the 11 group, N_n is the number of semester without a meal plan, and ϵ_n is the error term that is assumed to be independent and distributed $N(0, \sigma_n^2)$. We tested the hypothesis of normal errors with the Shapiro-Wilk W, Shapiro-Francia W, and the Skewness/Kutosis tests. All three do not reject the hypothesis of normal errors with a significance level of 18%. We tested the hypothesis of homoskedasticity with the Breusch and Pagan (1979)/ Cook-Weisberg test and rejected this hypothesis with a significance level of 4%.

The results using [White (1980)] robust regression that corrects for heteroskedasticity are shown in Table 6.5 below. As can be seen there is no

Table 6.5   Regression (6.1) Number tried: Number of obs = 88, F(2,85) = 3.36, and Prob > F < 0.04

Var	Coef	Std Err	t val	P > |t|
β	6.0	2.5	2.4	<0.02
δ	0.3	0.7	0.4	0.7
α	22.63	2.4	9.5	<0.001

significant upward trend in the number of restaurants tried with respect to the number of semesters without a meal plan. This supports the notion of efficiency that students should test alternative restaurants early to take advantage of the knowledge gained. The coefficient of 6 for the dummy variable reflects the fact that the 11 group survey had 21 more restaurants than the 07 survey.

Consumers do not use such a strategy once, but any time their circumstances change. Consider a beer drinker who started drinking inexpensive beers in college and through a STE strategy developed his preferences over them. After college he obtains a job and now has an income to upgrade his lifestyle. He might well use a STE strategy to determine his preferences over upscale beers. If a consumer relocates to a different city he made employ an STE strategy for many alternatives such as restaurants.

6.4   Forecasting with Data Provided by Others

Testing products usually provides information about their short term performance. For example, an STE strategy to test alternative restaurant meals does not provide information about the long term health affects. A test drive of a car does not provide data about its long term durability or resale value. Many forecasts require knowledge beyond what can be obtained either by testing or an STE strategy.

As a result, consumers make many of their judgments by acquiring knowledge and processing data provided by others. We shall use a very broad definition of data in this section and the rest of the book. In physical space, data includes conversations about products with friends, relatives, and sales people, magazine articles and ads, and newspaper articles and ads. In cyberspace it is any material provided by a site concerning products whether reviews, ads, blogs, or videos. In short, it is any material provided by others that a consumers could use to increase their knowledge and make forecasts.

Let us now examine data sources.

6.4.1 *Sources of Data*

The amount and type of data available to a consumer depends on the format and the data provider. We shall divide format into four categories:

1. Person to person interaction
2. Print: Newspapers, magazines, and books
3. Television
4. Internet.

We shall also divide data providers into four categories:

1. Second parties: manufacturers and sellers
2. Third parties: Individuals and private organizations that provide data, but do not directly sell products
3. Social media sites such as Facebook, Twitter, and blogs
4. Government: Data provided by government agencies or required by government acts.

Let us start by considering the category of person to person interaction. A consumer can obtain data from a sales person or a friend, acquaintance, or relative. In most cases the sales person would be a second party and the others third parties. The type and amount of data a consumer can obtain through human interaction depends on the training and experiences of the other person.

Next, we consider data available in the print category and start with second party providers. On products in stores, manufacturers generally provide a specification sheet listing the attribute values of the product. For some products like automobiles, they also provide a brochure describing the product and options. In newspaper classified ads sellers provide consumers with data briefly describing items available for sale. Manufacturers and sellers also buy print ads with pictures and generally a sales pitch.

Because millions of consumers search for similar goods, there are tremendous economies of scale for third parties to provide consumers with better data and the knowledge to interpret that data. One of the first third party organizations to provide consumer data covering a wide range of goods and services was Consumer Union, which initiated the publication of Consumer Reports magazine in 1936. For decades, entrepreneurs have created much more specialized "how to" books and trade magazines, providing reviews of technological products such as automobiles and electronic devices. Two such digital camera trade magazines are Popular Photography and Digital Camera World.

Television is a media that offers second parties the opportunity to create dynamic ads for consumers, but at a high cost. Given the high cost of producing TV content there is not much third party data provided on television. One example is Dr Oz, which offers data on medical conditions and maintaining good health through a proper diet.

The development of the interactive Internet, which provides a low cost opportunity to provide data in a multimedia format, has dramatically increased the amount of data available to consumers. Manufacturers provide consumers with much more data on their websites than they did in print or TV. For example, an auto manufacturer can post a video that enables a potential consumer to view the interior of a car. An industry that has greatly increased the information to consumers is the real estate industry. A consumer interested in buying a home can view many pictures of each property for sale, and increasingly, take a video tour.

The interactive nature of the Internet has enabled second and third party data providers to offer a new type of data not previously available in print or TV, the anonymous user review. The user rates the product on a five point scale from 1 to 5 with 5 being the highest rating and the site averages the users reviews. In many cases where the user provides a text evaluation of the product the viewer can read the text review from each user evaluator. Sellers such as Amazon.com provide consumers with user review data plus price search data through their marketplaces.

The Internet has created a major increase in the number and types of third party providers of data to consumers. Trade magazines that provide consumers product reviews, with few exceptions, have a Web site where consumers can find the reviews online. One example here is Consumer Reports Online. One type of site previously mentioned in Chapter 5 is the price search site, such as PriceGrabber.com. These sites, besides the prices of alternative sellers, frequently provide user reviews on both the reliability of the seller and the quality of the product. Sites that rely heavily on user reviews to provide data to viewers are travel, restaurant, and local service sites. Examples are TripAdvisor.com, which provides travel including restaurant data, Yelp.com, which provides reviews of restaurants and local services, and AngiesList.com, which focuses on local services such as plumbers and dentists.

With the rise of the Internet, entrepreneurs have created numerous review sites that provide consumers with comprehensive decision support for technology products, especially in electronics and automobiles. Let us consider sites that provide data on digital cameras, such as CNET.com, Consumerreports.org, Megapixel.net, DCResource.com, DPReview.com, Imaging-resources.com, and Steves-digicams.com. Such websites provide some or all of: (1) digital camera buying guides, (2) tables of camera attributes, (3) glossaries of terms, (4) camera reviews by professionals and users, (5) files of customer experiences with the cameras, and (6) galleries of pictures taken using the reviewed cameras. Items (1)-(3) are useful in step 2, the early stages of a search and (4)-(6) in step 3, the final step of a search. If, after reading the reviews, a consumer has made his choice and wishes to buy his choice, he can click on a link to Amazon.com marketplace, Pricegrabber.com or choose among a list of sellers.

The review site obtains revenue from the site where the consumer goes to buy the product. Successful sites can also obtain revenue by attracting advertisers. The rapid technological advance has increased the need for third party data. The low cost of internet sites, and opportunities to generate revenue have fueled the growth of third party review sites.

Entrepreneurs have created a new category of interactive sites on the Internet collectively called social media. The best known of these sites is Facebook.com. Facebook provides user reviews of products such as phone apps. Corporations and other organizations have pages on Facebook that provide consumers with information. Facebook offers users a new type of data. At various sites Facebook has a button with a thumbs up image. If a user clicks on the Facebook thumbs up button on a page in Facebook this data is communicated to friends of the user when they visit that page on Facebook.

Twitter is a communication site based on messages not exceeding 160 character . A firm can provide potential customers information such as the location of sandwich and fast food trucks. A firm can also use Twitter to provide short messages announcing the availability of products. Another social media site that has consumer information is YouTube.com, which displays videos created and uploaded by the individuals, firms, and other organizations. Videos include reviews of many products and demonstrations created by corporations.

Another category of social media sites that provide consumer information are blogs that review products. "Mommy blogs" review products of interest to mothers with young children such as toys. There are blogs on budgeting, automobiles, digital cameras and numerous other topics.

We will now discuss data provided by government, which, with the development of the Internet, is increasingly available online. Government required disclosure policies for sellers provide consumers with data. Let us start with the federal government and the Security and Exchange Commission that sets the requirements for public firm and mutual fund public disclosures. Publicly traded firms must file reports, which are public information, about their operations, management, financial condition, and contracts or lease agreements. The SEC also requires mutual funds to provide potential investors a prospectus with information to make an informed investment decision. The federal government performs safety tests and requires manufacturers to perform fuel efficiency tests on new cars, and this information is available at government websites and is displayed on the new car window sticker. There are extensive disclosure requirements for packaged food concerning calorie values and ingredients in the package. Recently the Obama administration made calorie information a required disclosure for restaurant meals. There are other safety required disclosures such as the component of a pesticide and a health warning for cigars and cigarettes. Required disclosures for a seller of real estate are covered by state law and vary widely among the states. States also have varying disclosure requirements for used cars.

One trend in online sites that needs discussion is the combining of data from various sources. For example, the real estate site Tulia.com provides both a list of public schools and their respective ratings that children who lived in a listed property would attend. Edmunds.com, a site that provides data about cars and pickups, includes gas mileage and safety data created by the government and the safety data created by the insurance industry car safety testing organization.

Currently most sites providing data to consumers are specialized. A notable exception, ConsumerReports.org provides consumer data over a wide range of goods and services, but only evaluates a subset of each market and frequently not every year. Most sites are much more specialized. Edmunds.com only provides data related to buying a car or pickup and DCResource.com only provides data about digital cameras. The consumer has a large number of specialized sites from which to gather data.

6.4.2 *The Information Value of Data*

The question is how much data should a consumer collect and process in order to be efficient. We shall use digital cameras to illustrate our qualitative analysis of this issue. In the case of digital cameras and other products undergoing rapid technological change, we consider the concept of perfect information questionable because acquiring and processing data is a costly activity. We will propose an alternative concept, the information value of data. This subsection is a minor revision of material in [Norman *et al.* (2008)].

6.4.2.1 *Processing cost*

The first factor limiting consumer data processing is cost. Even without acquisition fees, getting and processing data requires resources. Finding alternatives' specifications, for example, can require examining several brochures or visiting several Internet sites. In addition, if the consumer is faced with new technology or previously unknown choices, he may have to learn how to interpret the data. Consequently, the cost of data to the consumer should include not only the time and resources spent on acquiring the data, but also the cost of learning how to interpret the data, and the resources spent on interpretation.

Nevertheless, even with the aid of computers, more data, even if free, is not necessarily better than less data. Consider how much data could possibly be provided to a consumer in order to evaluate digital cameras. While a consumer has a limited ability to take pictures with a camera before purchase, in some cases a consumer could borrow a camera owned by a friend or look at pictures in the LCD screen of a demo in a digital camera store. A consumer could go to the manufacturer's site to examine the product description and the user's manual. A consumer could read all the reviews in magazines and at digital camera sites to see the results of the each reviewer's tests, which differ among reviewers.

This is still only a fraction of the data that could be supplied to the consumer. The potential buyer could be supplied with the detailed specifications of every component of the digital camera, the production details, the research and development reports, and the details of all the testing programs. The consumer could even be supplied with electron microscope pictures of the structure of the sensor. A data file describing the position of molecules on the sensor surface could be obtained. Indeed, the limit of data that could possibly be supplied to a consumer is only set by the Heisenberg uncertainty principle.

More data is not necessarily better than less: such a massive data set would be prohibitively expensive to obtain and would overwhelm the consumer's processing capabilities. Indeed, it might well intimidate consumers into making poor decisions. Although a computer-aided consumer can inexpensively process a great deal more data than a consumer without a computer, the amount of data that could be tractably processed is still **minuscule** in comparison to the potential limit. Indeed, given the cost of processing data, a consumer frequently processes a small fraction of the data available, such as reading only a small fraction of the product reviews available online.

6.4.2.2   *Capacity to discriminate*

Another important attribute of data is its capacity to help the consumer discriminate among alternatives' probable performance. [Akerlof (1970)] was the first to raise this issue in his discussion of the used car market, where buyers were unable to judge the reliability of a used car. [Spence (1973)] expanded the discussion by highlighting the market incentives of the market participant to provide signals to allow the other party to make a judgment of future performance. A good signal discriminates effectively with low processing cost. In the case of used cars, auto dealers have developed a certification program where used vehicles pass inspections and are backed by warranties. Some of the signals provided by manufacturers include a list of product specifications, such as a list including a digital camera's number of megapixels and size. Third parties also provide market signals. For example, Imaging-resource.com tests the focus time and shutter lag of a digital camera, and DPReview.com makes detailed picture noise measures for DSLR cameras.

In products undergoing rapid technological change, a consumer frequently lacks the knowledge to know which product attributes are needed for the intended product use. To better discriminate he needs knowledge to understand the functions of the attributes. For example, in the case of a digital camera, what is the function of an autofocus assist light and under what conditions in photo shooting is it really useful? Part of the data the consumers obtain from friends, salespersons, magazine articles, and online sites is knowledge to better understand what camera attributes are needed to take the desired type of pictures. Thus data can have information value if it enables the consumer to discriminate between the subset of alternatives to consider in greater detail, and its complement, not to consider further.

Once the consumer has found a small set of of digital cameras with the attributes needed for the intended use, he then needs to judge the performance of the cameras within this set. For this purpose, a consumer might use the brand such as Canon as a signal. This signal is not a perfect discriminator because not all Canon cameras are winners. To obtain a better discriminator the consumer might also read several reviews to judge performance or examine the picture and video galleries taken by a particular camera. There is frequently a tradeoff between the processing cost and the discrimination power of data. Data in comparing alternatives can discriminate if it enables the consumer to judge which alternative has the best performance in achieving the search goal.

6.4.2.3 *Reliability*

The final factor considered in the data's information value is its source's reliability. We shall consider two aspects of reliability. The first is whether the consumer considers the source trustworthy to provide unbiased data. In the next section we shall discuss the relationship between incentives and data bias. Even if a reviewer of a product has no incentive towards providing the consumer biased data, the question remains whether the reviewer is competent to provide an accurate assessment of a good or service. Consumers must make judgments concerning the reliability of alternative data sources in terms of trust and competence.

6.4.2.4 *Information value definition*

We will define the data a consumer obtains from a source as a *representation* of the good or service. The representations a consumer processes to select a preferred item will be called the *framing* of the item search. A representation contains a minuscule fraction of the data that could be included. For Internet representations and media ads this should be obvious. But, it is also true of a consumer's sensory interaction with a product or a recall representation of a prior act of consumption.

The *information value of data* is positively related to its reliability and ability to discriminate among alternatives and inversely related to its processing cost. The information value of data depends on what step the consumer is performing in an item search.

6.4.3   *Information Value Comparisons*

In order to improve their performance, consumers have an economic incentive to improve their forecasting skill through repeated searches. He learns which data has high information value for various types of item searches. In other words, through communication with friends and others, a STE strategy, and learning by doing, a consumer learns where to find reliable data that discriminates at a reasonable cost. In this section we qualitatively consider the information value of alternative data formats and data providers.

First let us consider the relative information value of the same data in cyberspace versus physical space. By the term *cyberspace* we mean the Internet. We shall define *physical space* to include print, TV, phone, and travel to the sellers's location. One example would by the magazine Consumer Reports versus Consumer Reports Online. Another would be conducting a price search at a price search site versus going from store to store or even phoning the various stores.

(1) **Travel**: It is cheaper to go from site to site in cyberspace than store to store in physical space.

(2) **Evaluation**: It is easier to find material on the Internet than it is in physical space. A good example of this is using a search tool at Consumer Reports online versus looking through published Consumer Report magazines to find a study about a product category.

(3) **Tools**: Cyberspace also dominates physical space in the provision of tools to consumers. Let us consider tables in physical space versus cyberspace. Magazine review articles frequently include tables with a side-by-side comparison of the discussed products attributes, but these tables are fixed. Websites can create personalized attribute tables of only those products that interest the visitor. These tables can also include links to reviews and current prices. Creating something nearly as useful in physical space would require acquiring and lining up the relevant tables in manufacturers' brochures, which lack a common format. Such cyberspace tools facilitate comparisons and discrimination.

(4) **Price**: It is much easier to perform a price search in cyberspace than in physical space. If a consumer knows what she wants to buy, she can input the product name into a search engine like Froogle.com, Price-Grabber.com, or Dealtime.com or scan the bar code with an app on her cell phone. This will return a price distribution of the product prices

through linked merchants. With a click, prices of the product including shipping costs can be ordered from lowest to highest. However, in both cyberspace and physical space, a deal can be "too good to be true." For example, in the case of digital cameras, a "too good to be true" price can mean the seller takes the camera out of the box and tries to sell the package components as extras. In cyberspace the customer has a readily available means of measuring the risk, an estimate, which is frequently given as a number of stars and testimony of previous customers, of the seller's reliability. Thus, a consumer can judge whether a low price is a legitimate offer. Obtaining such information in physical space from a large number of sellers would be prohibitively expensive because of travel costs or time delays in reaching a salesperson by phone and the lack of a readily available seller evaluation procedure.

(5) **Internet cheaper than print**: Because it is cheaper to present data on an internet page to thousands of viewers than provide the same material on print, data providers provide much more data on the Internet than in print. A good example here is classified ads on the Internet versus a newspaper. Apartment ads in print rarely provide photographs and detailed data, but this is commonplace on classified ads in Craigslist or online newspaper classified ads.

(6) **Video data**: While a video TV ad may have better resolution than a YouTube video, a consumer can obtain the YouTube video on demand, which is not the case for broadcast TV. In this sense, the same data on a YouTube video has higher information value than on a TV broadcast.

Now let use consider the comparison from the perspective of computational complexity. As we have asserted for an unaided human System 2 processor sublinear algorithms are tractable. For the server attached to a URL polynomial algorithms are tractable. Thus sites in cyberspace provide a polynomial assist to search in physical space.

Next let us consider the reliability attribute of information value. Consumers place their highest trust in the opinions of their friends; see [Nielsen (2012)]. Friendship creates an incentive to honestly reveal opinions. But, a consumer must also make a judgement concerning the competency of their friends opinions.

Consumers need to judge the reliability of online user reviews. In a [Nielsen (2012)] study, researchers surveying 26,000 Internet respondents worldwide found 70% considered user reviews trustworthy. User reviews do affect a business's profitability. As shown in [Luca (2011)], an extra star in a

Yelp summary of reviews for a restaurant can increase revenue by more the 5%. Hence, businesses have an incentive to manipulate these user reviews to increase their profits.

As discussed in [Fisman (2012)], should you trust these reviews? One example of manipulation of reviews was displayed when Amazon's Canadian site accidentally revealed that many book reviews could be attributed to the publishers or even the authors themselves. [Parsa (2009)] provides a second example of a Belkin development rep trying to hire people to write fake positive reviews. How common is such manipulation? [Kornish (2009)] found that while manipulation is not the dominant mode of behavior, it was prevalent in Amazon and iTunes data studied, but not in the Vanno data.

The reliability of third party sites depends on how the site gets paid for its services. ConsumerReports.org charges the viewer a flat annual fee to access the site and collects fees when the viewer is passed through to PriceGrabber.com to find a seller. Consumer Union buys all products they review. However, in most cases the third party site obtains the products to review free from the manufacturer. Most review sites collect fees in passing viewers through to sellers. They also make money through advertising and sponsorships. A review site gains a following by providing accurate, useful data. The bigger the following, the greater the pass through fees. Attracting a large following creates a strong incentive to maintain reliability.

Consumers also need to consider the reliability of ads placed by second parties in print or TV. [Nielsen (2012)] indicates that less than one half the respondents trust ads and their trust has declined since 2009. The profit incentive of second parties is to provide the data about the product in which it is superior to its competitors in order to sell the product. For example, Casio in promoting one of their cameras emphasized that the user could time date photographs in 160 cities around the world. For most consumers, while this is a neat trick, it is not as important as picture quality. In some cases ads misrepresent the product. For example, the UK Advertising Standards Authority deemed makeup ads using Julia Roberts and Christy Turlington had been airbrushed to the extent that they were misleading; see [Hazlett (2011)]. Second parties have no incentive to provide data that enables the consumer to reliably compare the product in the ad with alternatives.

In addition, consumers need to make a judgment concerning the capacity to discriminate between TV ads provided by second parties versus reviews provided by third party review sites. The typical ad shows how the product can solve a problem that the consumer is having. For example a drug that can prevent heart burn. A drug that prevents heart burn provides the consumer with knowledge that there is a solution to the problem, but not knowledge as to which alternative drug is the best solution. Ads rarely provide any data to accurately discriminate among alternatives. Instead, to sell the product they attempt to create a positive psychological feeling, called an affect in Slovic, Finucane, Peters and MacGregor (2006b), concerning the product. We will discuss the affect heuristic in greater detail in Chapter 9.

Facebook's business strategy of turning "likes" into ads is not without its defects, as shown in [Sengupta (2012b)]. Nick Bergus, when he found a 55 gallon drum of personal lubricant on Amazon.com posted a satirical comment on Facebook, "For Valentines day, And every day. For the rest of your life". Within days he found out that Facebook turned his comment into an ad paid by Amazon posted on Facebook pages. The ad contained his picture.

Third party review sites have a common format for reviews so that the consumer can easily compare the alternatives in the final set being considered. To attract a following the reviewer must consider factors important to the readers. Sites have alternative approaches to ranking alternatives. CNET.com uses a 1-5 scale so the viewer can compare the rating of the professional CNET reviewer with the average of user reviews. ConsumerReports.org ranks the alternatives on a 1-100 scale and has a special recommendation for products that have high quality at a reasonable price. Thus, third party reviews at sites with a large following have much greater capacity to discriminate than TV or Internet ads.

As pointed out, there are tremendous economies of scale in providing data for consumers· searching for products. Because it is much cheaper to provide such data through an Internet site than through a magazine published on paper, the growth in new data sources is primarily on the Internet. It is becoming much easier to find data with higher information value on the Internet than in physical space. It is common knowledge that consumers buying cars and other technological items are doing more of their background research on the Internet. This is a reflection of the growth of higher information value sources on the Internet. To what extent will technological advances enable consumers to obtain data with even higher information value in the future is a topic of Chapter 10.

6.5   Search Variation Across Consumers

Do consumers use the same judgment procedures? One case where they do is buying clothes. To judge whether clothes will fit, consumers generally try them on. This is more true for women than men because manufacturers of women's clothes in the US do not have a common standard for sizes. Each is unique. We shall consider the item search strategy for buying jeans in the next chapter. In this section we shall consider how students forecast performance in buying digital cameras. This material is from [Norman *et al.* (2008)].

How do students evaluate a digital camera? In order to construct a useful survey, we first interviewed 20 students. We then surveyed 27 students in 2003 and 40 students in 2006. Of the last group, 23 students were given a follow-up survey. Interviewed students were paid $10 for the interview. Surveyed students were paid $5 each and those that participated in the continuation survey, an additional $3. We shall focus on the last two surveys.

Subjects were given a list of possible data sources. For each source, subjects were asked whether they used it and if so, how useful it was where the response "not useful" was recorded as 1, the response "useful" as 2 and the response "very useful" as 3. The results are displayed in Table 6.6 below, where (a) on the questionnaire "Online Site" was "Online Site such

Table 6.6   Data sources and their usefulness.

Source	Type	Fraction	Usefulness
People	Friend or Relative	0.73	2.21
People	Sales clerk	0.6	2.30
Website	Manufacturer's Website	0.5	2.14
Text	Photography or PC magazine	0.28	2.5
Text (Website)	Consumer Reports	0.35	2.23
Website	CNET	0.25	2.44
Website	Online Site (See a below)	0.48	2.53

as DCResource.com, DPReview.com, Imaging-Resource.com, and Steves-digicam.com. "Fraction" is the fraction of the 40 subjects who used the indicated data factor. In addition, the fraction of subjects that used either a friend or sales clerk was 0.9 and the fraction that used at least one of the Text or Website sources was 0.75.

Let us consider how the three data properties of processing cost, discrimination, and reliability affected the subjects' search. Let us start with reliability. The subjects used an average of 4.2 sources suggesting the need to double-check the data from any one source and that using multiple data sources expanded the data coverage of digital cameras. Also, subjects found the data from 3rd party sites to be more useful than 2nd party sites. For example, the mean of Online Site, which is 2.53, is more than 3.5 standard deviations greater than the mean of Manufacturers Website, which is 2.14. We interpret the results to imply that the digital camera review sites presented data with the highest information value.

Now let us consider processing cost. Students searched an average of 9.8 hours over an average of 1.2 months to buy their camera. Search time ranged from 2 to 60 hours. DCResource.com has over 60 camera reviews of 15 pages or more. If the subject read these reviews at 20 pages an hour he would take 45 hours to finish. However, there are 6 sites with reviews and numerous articles and reviews in magazines and books. Even the subject who searched for 60 hours processed only a small fraction of the available data, which is a minuscule fraction of what could be provided.

To reduce their processing costs, subjects generally select a small set of cameras using the criteria listed below, and then evaluate this small set much more carefully. Consumer search procedures vary widely in buying digital cameras. In the second survey when asked:

> How many cameras did you evaluate closely? *(For example, evaluating closely might mean you examined the camera physically, read a review, took or looked at pictures — several minutes in each activity).*

One subject responded with "1"; twenty-five subjects responded with "2 or 3"; thirteen subjects responded with "4 to 6"; and, one subject responded with "more than 6."

Now let us consider the property of discrimination. In the market there are currently over 150 new digital camera models. How did consumers reduce this number to the number they listed above? In the continuation survey, subjects were asked to rank the following attributes in the order that they applied them to their decision:

(1) Size (Tiny, Small, Large)
(2) Type (Point and click, small with manual controls, Telephoto, prosumer, DSLR)

(3) Megapixel (2, 3, 4, 5 and so on)
(4) Brand (Canon, Nikon, Sony and so on)
(5) Special feature (Optical zoom, autofocus assist light, great video. Any special feature that camera must have such as external flash)
(6) Budget (Price must be less than budget)
(7) Style (Must be a fashion statement)

The ranking is shown in the Table 6.7 below. Importance and order are the

Table 6.7　Factors: Importance and order.

Factor	Size	Type	Megapixel	Brand	Special Feature	Budget	Style
Importance	1	6	2	4	5	3	7
Order	1	5	2	4	6	3	7

ordinal rankings of the averages. The inconsistencies can be attributed to allowing the subjects to list factors as ties. The top four factors were size, megapixel, budget, and brand.

There are a variety of ways students chose the small set that they closely evaluated. What is important to note is that specifying a size, megapixels, budget, and brand can define a small set. For example, a tiny Canon with 4 or 5 megapixels costing less than $350 gives you a small set.

The response to the question on the next page below the tables is shown in Table 6.8 below.

How did you judge the quality of the digital camera you purchased?

Table 6.8　Factors to determine the camera quality.

Factor	Fraction	Usefulness
Most megapixels for budget implies quality	0.85	2.21
Took the quality advice of a roommate, friend or relative	0.53	2.14
Took the quality advice of a sales person	0.52	2.29
Choose a particular brand based on reputation	0.8	2.38
Read review(s) of particular cameras	0.63	2.6
Judged quality of pictures via the LCD viewfinder pictures	0.4	2.1
Examined galleries of pictures	0.38	2.47

Fraction and Usefulness are defined in the same way as in the first table in this section. In order to interpret the table it is first noted that on average the subjects used 4.7 factors to judge the quality of their cameras. The most useful factor was magazine or online reviews with a mean of 2.6. Consider the nonzero responses of the subjects. If we consider pairwise the difference between the mean usefulness of reviews with the mean usefulness of the other factors divided by the largest standard deviation of the two, the usefulness of the reviews is more than 3 standard deviations better than most megapixels, advice of friend, and LCD monitor. It is more than 2.5 standard deviations better than advice of a sales person and more than 1.9 standard deviations better than brand.

For some product forecasts such as the fit of clothes, there is a standard way to judge the fit: either remember the size that fits or try on the clothes. For new technology there are a wide variety of ways to judge performance. Again, consider judging the performance of a digital camera. There are quick ways to make such a judgment by looking at summary tables of digital camera experts or asking the opinion of someone knowledgable about them. On the other hand, the consumer could spend a great deal of time carefully reading reviews and examining sample photos in galleries. Because there are numerous ways to judge the performance of a digital camera, from research on the Internet to talking with friends or sales person, there is little convergence in item search strategies for a digital camera. There is also unlikely to be any convergence in item searches where there are a large number of alternative procedures for judging performance.

If we were doing this survey today we would also question how much students used social media online to find data.

6.6 Conclusions

With the increase in the rate of technological change and the constant introduction of products that have new features or are entirely new, consumers must spend considerable resources to obtain data to evaluate the alternatives. Given the economies of scale in providing such data and the ability to obtain a return on their efforts, entrepreneurs have created many third party sites on the Internet to provide such data. In Chapter 10 we shall consider future developments in providing data useful to consumers.

Chapter 7

Repeated Item Search: Choice

7.1 Introduction

Consumers make item searches all their lives. Given the opportunity cost of an item search, they have an incentive to improve their search strategy performance over time. To be efficient they must develop different search strategies for different types of goods and services because of variations in the frequency of search, rate of technological change, and market organization. As was pointed out in the previous Chapter, variations in these factors determine the extent to which the consumer can rely on past experience versus collecting and analyzing data provided by others.

Consumers learn their search strategies through a sequential trial and error, STE, strategy and through input from others such as friends, relatives and experts. In this Chapter we focus on how consumers achieve efficiency in repeated item searches and in Chapter 9 we focus on how close consumers come to finding a preferred item.

We will argue that what makes consumers efficient in developing appropriate strategies for various types of item searches is the accumulation of a large body of knowledge concerning market organization and alternative products. As most of this knowledge is very prosaic, we shall call it consumer knowledge and resist the temptation to call it consumer capital. One common property of this knowledge is that it is useful in future searches.

We have assumed that preferences are learned and not obtained at conception. It is efficient for consumers to learn preferences over those aspects of searches that are repeated. We shall call this type of consumer knowledge search preferences. Examples here would be to develop preferences over which stores to search and over product attributes, such as color to reduce the number of alternatives to consider. To what extent is it efficient to learn preferences over specific market alternatives is a special case.

We start by repeating the brief overview of an item search, which generally has the following steps:

1. Start set based on a goal: The subset of all marketplace alternatives chosen to initiate the search
2. Sets then subsets: A consumer uses set rules to reduce the size of the set to be processed
3. Final set: A consumer evaluates the specific alternatives in this set one by one in order to obtain the preferred item

In our formulation an item search can be represented as a decision tree with the property that as the consumer proceeds, the number of specific alternatives at each step progressively decreases. Such an item search has been called a funnel search.

There are circumstances in which a consumer may reorganize the search resulting in an increase in the number of specific items under consideration. The less a consumer knows about the alternatives in the item search the more data he must acquire at each stage to make a decision. Under some circumstances he may find data at a stage of the search that when evaluated causes him to reorganize the search.

In the next two sections we consider how a consumer performs each step and how the consumer obtains efficiency in each step. In Section 2 we consider in detail Steps 1 and 2 involving sets. Generally, the more frequent the item search, the smaller the number of elements of the start set and the fewer type 2 steps before step 3. We show how learning search preferences increases set decision efficiency. In Section 3 we discuss Step 3: Finding a preferred item from the final set. We consider the conditions under which it is efficient to learn preferences over specific alternatives. There is tremendous variation among different types of item searches that a consumer performs. Also, there is tremendous variation in item searches among consumers for a similar type of item.

In Section 4 we analyze our survey of students buying jeans. The greatest gains in efficiency are realized in learning search preferences. We conclude in Section 5 by summarizing how the accumulation of consumer knowledge leads to search efficiency.

7.2 Steps: Sets

We shall consider two types of sets. The first type is a category or subcategory of goods in the marketplace, such as laser printers that the consumer might research on the Internet. A second type of set is a store set that is the goods in a category or subcategory carried by a particular store, such as the laser printers carried by a local electronics store. In this case the example of the second type is a subset of the first type. A start set is the set over which the consumer initiates an item search and it could be of either type.

Generally, a consumer starts an item search with several set steps before shifting to considering the specific alternatives of the final set. Let us consider an example of the efficiencies and issues of set steps. Automobile dealers in Austin, TX, have over 8000 new cars on display in their lots. A discriminating test of a car is a test drive, but if a test drive took on average 30 minutes, this would take 4000 hours or 500 days at 8 hours a day. If a consumers selects Chevrolet, Ford, Honda and Toyota, he has reduced the number of 8 hour days to test drive about 5400 days to 337 days.

If the consumer decides he wants a smaller fuel efficient car such as a Cruze, Fiesta, Civic, or Corolla he has reduced the number of 8 hour test drive days from about 670 cars to 42, a reduction by a factor greater than 10. As the consumer has the knowledge to realize that he only has to test drive one example of each model he has reduced the possible test drives from 8000 to 4, a reduction by a factor of over 1000. While the idea of even test driving every car on the lot may seem ridiculous, it illustrates a point. Set choices are useful to greatly reduce the effort expended in conducting time consuming tests. And as we shall see, this requires consumer knowledge.

7.2.1 *Start Set*

An item search starts with a goal. In the standard microeconomic consumer utility optimization problem, the consumer selects a bundle of goods from all goods in the economy. The goal is to maximize utility subject to the budget constraint. There is no search and no need to define a search goal. When one considers an item search, one needs to consider the search relative to a goal to distinguish among the various types of searches a consumer makes. The amount of effort a consumer expends in defining a goal varies greatly among different types of item searches.

Frequently in repeat purchases this occurs when the previous purchase or purchases has been consumed. A common example would be to initiate a grocery shopping trip when food supplies run low. Another example would be that when a product breaks down and is not worth repairing, a consumer starts an item search with the goal of replacing the broken item. Also, goals can be created when a consumer decides to upgrade a product, such as buying a new high definition TV. A consumer might deliberate such a decision several months with incidental learning before starting an active search. At the other extreme, a consumer might see an attractive display in a grocery store and place the item in his cart with very little System 2 deliberation.

Given a goal, a consumer starts a search with a set of alternatives to consider. To provide a reference point we assert that at birth a consumer faces all goods and services for a start set. From childhood on, a consumer begins narrowing the start set by learning which types of good satisfy which needs and search preferences over the attributes of these goods. The boundary between a fixed requirement to achieve a goal and these search preferences is fuzzy.

For most item searches, the start set is much smaller than the set of goods and services that could possibly satisfy a particular need. Let us consider a household buying a family car that can transport 2 adults and 2 children. If the household wants a car that has a fold down back seat in order to carry large packages, the start set is much smaller than the set of all cars that can carry four people. The imposition of a fold down back seat is an example of what we are calling search preferences. It reduces this particular start set to station wagons, minivans, or SUVs. The fold down back seat is an example of a fuzzy attribute that could be considered either a fixed requirement or a preference depending on the importance of carrying large packages.

The start set for an item search shall be defined as the set over which the consumer starts an item search, based on past experience, without gathering any new data. The start set could be a store, a category, such as large TVs. Finally, in general the more frequent the search, the fewer the number of specific alternatives there are in the start set. In some cases an item search is reduced to a replacement operation where the start set is the preferred item.

7.2.2 *Stores and Logistics*

To achieve efficiency in an item search in physical space a consumer must consider which stores to visit and the logistics of the search. Stores tend to specialize. Some tend to focus on the range of goods they carry such as electronics or sporting goods. Department stores tend to focus on a targeted income group. For example, a discount department store like WalMart focuses on basic, low cost products in comparison to an upscale department store, such as Neiman Marcus, which focuses on merchandize appealing to the higher income groups. From childhood on, consumers learn much more than just which stores carry what merchandize and store services, such as return policy, credit, and repair services.

Consumers learn which stores carry the preferred type of merchandize to achieve the search goal at a price they can afford. Store decision rules involve both compensatory and non-compensatory aspects. A non-compensatory aspect is to select stores that carry sets that might contain a desired item. Compensatory aspects are tradeoffs between quality, relative prices, travel cost to the store, and store services. The stores a consumer considers for a particular type of search is an updated list, as was discussed in Chapter 5. Again, generally the more frequent the search, the smaller the number of stores there are on the list.

In a physical space item search there are two logistics problems to solve in order to achieve efficiency. One is the aggregation problem of deciding what item searches to conduct on a particular trip to various stores. For example, most grocery trips involve buying several items. In shopping online a consumer must consider aggregating purchases to achieve cheaper shipping. The second problem is solving the mini traveling salesman problem of determining an efficient path through physical space. We assert that consumers generally solve these problems by intuitive sequential trial and error methodology.

In repeated item searches for a similar good a consumer generally develops a small list of stores or online sites to consider. One example was the use of a STE strategy in Chapter 6 to generate a small list of restaurants for lunch, and another is the list of online sites to search for textbooks discussed in Chapter 5. Later in this Chapter we shall present survey data about the number of stores students search for jeans. Generally such a list is organized as a decision rule that varies with the type of good, but with experience can be executed with very little System 2 thought. For groceries the decision rule might be the store to visit depending on the starting location of the search and the type of groceries. For clothes the decision rule might be the order of stores in which to search for a clothing item. Organizing a list of stores into a decision rule is an example of a heuristic based on search preferences. Developing such rules drastically reduces the number of stores to consider.

7.2.3 *Categories*

The number of category set steps that a consumer can execute in an item search for a product depends on market organization. The greatest number of steps is in the case of build or configure to order where the number of alternatives can be very large. Next is production for inventory where sellers maintain a large number of alternatives in inventory. Last is professional services, such as medical, legal, or artisan services such a plumber or other repair person.

Let us start with configure to order. On 27 Aug 08 I went to the Apple store online to examine the "configure your iMac 24-inch" page. On this page the customer was offered the indicated number of options in configuring the purchase: 2 processors, 2 amounts of memory, 4 hard drives, 2 Graphics cards, 2 Apple Mice, 4 keyboards. In addition, the consumer had a yes or no option in a modem, iWork 08, Final Cut Express 4, Aperture 2, Logic Express 8, and AppleCare Protection. Finally, the customer was offered 3 options in MobileMe Membership, and 4 options regarding HP printers. The customer could select one option in each category so that there were $2 \times 2 \times 4 \times 2 \times 2 \times 2 \times 4 \times 2 \times 2 \times 2 \times 2 \times 2 \times 2 \times 3 \times 4 =$ 393,216 alternatives. Making 14 one attribute choices sequentially is vastly more efficient than trying to construct, say, a binary comparison operator to evaluate the 393,216 possible alternatives. What makes this possible is that the final assembly is for final demand, not for inventory. The product is assembled once the order has been submitted.

This Apple site and currently a similar site at Dell are two examples of sequential decision processes. The decision task is greatly simplified for the consumer because at each stage the consumer is presented with the standard option and considers an upgrade, rather than being presented with a list of all possible combinations. Nevertheless, the choices are frequently not independent, as a customer who wants a more powerful processor is also likely to want a larger hard drive. Services, such as an insurance contract where the consumer fills in the options on a sheet of paper, are also sequential decision processes.

Now let us consider production for inventory such as in the case of cars, where the number of alternative cars for a model can run into the tens of thousands when one considers every possible combination of body type, engines, transmissions, colors, fabrics, and other options. As car manufacturers produce for inventory, they only produce those combinations that are likely to sell, and even a large dealer only carries a small fraction of the possible combinations on his lot. For example, in the search for a car a consumer can generally make the choice of a transmission prior to the selection of colors and fabrics. A dealer lot is generally organized by model and body style so that a customer can make at least two set decisions before considering the tradeoff among the alternatives in the chosen set. If the dealer does not have the desired color/fabric combination on the lot he sometimes can obtain it from another dealer in the state for a cost. If the consumer is willing to wait several weeks, he could order it from the manufacturer using a sequential decision process through all the attributes.

In selecting a professional service such as a lawyer or artisan service such as electrician, the start set is frequently the only set operation. The start set might be recommendations from friends, relatives, or neighbors or a list in the yellow pages or online.

The decision rule for a category or subcategory could be non-compensatory or compensatory. One example of a non-compensatory rule would be to impose a budget constraint on the search, such as only looking at items within a specified price range. Another example of this type of rule is to select cars that seat four, because the family has four members, and not to consider sports cars that only seat two. The choice among sets could also be a compensatory rule like weighing the purchase and operating cost, size, comfort, and safety of small Corolla or Civic sedans with larger Camry or Accord sedans. Given market organization, the execution of such a rule would be at the set level and would not require one observation per member of various sets.

In general, the higher the rate of technological change and the greater the interval between purchases, the more effort a consumer must make to create a category decision rule. For example, with a high rate of technological change, a consumer may not even know from experience which attribute values best suit his intended purpose. With the rapid advance of microelectronics, items such as computers and televisions can go through many product cycles between buying cycles. Simply identifying the alternatives can require effort. Consider a consumer replacing a cathode ray tube, CRT, television after, say, six years. Television is undergoing a shift from 4 by 3 aspect ratio screens to those 16 by 9 aspect ratio. Television is also shifting from analog to digital to high definition digital signals. There are also various types of projection systems. In order to find a preferred item the consumer must forecast the future behavior of the alternative categories in household entertainment processes. This requires gathering new data from outside sources because previous the experience with a CRT television is outdated and not much use in evaluating plasma TVs. Also, if the consumer is considering a 3D TV, he must consider the availability and cost of 3D programing. This is the type of search that is most likely to be reorganized during the search.

Category decision rules are useful in future item searches to the extent that the properties of the sets over which they were determined remain unchanged. These decision rules are based on search preferences. Manufacturers of many products release new models once a year or in some cases, like digital cameras, more frequently. While the attributes of the new models can change, the general properties of the categories are generally much more stable. While the size of a compact Corolla or Civic has increased over time their size has remained smaller than the midsized Camry or Accord. From experience a consumer may well have established a search preference over the two relative sizes of products. Another example of a search preference is a preference over the attributes of a product. With changing fashion, the clothes a consumer considers in the next purchase are generally different from the last purchase. What is unchanged are color combinations, brands, sizes, and styles. In section 7.4 we shall analyze the efficiency gained by establishing search preferences over attributes of clothes.

In general, the more frequent the search, the fewer the number of set steps there are. Steps are combined and executed almost automatically. That is, the more frequent the search, the less System 2 thought is needed to perform each step. Consider a consumer who relocated to a new town a few years back and buy groceries, once a week. Initially the consumer evaluated the alternatives with System 2 operations and decided what groceries to buy at which stores. Over time grocery buying becomes routine, so that the first time the consumer consciously considers alternatives might be a choice of jam from the jam display. For some items on a grocery list, the item search can be reduced to a replacement operation.

However, the number of steps can also increase if circumstances change requiring a new evaluation. Examples would be the opening of a new grocery store near the consumers residence and a new type of product entering the marketplace.

7.3   Steps: Preferred Item From Final Set

At some point in a search, consumers switch from processing alternatives as sets to processing each alternative individually. We call the set at which this happens the final set. In some cases this final set could be the start set. Consumers use the decision rules discussed in this section and in Chapter 4 to process this set. How consumers process the final set depends on the size of the final set. Generally, the more frequent an item search for a particular goal, the smaller the final set. The greater the number of alternatives in the final set, the more likely the consumer will start with a non-compensatory decision rule, such as elimination-by-aspects. When the final set has a few alternatives, either initially or after repeatedly applying non-compensatory decision rules, a consumer will generally use some form of a compensatory decision rule. Such a strategy reduces the amount of information processing to find a preferred item in the final set, [Payne *et al.* (1993)].

The last decision to make in an item search is how much or how many of the item to purchase. This amount is usually determined by heuristics. Consider purchasing gasoline for a car. A consumer frequently fills the tank to capacity when purchasing gasoline. In purchasing groceries, the amount is frequently an estimate of the household needs for a meal or until the next grocery trip. This is not to state that the amount is insensitive to price. If the price of gasoline rises, a consumer will frequently reduce the amount of driving for pleasure so the gas tank will be filled up less often. In selecting among close substitutes, price is one aspect of the decision process. Changes in relative prices can result in a buy or no buy scenario. If a grocery store offers a special sale on steak, it increases the probability that a consumer will make steak one of the meat selections in the shopping trip.

A central issue of this chapter is: To what extent is it efficient for consumers to define their preferences over specific alternatives in a item search? Let us consider a first time search for a good with a start set containing m alternatives. For the traditional bundles model of a consumer, consumer preferences are assumed to satisfy three axioms: completeness, transitivity, and reflexivity. We shall interpret completeness to mean that if a consumer is presented with two of the m alternatives, the consumer can rank them.

What fraction of the $m \times (m-1)$ pairs of alternatives is it efficient for a consumer to actually rank. Assume the item search is correctly executed and the consumer selects an alternative. This means that the selected item is preferred or at least not inferior to all the alternatives not in the final set. In the final set the execution of a non-compensatory rule means the selected item is preferred to the dropped item. The execution of a compensatory rule over two alternatives in the final set ranks the two alternatives. This means that the number of pairs of alternatives actually compared is equal to the number of compensatory rules executed in processing the final set. Generally, this will be a small fraction of the pairs in the start set.

There is a new approach to the axiomatic consumer in which a dominance relationship is introduced, [Fuchs-Seliger and Mayer (2003)]. A consumer does not have to establish preferences over any pair of alternatives that is dominated. If we assume that the set operations in the earlier stages of an item search satisfy the dominance relationship, then only the preferences over the final set matter.

Now let us consider repeated item searching. We shall distinguish between established preferences and constructed preferences as follows: if a consumer can determine a preference between two alternatives by recall from memory, without having to forecast the performance of the two alternatives, then the consumer has an established preference over the two alternatives. From experience the forecast of the two alternatives has been encapsulated into the utility measures of the two. In such a case the only data a consumer would gather about the two alternatives is the minimum necessary to identify the two alternatives. If a consumer gathers data to forecast the future performance of two alternatives, the consumer is constructing a preference between the two. Given the rate of technological change and the rate at which new products are introduced into the marketplace, constructing preferences is very common.

It is efficient to establish preferences over pairs of items that will be encountered in the final set of future item searches to reduce the processing effort. This means remembering the constructed preferences. As processing the final set to find a preferred item and ordering them are both linear process it would be efficient to order them if the consumer expects to encounter variable prices or availability. For example, a partial ordering over beers would be of use to a beer drinker, but if he just bought a new car, a partial ordering over new cars would not be of use for the next purchase.

Now let us consider the effort required to process the final set of an item search. Being able to use preferences established in previous item searches in the current search reduces the effort. The extent to which this is possible is dependent on the frequency of the search, the rate of technological change and the cost of the two alternatives being considered. We shall consider four categories in terms of decreasing frequency of purchases: food, clothes, electronics, and houses.

Let us start by considering food purchases, groceries and restaurant meals. Given the frequency that we purchase food, groceries that are manufactured foods whether canned goods, frozen goods, or in cartons vary little from purchase to purchase. The variance in restaurant meals is greater, but the same item ordered from a menu generally has little variation. The types of food with the greatest variance between purchases are fruit, vegetables, and meat. Using a STE strategy a consumer establishes preferences for the final set of various types of food purchases. In the case of fruit it would be for an idealized ripe fruit. A consumer develops heuristics based on color, softness, and smell to forecast the ripeness of the alternative fruits under consideration. Simple heuristics are also applied to vegetables and meat. Some consumers are concerned with their diet. The items considered in their STE strategy could be restricted to those that meet, for example, fat, salt and sugar requirements.

Because of varying prices and availability such preferences are organized as a partial ordering, so that the only data a consumer must acquire in the case of manufactured food or restaurant meals is that needed to positively identify the alternatives. In the case of fruit, vegetables, or meat, the consumer must acquire data to judge the quality of the alternatives. In the case of food, a heuristic to select between the final alternatives requires very little mental effort.

For most consumers, clothes are purchased less frequently than food. To forecast the performance of alternative clothes, fit is the most important variable. In the United States, manufacturers of clothes for women do not share a common system for size, so the numbers representing size are not useful for forecasting fit unless the women has considerable experience with the brand. Moreover, manufacturers sizes are growing in response to increasing obesity. In contrast, clothes for men have a common system of measurement, but there is some size creep due to increasing obesity. The fundamental aspect of most search strategies for clothes is the need to try on the alternatives, an expensive operation in terms of time.

How do consumers achieve search efficiency in buying clothes? In a few cases the search is reduced to a replacement operation. For example, one male member of our current research group buys Wrangler jeans in his size without trying them on. Women concerned with fashion are less likely to buy clothes as a replacement operation than men. They can achieve search efficiency in buying clothes by establishing search preference over various attributes of clothes such as stores, price range, colors, fabrics, styles, and brands. In the next section we shall consider this gain in efficiency in detail by describing how students search for a pair of jeans.

Electronics is a category of goods where most consumers make infrequent purchases. Also, there is a rapid rate of technological advance in electronic products. For electronics, experience with past products frequently yields little benefit in forecasting the current products on the market. For example, previous experience with a VCR does not provide much insights into selecting a DVD player. A typical consumer must perform research to gain knowledge needed to forecast the performance of alternatives. As was pointed out in Section 6.2.2 Data, there are many alternative knowledge sources and forecasting techniques a consumer could use and there is tremendous variation in the effort consumers take in determining their preferences in the final set.

The effort required to establish preferences in the final set is a function of the cost of the items in the final set. The greater the cost, the greater the effort is given to justifying the final choice. Let us consider three theories posited by decision psychologists, [Bettman *et al.* (2006)], [Montgomery (2006)], and [Svenson (2006)]. We summarize the theory of [Bettman *et al.* (2006)] as follows: consumers expend effort in (a) increasing the accuracy of the choice, (b) reducing cognitive effort, (c) reducing the experience of negative emotion when making the choice, and (d) increasing the ease of justifying the the decision. In this book we argue that consumers in repeated item searches have an incentive to improve the efficiency of their item searches, which is supported by (a) and (b).

Two additional theories for dealing with difficult major purchases are search for dominance structure by [Montgomery (2006)] and Diff Con theory of [Svenson (2006)] about pre- and post-processing. In the former, consumers are assumed to continue to process the acquired data about their alternatives until one alternative dominates the other. The Diff Con theory is similar to Montgomery's search for dominance theory in that the consumer wants to create a superior alternative through processing. After the decision, processing continues to support the chosen alternative.

In this book we assume consumers create their preferences to the extent that they are useful in repeated searches. Constructing preferences has been a topic in decision psychology for some time, for example see [Lichtenstein and Slovic (2006)]. From the perspective of this book, the approach of decision psychologists needs some explanation. They focus on the selection of a preferred item from the final set, not the sequence of decisions from the start set. Also, they do not discuss how a consumer creates preferences that satisfy an axiomatic system, but rather the decision process to find a preferred item. Finally, the focus is on infrequent, costly decisions such as buying a car or house.

7.3.1 *Steps: Stopping Rules*

In an item search a consumer must develop stopping rules for many aspects of the search such as ending an Internet background research, deciding not to visit another store or online site, and deciding not to evaluate additional sets or individual alternatives. As pointed out by [Gigerenzer and Selten (2002)] consumers use simple stopping rules, which are heuristics. One of the first economists to develop such a theory was [Simon (1955)]. He presented his model of bounded rationality in which consumers stop when they have achieved satisficing performance based on the aspiration level. [Gigerenzer (2002)] discusses several stopping heuristics. Our addition to the list of stopping rules is a marginal cost-benefit heuristic learned in a STE strategy for improving search strategies. For example, in creating an updated list for clothes shopping, a consumer has learned that it not worth the effort to consider stores outside the list. We consider this heuristic in the next section.

7.4 Search Efficiency: Jeans

An item that students at our university buy frequently, but not as frequently as food, are jeans. In this section we focus on how students achieve search efficiency in buying jeans. To obtain data on their jean search strategies we created a questionnaire that 150 students in a large Introduction to Macroeconomics class answered in the spring of 2011. They were paid $5 for their efforts. On average these students had completed 1.55 semesters of college. Of the 150 students, 88 were male and 62 were female. On a budget survey given in the spring of 2012 to 97 students either in an upper division economics class or attending a meeting of the UT economics association, we asked two questions regarding their search for jeans to clarify a couple of points raised in the earlier survey.

In selecting a pair of jeans, a student has potentially thousands of pairs of jeans to consider. For example, in Austin the research group determined that 45 stores sold jeans and that there were 173 brands of women's jeans and 145 brands of men's jeans. In addition, there are at least 10 jean colors and 10 styles of jeans. Given the very large number of potential purchases, how do students achieve jean search efficiency in repeated searches?

The two major costs of jean search are the travel costs to the stores selling jeans and the time cost of trying them on in order to determine how well they fit. Jeans are a frequently purchased item with which students have a great deal of experience. Students were asked the following two questions:

In cool weather in the Winter how many days a week do you wear a pair of jeans to school ____ (include weekends if you come on campus so answer is from 0 to 7)

10. In the past 2 years how many pairs of jeans have you bought? ___

The responses are shown in the Table 7.1 below. In cool weather, jeans

Table 7.1   Days worn/week and number bought ($n = 150$).

Variable	Mean	Std err	Median	Mode	Range
Day worn	5.41	0.12	5	5	1-7
No. Bought	7.77	0.49	6	5	0-40

are worn frequently. The number of jeans bought has a tail to the right with the five largest numbers of jeans bought being 20, 25, 30, 40, and 40. Given the number of purchases, students are able to improve their search efficiency using a STE strategy based on going to different stores and trying on different brands and styles of jeans.

To determine just how many stores students searched and how many pairs of jeans they tried on we asked the following question displayed in Figure 7.1 on the top of the next page. We first looked at the averages for stores visited and brands, styles, and total jeans tried on using the data from the 136 who supplied usable data for the three jean item searches. The results are displayed in Table 7.2 on the top of the next page. A 0 entered for stores visited means the student bought the jeans online and a 0 for the various categories of tried on means the students bought the jeans without trying them on. It is important to note that these distributions all have a tail to the right. Consider the number of stores visited: While the mean is slightly greater than 2, the top five numbers of stores visited are 7, 8, 10, 10, and 21.

14. Consider that last three successful shopping trips to buy jeans starting at the most often point checked above in Question 11. Please fill in the following table: If you bought jeans without trying them on then enter 0 in 3 boxes with the word tried on.

Trip	# stores visited	# brands tried on	# different styles tried on	# jeans tried on (total)	Success (y/n)
Last					
2ⁿᵈ to last					
3ʳᵈ to last					

Fig 7.1:   Question 14

Table 7.2   Stores, brands, styles, tried on, and success ($n = 136$).

Variable	Mean	Std err	Median	Mode	Range
Stores visited	2.11	0.09	2	1	0-21
Brands tried on	2.19	0.08	2	1	0-10
Styles tried on	2.29	0.10	2	2	0-21
Jeans tried on	3.91	0.18	3	3	0-40

We now consider two factors that influence the numbers. The first factor is that we expect women to try more stores, brands, styles, and to try on more jeans in total. A second factor is presented in the following question we asked students on the survey: "Do you wear different brands or styles of jeans for different purposes, for example a work detail, class, and a date? Yes __; No __", 96 responded with a "Yes" and 54 with a "No". We expect the numbers for the Yes responders to be greater than those for the No responders.

In Table 7.3 at the top of the next page, 136 students supplied usable data for three trips. For each student we averaged the data for the three trips and the results presented below are the average for the 136 students, the 81 males, the 55 females, the 91 Yes responders (different jeans for different purposes), and the 45 No responders (same jeans for different purposes): Students search for jeans in a small number of stores and try on a small number of jeans in a few brands and styles. The Sig:W>M row is the significance of a one tail t test with unequal variances that the indicated mean for women is greater than the corresponding mean for men. We did not test the % success. The Sig:Y>N is the significance for the one tail t test with unequal variances for the Yes responders being greater than the

Table 7.3   Jean search: Averages for past 3 searches.

Group	n	# stores	# brands	# styles	# jeans tried on	% success
Men	81	1.92	1.94	2.08	3.21	84
Women	55	2.38	2.57	2.61	4.91	76
Sig:W>M		0.03	0.003	0.04	0.002	—
Yes	91	2.14	2.33	2.43	4.18	—
No	45	2.04	1.92	2.00	3.34	—
Sig:Y>N		No	0.02	0.03	0.05	—

No responders.

The next question to ask is whether these search preferences are stable over time or do they change. In the supplemental survey we asked the following two questions:

21. Buying jeans–Stores: Consider the stores you shop for jeans in the area you usually shop in (i.e. Austin, Houston, your hometown etc). Check all that apply:
a. I have gone to the same store(s) or online sites for the past two trips _(73%)_
b. I tried a new store because it had a sale _(42%)_
c. I tried a new store because it was recommended by a friend _(24%)_
d. I tried a new store because I started my shopping trip from a different location than usual _(9%)_
e. I tried a new store for the following reason _(0%)_____

22. Buying jeans–Brands: Consider your last trip to buy a pair of jeans. Did you try them on before buying them? Yes ___ No___ "
If yes, answer the following: Consider the brands (for example, Levi, Gap, Wrangler, .) you tried on in your last search for jeans. Check all that apply:
a. I tried on the same brands that I have tried on before _(82%)_
b. I tried on a new brand because it was on sale _(50%)_
c. I tried on a new brand because it was recommended by a friend _(23%)_
d. I tried on a new brand because it looked good _(53%)_
e. I tried on a new brand because I saw an ad I liked _(11%)_
f. I tried on a new brand because the new store sells brands that I have never tried on before _(10%)_
g. I tried on a new brand for the following reason _(3%)_____

The percent of the 95 students who answered question 21 is contained in the () for each alternative. For example, the data shows that 73% went to the same store(s). The percent of the 92 students who answered the second part of question 22 is contained in the () for each alternative. For example, 82% checked that they had tried on the same brands before. The data contained a few inconsistencies. The data indicates that students modify their searches with "responding to a sale" being the reason with the greatest number of checks for question 21 and "looked good" being the reason with the greatest number of checks for question 22. On average students check out few stores, try on few brands of jeans, and they try new alternatives less than 30% of the time.

Given that students reported buying on average 7.77 pairs of jeans in the past 2 years, it would appear that their knowledge of jean sizes should be sufficient that they could buy jeans without trying them on. This is definitely not the case. Of the 335 jeans searches for which we have data, students tried on at least one pair in all but 13 cases, of which 10 were men and 3 were women. To make sure this estimate was accurate we asked the following question on the supplemental survey:

22 . Buying jeans–Brands: Consider your last trip to buy a pair of jeans. Did you try them on before buying them? Yes ___ No___

Of the 95 students who answered the question, 6 checked "No." This is 6.3%, but if we correct for inconsistencies on the second part of the question we have only 3 consistent "No" answers. The percentage of students who buy jeans without trying them on is small.

Now we need to consider why students, with few exceptions, try on a pair of jeans before buying them. One fact is the importance of a good fit. When asked, "I would only consider buying a pair of jeans that is a good fit," 95% responded with a Yes. Another factor is the importance of keeping up with the change in fashions. Students were asked the following question about what motivates them to buy a pair of jeans.

8. What motivates you to start a search for a new pair of jeans? (Check all that apply)
(1) Change in fashions and I want the new fashion ___
(2) Current pair or pairs are nearly worn out and need to be replaced ___
(3) I buy jeans on a regular basis such as bimonthly ___

The results in percent for all 150 students, each of which checked at least one response, are shown in Table 7.4 at the top of the next page. While keeping up with changing fashions is important for women, it is also important

Table 7.4   Motivation to initiate a jean search.

Group	n	Fashion	Worn out	Regular
All	150	44%	86%	8%
Men	88	35%	94%	6%
Women	62	56%	74%	11%

for men, though not as much. A new fashion can have changes in shape, so to predict whether it will fit, trying it on is the best predictor. Each manufacturer of women's jeans has its own system of measurement, so women must learn a measurement system for each manufacturer whose brands she is interested in trying on to reduce the number she needs to try on. Men's jeans have a common measurement system. In both men's and women's clothes there is an obesity creep as manufacturers make recorded sizes bigger to flatter their potential customers; for example, see [Camber (2007)]. Also, if a customers body is changing shape, trying on a pair of jeans is again the best predictor of a good fit. Efficiency is achieved by only considering a small number of jeans to try on.

The first factor in achieving jean search efficiency is to only consider a price range of jeans that is affordable. In our online investigation, the price of new jeans, not on sale, varied from \$14.70 to \$745.00. Concerning prices, the subjects were asked:

11. Consider the last 3 pairs of jeans you bought: (give dollar amount for each)
(1) Lowest price \$ ___
(2) Middle price \$ ___
(3) Highest price \$ ___.

12. For how many years have you been buying jeans in that price range?
___

The lowest price recorded for (1) was \$3, and the highest price recorded for (3) was \$350. The average for (1) was \$27.60 and the average for (3) was \$69.80. In Table 7.5 on the top of the next page, we display some descriptive statistics about the price range and the number of years buying in that price range: Again, both of these distributions have a tail to the right. The top five in the price range data are 155, 160, 170, 270, and 270. (Yes, I checked to make sure the two students reporting 270 were different people.)

Table 7.5   Price range [(3)-(1)] and years bought price range ($n = 150$).

Variable	Mean	Std err	Median	Mode	Range
Price Range	42.15	3.57	30	30	0-270
Years Bought	5.28	0.26	5	10	1-19

Now let us consider the variation in the range of purchase prices for the indicated grouping of students with complete data as is shown in Table 7.6 below. Yes and No refer to the students' responses to whether they wear

Table 7.6   Range in average purchase prices by indicated group 1 and 2.

Gr 1	No. Gr 1	Gr 1 Ave	Gr 2	No. Gr 2	Gr 2 Ave	Sig(1-2)
Male(all)	82	$36.94	Female(all)	60	$49.15	0.06
M&F:Yes	95	$49.83	M&F:No	47	$26.46	<0.01
Male: Yes	56	$41.75	Male: No	26	$26.58	0.006
Female: Yes	39	$61.44	Female: No	21	$26.33	0.006
Male: Yes	56	$41.75	Female: Yes	39	$61.44	0.04

different jeans for different purposes. For example, Male: Yes is the subset of male subjects who wear different jeans for different purposes. The difference in the means for all cases had the correct sign and was significant for a one tail t test with unequal variances at the α level shown in column Sig(1-2). Given the fact that the average range on purchase prices for Male: No was almost equal the average range on purchase prices for Female: No as shown in the table, it is not surprising that the difference was not significant. The price of most jeans in the marketplace lies between $10 and $250. If we assume that the price spread that the subjects considered was no more than the purchase price spread + $20 then on average men considered less than 1/4 of this $240 price range and women considered less than 1/3 of this price range.

We assume that students through a sequential trial and error process find stores that sell jeans in their price range and sell brands with the styles and fit they desire. When asked "List the store you go to: 1st, 2nd, and 3rd (You may list less than three but no more than three)", of the 136 students with complete data 1% left the question blank, 10% listed one,

24% listed two, and 64% listed three. When asked "Check if you generally go to these stores in the same order each shopping trip __". 44% responded with a check. The final question relating to selecting stores with the % of the 136 students with complete data in () was:

17. Check which store do you generally go to first?
(1) The one with the greatest probability of successful purchase? __(82)__
(2) The store closest to home? __(23)__
(3) Other __(5)__ Please describe __(price or deals)__.

The fact that 82% go first to the store with the greatest probability of success is a clear indication that they develop a knowledge base about stores in repeated item searches for jeans.

Now let us consider brands. When asked to "list these brands in order of preference (You may list less than three but no more than three)", of the 136 students with complete data 0% left the question blank, 7% listed one, 26% listed two, and 68% listed three. Some descriptive statistics for the question, "How many years have these brands been your favorites __?" are shown in Table 7.7 below. Only 13 students indicated less than 2 years

Table 7.7   Years brands have been favorites ($n = 136$).

Variable	Mean	Std err	Median	Mode	Range
Years Favorites	4.10	0.21	4	2	0-10

for this question, which means that for most, their search preferences have been established.

Consumers have an incentive to establish preferences over attributes that they will likely encounter in future item searches. In this regard let us consider first style and then color. Subjects were given 10 styles: Boot-cut, Straight leg, Skinny, Flare leg, Low-rise, Ultra low-rise, High waist, Stone washed, Distressed, and Other (please specify _____). They were first asked to partition them into three categories; Normally consider, Might consider, and Never consider. Then they were asked to rank the styles in the Normally consider category. The results of this question are shown in Table 7.8 on the top of the next page for males versus females and the significance of a one tail t test with unequal variances is shown in the column Sig (M - F). The difference in means had the correct sign because, as might be expected, there are many more styles that men on average would not consider than women on average would not consider.

Table 7.8   Style.

Category	All Subjects (150)	Male (88)	Women (62)	Sig (M-F)
Ordered	2.8	2.3	3.4	<0.001
Might	2.1	1.8	2.6	0.002
Never	4.0	4.9	2.7	<0.001

Subjects were also given 10 colors: Dark Blue, Blue, Pale Blue, Black, White, Tan, Grey, Olive, Unconventional e.g. yellow, pink, Other (please specify _____). They were first asked to partition them into three categories; Normally consider, Might consider, and Never consider. Then they were asked to rank the colors in the Normally consider category. Then Table 7.9 below contains the results of this question for males versus females and the significance of a one tail t test with unequal variances is shown in the column Sig (M - F). The difference in means had the correct sign because,

Table 7.9   Color.

Category	All Subjects (150)	Male (88)	Women (62)	Sig (M-W)
Ordered	2.7	2.6	2.9	0.1
Might	2.1	1.7	2.7	<0.001
Never	4.2	5.0	2.9	<0.001

as might be expected, there are many more colors that men on average would not consider than women on average would not consider.

How do students achieve search efficiency in repeated item searches for jeans? Consumers have incentives to reduce their item search costs given the opportunity costs of such searches. Through repeated searches, they learn to drastically reduce the start set from the potential start set of all jeans in the city where the search is being conducted. Also they gain a good estimate of what size fits. In addition, they establish search preferences over stores, brands, styles, and colors.

Of the 138 students with usable data for the 3 jean item searches, 92 visited 2 or fewer stores on each of the 3 trips. These students tried on average 1.7 brands and 3.1 jeans per trip. If we consider the 15 students in the tail of the distribution, who visited on average 4 or more stores per trip, they on average tried on 3.8 brands and 7.1 jeans per trip. Even the tail of the distribution only considers a small fraction of stores, brands, styles, and colors of jeans.

We assert this reduction takes place without a great deal of deliberation. Students remember and use those aspects of previous successful searches that reappear in the current search. We assert that this happens automatically without much System 2 effort. Given 117 out of the 150 start their search from their parents home and that they on average have bought 7.7 pairs of jeans in the past two years we assert that they have established search preferences that require very little System 2 effort to evoke. We also assert that search preferences are organized to execute search heuristics. For example, students might well have one established route through stores to buy jeans for class and another route to buy jeans for a date.

The last point we wish to make about the search for jeans is to provide some evidence that through repeated item searches, consumers learn when to stop. Students were asked:

22. If you failed to buy a pair of jeans in the past two years, why? Give the number of times for reasons below.
(1) Time constraint. If I had searched more in the stores I normally go to I probably would have found a pair. ____
(2) I checked the stores that I normally go to and did not buy a pair. From previous experience I knew no other stores nearby carries the jean brands I like ____
(3) Decided to go to another set of stores in a different mall, location, or city. ____
(4) Other ____ Please explain _____.

Of the 136 students with complete data, 87 reported at least one failure of which 48% responded to (1), 64% responded to (2), and 29% responded to (3). The option (2) is a statement that the marginal benefit of going to another store would not be worth the anticipated effort, learned from experience in repeated item searches for jeans.

7.5   Conclusions

For procedural economics the focus of consumer item search is the associated search strategy. In this Chapter we have focused on the steps in an item search strategy and how consumers learn to achieve efficient strategies.

Consumers learn efficient search strategies by accumulating a large body of consumer knowledge in the form of objective facts about products and market organization and subjective search preferences over those aspects of an item search that are likely to be repeated. Search preferences are used in constructing decision rules to drastically reduce the number of alternatives to be considered.

What we have not considered is how close to optimal does a consumer achieve in an item search. Before considering this issue we will consider budgeting, which is an important aspect of achieving consumer performance.

Chapter 8

Budgeting

8.1 Introduction

In this Chapter we consider how consumers budget. In order to simplify the consumer optimization problem, we have argued that consumers search for their purchases item by item. The study of student budgeting is the study of how students finance their sequential item searches that repeat at different frequencies. We assert that students use an incremental adjustment process to develop budgeting procedures. The more frequent the purchase the greater the number of opportunities to make an adjustment. For example, food purchases repeat much more frequently than tuition payments.

To study budgeting procedures we performed several budget surveys of students at our university who were living in rented apartments. College students are good subjects because they are just starting to learn how to budget over frequently repeated purchases, such as food. In Section 2 we present our survey data showing that students have the greatest budget responsibilities in food, clothing, and entertainment. Students make frequent purchases in these categories.

We consider student budgeting procedures in Section 3. Three factors we examine are the frequency of budgeting, what procedures students use to budget, and the extent to which they specify fixed amounts of expenditures per category. We find that student budgeting is characterized by flexibility in expenditures per category. We examine two indices, budget self-rating and financial hardship, that can explain the variation in student procedures.

The basis for incremental adjustment is monitoring the flow of funds. In Section 4 we consider the frequency and method students use to monitor the flow of funds in their checking account. We relate this data to the budget self-rating and financial hardship indices.

In Section 5 we argue that monitoring the flow of funds creates the basis for a feedback incremental adjustment heuristic for budgeting. We provide many examples of adjustments, which include altering the household production function for food. Balancing the flow of expenses with the flow of income is difficult because many students tend to run out of money before the end of their budget period. Some students have a feast or famine budget style where they spend more early in the budget period and cut back when they start to run out of money.

In Section 7 we compare our results to the previous results of [Thaler (1991)] and [Heath and Soll (1996)]. Our research shows students are more flexible in their budgeting than the previously reported studies suggest.

8.2 Budgeting Surveys

In order to investigate budgeting, we conducted surveys of undergraduates at our university who lived in rented apartments or houses and were responsible for preparing or buying meals without a meal plan as shown in Table 8.1 below. Sem Coll is the average number of semesters the subjects

Table 8.1   Budget surveys: Year and number of subjects.

Survey	1	2	3	4	5	6
Year	2000a	2000b	2006	2007	2010	2012
Subjects	85	25	49	50	125	97
Sem Coll	6.4	5.0	7.3	6.1	4.2	3.3

in the respective survey were college students. We will discuss the impact of the variation later. Subjects in the 2000a, 2000b, and 2012 surveys were paid $5 each and subjects in the 2010, 2007 and 2006 surveys were paid $1/page plus $1. Questions on the surveys varied because we focused on different aspects of budgeting in each survey.

Students generally live in a dorm the first year of residence and thereafter move into a rented apartment or house, where the number of categories that they must budget increases. We were interested in knowing the split between bills the parents pay directly and bills that the students pay directly regardless of the source of these funds. We asked several versions of this question and the least ambiguous was presented on the '07 survey.

This version was repeated on the 2012 survey. On this survey we first provided students with definitions concerning responsibility and then asked the following question:

Who pays: We are interested in what fraction of your total educational expenses passes through your account.

You pay if money passes through your account. That is, you write a check on your account, pay cash, or use a debit/credit card on your account to pay your bills. (You pay even if your parents make a direct deposit into your account or send you a check to deposit. Note: we are not asking where the money in your account comes from–just what bills you pay from your account.) For example, you pay 100% of your rent if you write the check, regardless of the fact that 100% may be money from your parents.

Parents pay if they write the check, or if you or they use a credit card for which the bill is paid by your parents. For example, if your parents pay your tuition bill from their account and the money does not pass through your account, then parents pay 100%. If parents deposit extra money in your account so that you can buy your textbooks, then you pay 100%, but if you buy your textbooks with a credit card where the bill goes to your parents, then parents pay 100%.

Mixed pay if you buy 20% or your clothes you use at UT with money from your account and your parents use their credit card to pay for 80% at home before school, then you pay 20%. If you pay for most of your food at UT, but your parents buy some of your groceries, then you need to estimate what fraction of your food budget goes through your account.

15. To the nearest 10%, estimate how much of each of the following expenses you pay Tuition _(44) _ Rent _(61)_ Auto _(35)_ Textbooks _(60)_ Utilities _(64)_ Food _(70)_ Clothing _(65.4)_ Entertainment _(82)_ Cell phone _(20)_ Other (specify) _(4 for Fraternity or Sorority)___

Note that for the 2012 survey students were asked to report how much they paid to the nearest 5%. The percent is indicated in the () for the 140 students in the two surveys that provided usable data. Why is the percent that passes through a student's account important? These are categories that the students must consider when budgeting. The two categories with the highest percentages are Entertainment with 82% and Food with 70%. Entertainment is a category that students generally have had prior budgeting experience, but food is generally new.

   The average data has a major defect in that a large number of students record 100% and a much smaller number record 0%, so the average data is not too revealing. Another way of looking at the data is to determine the percent of students who paid 100% in a category and the number who paid a positive percent less than 100%. The results are displayed in Table 8.2 below. The three categories where students must budget the greatest

Table 8.2   Budget responsibilities by category ($n = 140$).

Category	% who pay all	% at least part
Tuition	41	50
Rent	59	67
Auto	26	50
Books	69	57
Utilities	61	69
Food	59	91
Clothing	50	84
Entertainment	71	90
Phone	18	24

amount are food, clothing and entertainment. We shall focus most of our attention on how students budget for these three categories.

Finally, we investigated whether the two surveys were statistically different. We added the percent students paid in food, clothing, and entertainment together. The average for the 2007 group was 233.3 and for the 2012 group was 208.7 and these means are different with a two tailed t test with an α of 10%.

What accounts for the difference? There is great variation in student budget responsibilities. A few students have a debit card or credit card to buy food, clothing, and entertainment where the bill goes directly to the parents. In the 2007 survey only 1 student had a sum statistic of the three categories of less than 30 and in the 2012 survey 12 students were less than 30 in this statistic. The 2012 survey had a much larger percentage of students with few budget responsibilities. We attribute this to the fact that the average number of semesters students in the 2012 group was 2.8 less than the 2007 group. The data from the various surveys revealed that the percent students pay in these categories tends to increase with the number of semesters the student is a college student.

8.3 Budget Procedures

In this section we examine budgeting procedures such as the frequency and methodology of budgeting. Students varied greatly in these two factors of budgeting. In the surveys we asked students to subjectively rate their budgeting performance. We hoped that these statistics would be useful for interpreting the variation in budgeting procedures.

Let us start by considering the variation in budget procedures. We asked questions concerning whether they paid their bills on time, the frequency of budgeting, record keeping, and budget methodology. On the 2000a, 2006 and the 2007 survey gauged the extent to which students paid their bills on time as shown below:

44. Do you pay your bills on time?
Always ___ Almost always ___ Occasionally late ___ Frequently late ___

The responses for the 2000a and 2006 data are combined, but for a reason to be discussed later the 2007 was kept separate. The data is displayed in the Table 8.3 below.

Table 8.3   Pay bills on time.

Group	Obs	Always	Almost	Occ late	Freq late
2000a and 2006	132	48%	39%	9%	5%
2007	49	45%	49%	4%	2%

On the 2007 survey we first defined budgeting and then asked a question about budgeting frequency:

Current Budgeting: Do you consider your expenses and account balance before planning for the future? This could be done formally (in a spreadsheet) or intuitively (like looking at your account balance and deciding to eat ramen for the rest of the month).

18. Check all that apply concerning how often you budget or plan.
a. Weekly? Yes __ No __
b. Monthly? Yes __ No __
c. Each semester or summer session? Yes __ No __

On the 2000a, 2006, and 2012 surveys we asked variations of this question. The results are listed in Table 8.4 on the top of the next page. The fact that the values from the 2006 survey are lower may be attributed to the fact that

Table 8.4   Budget frequency.

	2000a	2006	2007	2012
Week	62%	22%	50%	56%
Month	71%	51%	62%	58%
Semester	62%	43%	58%	39%

we did not define budgeting before asking the 2006 survey students about the frequency of their budgeting. Our definition included both informal and formal procedures for budgeting and the 2006 students without our definition may have only considered formal procedures for budgeting.

Now let us consider record keeping. On the 2000a survey we asked the following question:

15. **Check all that apply** about how you maintain records of your expenditures:
[1] No objective or intuitive records __ (8)
[2] Intuitive records in your head __ (60)
[3] On paper __ (47)
[4] With a computer program __ (12)

The percent checking each response is shown in the ().

On the 2012 survey we asked a more extensive version of this question that included procedures used in budgeting. This 2012 version is as follows:

11. Budget methodology: Check all that apply:
a. I anticipate future expenses __ (59)
b. Based on my bank balance, I intuitively decide what needs to be done __ (53)
c. I check my bank account and see what bills have been paid. __ (39)
d. I keep a written or computer record of all my expenses by category __(23)
e. I write down my budget on paper __(03)
f. I input my budget into a spreadsheet or computer software program __ (22)

The percent checking each response is shown in the ().

Budgeting methodology is covered in the following question asked on the 2007 survey:

21. Besides monitoring your bank and credit cards plus anticipating future expenses, do you use one or more of the following methods to control your expenses?

- Method A: I develop intuitive rules to control the amount of money I spend on each individual purchase. I do not keep records by category or expenses. For example, I determine how many times a week that I can afford to eat at restaurants and the range of prices I will pay for a meal.
- Method B: I budget for various categories of expense, either on paper, on a spreadsheet, or in a program like Quicken. Then I predict my expenses in each category, and if there is a discrepancy between my expense forecast and how much money I have, I plan how to bring the two in line.
- Method C: Rent is fixed, utility bills are basically predictable, food varies somewhat, but I am flexible in eating out, entertainment expenses, and car expenses (if applicable). I adjust expenses intuitively.
- Method D: Once a week (or other regular period), I check my account balance, determine what bills have been paid, anticipate what needs to be paid, and intuitively consider how to adjust my flexible expenditures (such as food and entertainment).
- Method E: As long as the credit card bill that my parents receive this month isnt too much more than they got last month, I dont need to worry much about controlling my expenses.

Check **all** your methods: Method A __, Method B __, Method C __, Method D __, Method E__.

We asked the same question on the 2006 survey without the D option. The percent responses for these two surveys is indicated in Table 8.5 below.

Table 8.5   Budget methods.

Survey	Num Obs	Meth A	Meth B	Meth C	Meth D	Meth E
2006	49	35%	6%	82%	n/a	20%
2007	50	50%	16%	82%	50%	12%

In the 1930s a form of budgeting known as tin can or envelope budgeting was common. Budgeters put cash into containers for each category of expenditure. They then only spent what had been allocated for that category and did not move cash from one category to another. The percent who responded to Method B, a variation of tin can budgeting, in either the 2006 or 2007 survey was less than 20%. A similar question in the 2010 survey also revealed that less than 20% used a form of tin can budgeting. Students in our surveys indicate that they are much more flexible than would be the case under tin can budgeting.

To explain variations in budget procedures we constructed budget self-rating statistics. In the 2000a and 2006 surveys students were asked the following question about their qualitative budgeting self-rating:

> 30. Based purely on your subjective option, how well do you budget.
> 1. Poorly. ___ 2. Poorly, but improving ___
> 3. Adequately ___ 4. Adequately and improving ___ 5. Very well___

For this subjective index we gave each student the numerical value of the option they selected. In the 2007 and 2012 surveys, students were asked to give a quantitative self-rating as follows:

> 20. How well do you budget (based purely on your subjective opinion)?
> **Key**: Use a 0 -10 range, where 0 indicates that you have no grasp of your expenses and 10 indicates that you always know whats going on and allocate money wisely among alternatives. Remember it is not how much money you have to spend, but how wisely you spend what you have. Your self-rating _____

Now we consider the relationship between these self-rating statistics to budget performance. Let us start by considering the relationship to these statistics with paying bills on time, for which the data is shown in Table 8.4 above. This data is combined into two groups: the students who always paid their bills on time and those who were less punctual. The results are shown in Table 8.6 below with the α significance level. The 2007 group used

Table 8.6　Budget self-rating and paying bills on time.

Group	Mean: Always	Mean: Less Than Always	Sig at α of
2000a and 2006	3.3	2.8	0.004
2007	7.4	6.5	0.04

a different budget self-rating statistic from that of the other two groups, but in both cases the mean of those students who always paid their bills on time was significantly higher than those that did not with an α of less than 0.05. We also asked the 2007 students, "Since becoming a student: (f) Number of times you have maxed out a credit card: ___". In response to this question, 26 responded with a 0, and 10 with 1 or more, and the others left it blank. The mean self rating of the students with 0 max outs is 7.54, which is significantly greater at a significance level of 0.0005 than 6.1, the self rating mean of the 10 students with 1 or more credit card max outs.

To examine the relationship of the self-rating statistics to the frequency of budgeting, record keeping and budget methodology we created indices in order to employ regression analysis. From the data on frequency of budgeting in Table 8.5, we created a budget frequency index BF_n where $BF_n = 0$ if students did not budget regularly in any period, $BF_n = 1$ if they budgeted in 1 of the periods, 2 if they budgeted regularly in any two periods, and 3 if they budgeted regularly in all three periods. For the record keeping question, number 15 from the 2000a survey, we constructed a records index R_n based on which response the subject checked, which would be 1, 2, 3, or 4. If a student checked more than one response such as 3 and 4 we assigned the student the higher number.

For the first question on methodology, which is question 11 on the 2012 survey, we constructed a methodology index, M_n that equaled the sum of the number of responses checked. For example, if a student checked a, c, and e, the index value was 3. The last index we constructed was a control index C_n for Question 21 of the 2007 survey. C_n equals the sum of the number checked for A,B, and C for both the 2006 and 2007 data. We also created a second value for the 2007 data based on the sum of the number checked for A through D.

We postulated the following regressions:

Frequency regression $\qquad BF_n = \alpha + \beta SF_n + \epsilon_n$ $\qquad$ (8.1)

Records regression $\qquad R_n = \alpha + \beta SF_n + \epsilon_n$ $\qquad$ (8.2)

Methodology regression $\qquad M_n = \alpha + \beta SF_n + \epsilon_n$ $\qquad$ (8.3)

Control regression $\qquad C_n = \alpha + \beta SF_n + \epsilon_n$ $\qquad$ (8.4)

where BF_n is the budget frequency index, R_n is the record index, M_n is the methodology index, C_n is the control index, SF_n is the self-rating index, and ϵ_n is the error term that is assumed to be independent and distributed $N(0, \sigma_n^2)$. We ran these regressions (8.1) - (8.4) using the appropriate data. For each regression we tested the hypothesis of homoskedasticity with the Breusch and Pagan (1979)/ Cook-Weisberg test and tested the hypothesis of normal errors with the Shapiro-Wilk W, Shapiro-Francia W, and the Skewness/Kutosis tests. In those cases where the hypothesis of homoskedasticity was rejected with a significance level of 5% we performed the regression using [White (1980)] robust regression that corrects for heteroskedasticity.

Table 8.7 Budget procedure regressions.

Reg	Survey	Obs	reg F	β(val)	β(P-val)	H	N1	N2	N3
8.1	00a + 06	130	7.53	0.25	0.001	R	R	R	R
8.1	07 + 12	143	16.38	0.18	<0.001	R	N	N	N
8.2	00a	85	6.1	0.17	0.02	N	N	N	N
8.3	12	96	10.5	0.23	0.002	N	N	N	N
8.4	06(A-C)	49	2.72	0.11	0.105	N	R	N	N
8.4	07(A-C)	49	3.23	0.09	0.08	R	N	R	R
8.4	07(A-D)	49	14.6	0.20	<0.001	R	N	N	N

The results are shown in Table 8.7 above where Reg is the indicated regression, Survey is the data and the year is abbreviated, Obs is the number of observations, reg F is the F statistic for the regression, β(val) is the value of the coefficient, β(P-val) is the significance value. The H column presents the results of the test for homoskedasticity. R means rejected at a significance of 5% and N means not rejected. N1, N2, and N3 present the results for the three normality tests in the order given using the same conventions.

The results for regression (8.1) clearly indicate that the higher the budgeting self-rating, the more frequently the student budgets on a regular basis. The results for regression (8.2) indicate that the self-rating index can explain the extent to which a student keeps a record of budgeting. The higher the self-rating, the more steps a student employs in budgeting as the results for regression (8.3) indicate. The results for regression (8.4) indicate that Method D is most closely related to budget self-rating. This is consistent with our previous result that the budget self-rating index is related to the frequency of budgeting. Overall, the budget self-rating indicies appear reasonably robust and are a useful way to organize the variation in budget frequency and procedure.

8.4 Monitoring

Students make frequent sequential item searches. We investigate how active students were in monitoring the flow of funds in their bank accounts while making these item searches.

In order to determine how frequently subjects monitored the flow of funds, we asked students on all but the 2000b survey a question about knowledge of the balance in their checking account. The subjects in the 2006 survey were asked the following monitoring question:

22. Answer this question if you have a checking account, debit card, or credit card. How often do you check on the items in a, b, and c below? If you know your balance (or status of checks) at all times, put 0. If you check every couple of days, put 2 or 3. Once a week, put 7. When you receive your statement, put 30.
a. Checking account balance? _____

There were slight differences in how we asked this question in the various surveys, but because the differences were minor, we decided to combine the answers for the 298 students with complete data into the Table 8.8 below. We shall consider those students who monitor their bank account more

Table 8.8 Frequency that bank account is monitored in percent

Every _ Days	S2000a	S2006	S2007	S2010	S2012	Sum
Num Obs	80	49	49	120	96	294
0-2 days	43.8%	44.9%	51.0%	42.5%	33.2%	41.6%
0-7 days	82.5%	79.6%	77.6%	79.2%	89.6%	82.2%
8-29 days	6.3%	12.2%	4.1%	7.5%	5.2%	6.9%
30+ days	11.3%	8.2%	18.4%	13.3%	5.2%	10.9%

frequently than when they receive their statement as "active" monitors and those that do not as "passive" monitors. What Table 8.8 clearly indicates is that most students actively monitor the flow of funds – while 11% wait until they receive their bank statements, 82% check their balance at least once a week.

Most students use more than one method to monitor their bank accounts. On the 2010 survey students were asked the following question with the % of the 125 students responding Yes to the various options in ():

12. How do you check your checking balance? (More than one way is certainly possible!)
(a) Every time you withdrawal funds via ATM or at bank? YES_(60)_ NO_

(b) Using your bank website with your computer? YES_(88)_ NO__
(c) Using an app on your iPhone, Blackberry, or cell phone? YES_(28)_
NO__
(d) When you see your bank statement? YES_(47)_ NO__

Most students use more than one method to monitor their account as 78%
indicated on this question. Why is monitoring the flow of funds so important? One reason is that bouncing a check generally costs a student $25
or more. We assert that learning to budget is an incremental adjustment
process, and given the frequency of food, entertainment, and clothing purchases, students can learn using a sequential trial and error process based
on monitoring their accounts.

A question on the 2010 survey that supports this claim is:

28. Since starting college, I have improved my budgeting and the control
over my expenditures. YES _(86)_ NO _(14%)_ If YES, please check all
that apply
(a) I check my checking account balances more frequently _(90%)_
(b) I monitor my credit card debt more frequently _(50%)_
(c) I budget more frequently _(70%)_
(d) When I budget I spend more time considering my alternatives _(72%)_
(e) I now use a budget aid such as a app, spreadsheet or software program
_(20%)_
(f) Other _(5%)_
Please explain _____
(g) I started improving my budgeting in my _(1=62%) _(2=29%) _(3=8%)
_(4=2%)_year in college. (1, 2, 3, or 4)

The % in the Yes/No question is based on the 125 subjects who filled
in the 2010 questionnaire. The % in (a) through (f) is based on the 107
students who answered Yes and the % in (g) is based on the 93 students
who responded to this option. As indicated, 90% who have improved their
budgeting checked that they check their account balances more frequently.
Because 62% indicated that they start improving in their first year, the
data from the 2010 survey from a first year economics course with lower
and upper division students is more representative of student learning than
the other surveys, which had mostly upper division students from an upper
division class.

In the rest of this section we postulate three regression for which we
test the hypotheses of homoskedasticity and normal errors with the tests
mentioned in the previous section. In all cases the maintained hypothesis
was rejected with a significance level of 5%. We performed the regressions

using [White (1980)] robust regression that corrects for heteroskedasticity. In the first regression we postulate that monitoring the flow of funds is learned behavior:

$$D_n = \alpha + \beta S_n + \epsilon_n \qquad (8.5)$$

where D_n is the monitoring frequency in days, S_n is the number of semesters as a college student, and ϵ_n is the error term that is assumed to be independent and distributed $N(0, \sigma_n^2)$. The results are presented in Table 8.9 below, where 2010 is all complete data from the 2010 survey, All is all com-

Table 8.9   Monitoring frequency by semesters as college student regression.

Data	# Obs	F stat for reg	β(value)	β(P-value)
2010	116	5.37	-0.78	0.022
All	389	2.67	-0.20	0.10
All(-1)	388	6.14	-0.27	0.014

plete data, and All(-1) we dropped one observation who reported passive monitoring of 60 days as unrealistic.

The 2010 data and the All data support our hypothesis that the coefficient β should have a negative value. The 2010 survey was conducted in an Introduction to Macroeconomics class and 25 of the subjects had completed fewer than 2 semesters. In this group 10 reported monitoring frequencies greater than 7; of these, 5 were passive monitors. In the All data the number of students who had fewer than 2 semesters was 36, and of these the same 10 had a monitoring frequency greater than 7. Most of the students in the non-2010 surveys were juniors and seniors. We assume that the slope is less negative for the All data because there are proportionately fewer freshmen when learning how to monitor begins. The fact that dropping one passive monitoring observation has such a large effect on the significance levels shows that the results are sensitive to the number of passive monitors.

Now let us consider the relationship between monitoring and budget self-rating. We postulate that the higher the value of the self-rating the more frequently the student monitors the flow of funds in the following regression:

$$D_n = \alpha + \beta SF_n + \epsilon_n \qquad (8.6)$$

where D_n is the monitoring frequency in days, SF_n is the value of the self-rating, and ϵ_n is the error term that is assumed to be independent and distributed $N(0, \sigma_n^2)$. The results are presented in Table 8.10 below, where

Table 8.10 Monitoring frequency by self-rating regression.

Data	# Obs	F stat for reg	β(value)	β(P-value)
2000a + 2006	134	0.56	-0.50	0.46
2000a+2006(Active)	121	5.61	-0.59	0.02
2007+2012	137	3.98	-0.95	0.05
2007	47	6.78	-2.19	0.012
2012	90	0.000	0.001	0.997
2012(filtered)	42	10.34	-1.42	0.03

2000a + 2006 is all complete data from the two surveys, (active) means fewer than 30, 2007 + 2012 means all data from those two surveys, and 2012(filtered) means observations in the 2012 data for which students were responsible for more than 50% of their food budget and did not ask their parents for more money when they were low on funds.

The regression results are sensitive to the distribution of the passive monitors. The 2007 data is the only set with a significant relationship by itself. This data had 10 passive monitors and none of them were associated with values of self-rating of 8,9, or 10. The fact that the 2000a + 2006 regression was not significant can be explained by the distribution of the passive monitors for which the self rating budget value of 1 had 1 passive monitor, the values of 2, 4, and 5 each had 2 passive monitors, and the value of 3 had 5 passive monitors. The 2012 data had 4 passive monitors and 3 of them were associated with self-rating values greater than 7. If we filter the 2012 data to remove students who can count on their parents to provide additional funds and are responsible for less than 50% of their food budget, 3 of the passive monitors are eliminated and the filtered regression is significant.

Let us consider another index that relates to monitoring frequency. On the 2000a and 2006 surveys students were asked the following question about their finances:

17. Would you say that your total income for the year is;
[1]. Barely enough to get through the year without car expenses _(19.8%)_

[2]. Enough to live adequately without car expenses ـ(23.7%)ـ

[3]. Barely enough to get through the year including car expenses ـ(17.6%)ـ

[4]. Enough to live adequately including car expenses ـ(22.9%)ـ

[5]. Enough to have a great life including car expenses ـ(16%)ـ

We postulate that the fewer financial resources a student has, the more frequently he will monitor the flow of funds with the following regression:

$$D_n = \alpha + \beta P_n + \epsilon_n \tag{8.7}$$

where D_n is the monitoring frequency in days, P_n is the value of income index and ϵ_n is the error term that is assumed to be independent and distributed $N(0, \sigma_n^2)$. The results are presented in Table 8.11 below.

Table 8.11   Monitoring versus income regression.

Data	# Obs	F stat for reg	β(value)	β(P-value)
2000a + 2006	131	7.38	1.65	0.007

The fewer resources students have to finance their life at college, the more frequently they monitor the flow of funds.

Reviewing the data, we can say that there is no simple theory based on a single variable that will explain why some students are passive monitors of budget flow. For variables we examined, such as % budget responsibility, we always found exceptions. Nevertheless, monitoring the flow of funds at least once a week is important for over 80% of students surveyed.

8.5   Adjustment Process

Our theory is that students learn to budget by an incremental adjustment process, a type of sequential trial and error or STE strategy. The rate at which they can make adjustments depends on the frequency of the purchase. Two annual purchases are the contract to rent an apartment or house and the associated utilities. Two semester decisions are paying tuition and buying textbooks. Categories of goods and services with more frequent purchases are clothing, travel, auto, entertainment, and food. The most frequent is food followed by entertainment is second. As we shall see, these two categories are central to students making adjustments.

8.5.0.1   *Adjusting budget estimates*

Students generally budget intuitively with a minority making formal budgets in a spreadsheet or budget software program. Now let us consider some reasons for making adjustments in these budgets. Students need to adjust their budgets when their estimates were either too high or too low. Let us consider the questions addressing this concern on the 2007 and 2010 surveys:

[2007] 22. Were your September 06 estimate on expenses (formal or intuitive expectations) for the academic year 06 - 07 too high or too low? Key: Write H if high; L if low; N if no estimate; Blank if correct
Tuition ___ Rent ___ Auto ___ Textbooks ___ Utilities ___ Food ___ Clothing ___ Entertainment ___ Cell phone ___ Other (specify)_____

[2010] Adjustments: For questions 23 - 25, we want you to compare your current budget with the budget you made prior to entering UT this fall.

23. Did you underestimate your expenses or spend more than you intended in one or more of the categories listed in Q9
YES_55%_ NO_45%_ If YES, which categories _____
24. Did you overestimate your expenses or spend less than you intended in one or more the categories listed in Q9 YES_26%_ NO_70%_ If YES, which categories _____

The responses to the Yes/No part of 2010 questions 23 and 24 are shown in % of the 125 students who filled in this questionnaire. Some students left the Yes/No question blank. Table 8.12 on the next page displays the responses in % for question 22 from the 2007 survey and questions 23 and 24 from the 2010 survey.

Of the 2007 students 76% estimated at least one category too high and 82% estimated at least one category too low. The response to this question depends on how it is asked. On the 2010 survey 55% of the respondents indicated that they underestimated one or more categories. A factor why the response rate was less than the 2007 survey may be that subjects had to shift back and forth between page 2 and page 5 and some students may have simply ignored the question.

Of the categories that a student can change at most once a semester, utilities and textbooks were frequently in error. The two categories with the most frequent purchases, food and entertainment, give students the most trouble in making estimates.

Table 8.12   Adjustment categories (by % responding).

Survey	2007	2007	2007	2007	2010	2010
Question	22 Hi	22 Lo	22 No	22 Bl	23	24
Rent	8	4	2	86	2	2
Utilities	28	22	4	46	5	4
Textbooks	44	18	6	32	9	8
Cell	18	1	32	40	0	0
Meal Plan	n/a	n/a	n/a	n/a	5	8
Clothing	22	14	24	40	8	5
Travel	n/a	n/a	n/a	n/a	3	2
Auto	6	22	8	54	3	5
Entertainment	28	32	8	32	26	5
Food	26	34	8	32	33	6

Now let us consider questions on the 2007 survey that relate to the frequency, motivation, and categories of adjustments:

23. Since Sep 06, how many adjustments to your spending patterns or income? None _2%_ Few_74%_ Several_20%_ Many _4%_ Note: If estimates high or low you must have made adjustments.

Reasons to adjust expenses: For questions 24-28 the categories to consider are: tuition, textbooks, rent, utilities, food, entertainment, clothing, and auto. Answer those questions that apply to you.

24. In order to reduce overall expenses to income I cut back on overall expenses? Yes _70%_ No _30%_ If Yes in the following categories

----

25. In order to balance expenses and income, I increased my income Yes _46%_ No _52%_

26. Did you cut expenses in one category in order to increase expenses in another? (For example, cutting food costs to free up money for entertainment.) Yes _56%_ No _38%_
If Yes, fill in categories: Cut _____ to increase _____

27. I have increased or plan to increase expenses in one or more categories because I have or will have more money to spend (includes budget estimate too high). Yes _26%_ No _70%_ If Yes, list these categories _____

28. If at the end of the month (or other budget period) you tend to run out of money and cut back to make it to the next period, what categories do you cut? _____

The responses, where possible, are shown in % of the 50 students who filled in this questionnaire. Some students left the Yes/No question blank. As can be seen by question 23 almost all of the 2007 survey students are making adjustments. Let us consider the categories involved in making adjustments as shown in Table 8.13 below. The two most adjusted categories reported

Table 8.13   Adjustment categories [2007 $n= 50$] (by % responding).

Question	24	26 Cut	26 Inc	27	28
Tuition	0	0	0	1	0
Rent	2	0	6	1	0
Utilities	2	2	1	1	2
Textbooks	0	4	8	0	2
Cell	2	0	0	0	0
Clothing	18	8	6	1	1
Auto	4	2	8	2	0
Entertainment	42	22	24	8	46
Food	46	26	1	1	32

by students in Questions 24, 26, 27, and 28 are Food and Entertainment, which are the most frequent expenditures.

The next question to consider is how do students make adjustments to various categories in their budgeting process? We asked the 2007 students the following question:

Adjustment method
41. How did you make the adjustments? Check all that apply:
[1]. Intuitively adjusting spending in various categories without making an explicit budget. _(26%)_

[2]. Made a budget in my head to adjust expenses. _(36%)_
[3]. Made a budget on paper to adjust expenses. _(18%)_
[4]. Made a computer budget to adjust expenses. _(20%)_

The responses are ordered by effort and formality. The numbers in () are the % of the 50 students taking the 2007 survey who checked this response or a less formal response. For example, some students who checked [4] also checked [3]. What this question indicates is that over half the students are using intuitive methods to make adjustments. On the 2010 survey we asked the following questions about how students adjusted their budgets with the Yes responses of the 125 students indicated in ():

25. If you underestimated expenses or spent more than intended, what action did you (or will you) take (can be more than one)?
(a) Did you have to learn how to cook (includes microwave dinners) at home to cut down on eating out at restaurants? YES (56[81%]) NO
(b) Got a job or increased the number of hours I worked? YES (38[55%]) NO
(c) Obtained more money through parents, loans, or credit card? Yes (45[65%]) NO
(d) Sat down and recalculated my budget? YES (47[68%]) NO
(e) Cut expenses without recalculation of my budget. For example, ? less entertainment, less eating out, or when eating out less expensive restaurants? YES(71[103%]) NO
(f) Do you think your cutting expenses could be characterized by a simple rule such as I cut back on luxuries in several areas? YES (74[107%]) NO
(h) I plan to get a less expensive apartment next year YES (31[45%]) NO

Let us interpret a number like (nn[mm%]) above. The number nn is the number of students who checked the response and the number mm is the % of the 69 students who answered Yes to Question 23 in the 2010 survey. The fact that the % for both (e) and (f) is greater than 100 indicates more than 69 students answered this question. What is important is that adjustments are made with simple heuristics rather than with extensive calculation of all possible alternatives.

One approach to balancing expenses with income is to increase income. Question 25 of the 2007 survey indicates that for almost half of the 2007 students, obtaining more money was a part of balancing expenses and income. In the 2010 survey over half the students who underestimated one or more categories, obtained more income as indicated in (b) and (c) above.

Now let us consider specific steps students took to adjust their food budgets. The price of a meal can vary by more than a factor of 5 between preparing a meal at home and going to a restaurant. Students adjusting their food budgets do more than simply buying cheaper meals at restaurants. They must also decide how much food they plan to prepare in their residence. On the 2007 budget survey we asked the following question:

29. Will you adjust food expenses? ____ If "M" or "L", check all that apply: [Learn to cook (M = Yes)__] [Eat out __] [Select __ expensive restaurants] [Select __ expensive choices from menu] [Buy __ expensive groceries] Other (specify) _____

Prior to this question students were informed that "M" meant more or up and "L" meant less or down. The results for the 50 students are shown in Table 8.14 below.

Table 8.14   Food adjustments.

Category	Adj Food	Cook	Eat Out	Select res	Select meals	Groceries
Less	35	3	27	23	23	20
More	5	31(yes)	5	1	0	5

What this table indicates is that 35 out of 50 students wanted to adjust their food budget down and did so by some combination of leaning to cook, eating out less, and selecting less expensive restaurants, meals and groceries. These thirty five students also indicated that they either underestimated their food budget, and made subsequent cuts in food to reduce overall expenses to income, or cut expenses in food in order to be able to increase expenses in another category. Of the 69 out of 125 students who indicated that they underestimated at least one category of their budget in Question 23 of the 2010 survey, which is presented several pages back, 41 indicated underestimating their food budget. In learning how to cook as a response to adjusting their budget in Question 25 above, 56 responded yes; of these, 25 had indicated that they had underestimated their food budget.

In order to investigate learning to cook further, we asked the following question on the 2012 survey:

20. How have your cooking skills changed between high school and now? Check the boxes under HS that show the level of your cooking skill as a senior in high school and do the same for NOW that show your cooking skill level now
a. No cooking HS__ NOW __

b. Prepared food such as milk and cereal or TV dinner HS__ NOW __
c. Cook simple meal such as hamburger or fried eggs HS__ NOW __
d. Can cook a meal from a recipe HS__ NOW __
e. Gourmet cook HS__ NOW __

The % of the 93 students who gave complete data for the question is shown in Table 8.15 below. The table indicates that students increase their cooking

Table 8.15   Cooking skill: HS and now.

Level	High School	Now
a	11	0
b	31	2
c	22	13
d	28	59
e	6	24

skills considerably to decrease their food budget. Reducing expenses can require learning skills to change the Becker's household production function. A couple buying a home in the suburbs faces the same problem in terms of cutting the lawn, gardening, painting, and repairs. How much do they want to use their own labor and how much would they rather hire an artisan?

Now let us consider entertainment and clothing. There is also a large variation in entertainments costs. Going to the movies is an example where students have a menu of choices such as going to a movie theater, $8+, renting a DVD, $1-3, or checking out a DVD from the library, $0. These are the most frequent student purchases so that they can use a STE strategy. Of the 31 students adjusting entertainment expenses on the 07 budget survey, 19 would spend less and 12 would spend more. When considering entertainment details, 8 would date less and 10 more, 18 would go out less and 11 more, and finally 24 would go to less expensive events and 3 to more expensive events. Clothing has an option for reducing expenses by delaying new purchases. Of the 23 students adjusting clothing expenses on the 2007 budget survey, 17 would wear their clothes longer before replacing them.

Students also adjust less frequent purchases. Another example besides learning to cook, where students can use more labor to reduce expenses, is to buy textbooks online instead of from the UT bookstore. Thirty one 2007 students indicated they planned to buy textbooks online in the future. The less frequent the purchase, the less opportunity a consumer has to make a budget adjustment. For students renting an apartment or house this is generally a once a year decision. At our university it is cheaper to rent south of the river transversing the city, but it can be time consuming taking a bus in rush hour traffic. Living in West Campus is the most convenient, but also the most expensive. Living north of campus is a compromise between the two. Students do make annual adjustments in how much to budget for rent. Of the 69 students who underestimated their expenses on the 2010 survey, 30% plan to get a less expensive apartment next year. On the 2007 survey 19 students planned to rent a less expensive apartment next year, and 9, a more expensive apartment. On the 2010 survey, 31 out of the 125 students plan to rent a less expensive apartment next year.

Question 28 asks whether the subject had to cut back expenses at the end of the month (or other budget period). Of the 50 students filling in the 2007 survey, 39 had to cut back in at least one category. This indicates that balancing expenses with income is not an easy task. We postulated the following regression:

$$N_n = \alpha + \beta M_n + \epsilon_n \qquad (8.8)$$

where N_n is the number of categories adjusted at the end of the budget period, M_n is the adjustment method listed in Question 41 of the 2007 survey above and ϵ_n is the error term that is assumed to be independent and distributed $N(0, \sigma_n^2)$. We tested the hypothesis of homoskedasticity with the Breusch and Pagan (1979)/ Cook-Weisberg test and did not reject this hypothesis with a significance level of 80%. The results of the regular regression are indicated in Table 8.16 below.

Table 8.16   Number adjustments and adjustment method.

Survey	Num Obs	F stat for reg	β(value)	β(P-value)
2007	50	4.7	0.24	0.03

We tested the hypothesis of normal errors with the Shapiro-Wilk W, Shapiro-Francia W, and the Skewness/Kutosis tests and did not reject the hypothesis of normal errors for each regression with a significance level of 30%. What this regression suggests is that the more trouble a student has in balancing expenses with income, the greater the inclination to use a more formal method of budgeting.

The adjustment process involves adjusting income, labor input and choices and also requires time to achieve an adjustment. When the 2007 budget survey students were asked, "How long did it take you to adjust your budget?", 15 responded "a week", 16 responded "a month", 5 responded "a semester", and 14 indicated that they were "still adjusting". This indicates that 38% were taking more than a half year to adjust. Next, we consider a type of budgeting we call feast or famine budgeting.

8.5.1 *Feast or Famine Budgeting*

The feast or famine adjustment process is best defined as answer b in the following question in the 2006 survey that is shown below with the responses for the 49 subjects shown in ():

End of pay period adjustment
26. Check the response that best typifies the type of budgeter you are:
a. I budget to spend uniformly throughout the period between pay or allowance checks. __(22)_
b. During the first week or two after I get my paycheck or allowance from parents, I enjoy life. The week before the next check, I cut back on expenditures to avoid overdrawing my account. __(26)_
(1) If you cut back the last week, check all that apply: (a) Eat out less __(31)_ and when I do I order cheaper meals __(24)_
(b) Buy cheaper products and fewer luxuries at grocery store __(27)_
(c) Less entertainments expenses __(32)_ (6th street, movies, dates or cheaper dates) (d) Other (describe) ___cheaper beer (1)___no clothes shopping (2)

Of the 26 students who checked b, 4 also checked a, an inconsistency, but these students also checked at least one response under (1). This question on the 2006 survey had the highest response for feast or famine budgeters with over half indicating this type of behavior; on the 2010 survey only 18.5% or 23 out of 124 subjects indicated feast or famine behavior on a similar question.

The self-rating index of students who do not feast or famine budget is higher than those that do, but a t test of the difference is not significant. The one significant relationship we found is the income index, which describes how much money a student has for expenses. The income index of feast or famine budgeters is 3.5 while those who do not budget this way is 2.6 and a t test of the difference is significant with an α of 0.02. This result suggests that poorer students can not feast or famine budget because they are in famine mode the entire budget period.

8.6   Conclusion

In this section we focus our attention on comparing those aspects of the previous research of [Thaler (1991)] and [Heath and Soll (1996)] that were topics of our research.

[Thaler (1991)] asserts that the substantive consumer model implies that money should be fungible, that is, money should not have labels attached to it. Our research provides further evidence that money is not fungible. On the 2007 survey we asked the following question and the response of the 50 students is indicated in ():

> 49. Do you treat money you earn yourself differently from money you get from your parents?
> Yes _(34)_ No _(15)_ If Yes, check all that apply a. I am more frugal with my money because I earned it _(22)_ b. Money I get from my parents is earmarked for specific items and the money I earn is for entertainment _(29)_ c. Discuss: (one student wrote "groceries only for parents money")

Another example is that parents who give their children a credit card where the bill goes to the parents generally restrict its use, for example, for emergencies only. Thaler adapts the prospect function to budgeting. The logic of the prospect function indicates that budgeters adjust their memory of experiences to increase their utility. We did not investigate this phenomenon.

[Heath and Soll (1996)] have assumed that subjects in their budgeting have designated fixed amounts for such categories as food, entertainment, and rent. Our data indicates that most student budgeters are flexible.

Students simply do not have the computational resources to consider every budget alternative. They can pay their semester and monthly bills up front and learn to adjust the flexible expenses such as food and entertainment. Successful informal budgeters can use this method of budgeting throughout their lives. Two infrequent purchases are buying a car and buying a home. If the consumer had to borrow money for such a purchase, traditionally the budget amount was determined by the lender. I assume the recent housing bubble and collapse represents a temporary suspension of the traditional role of the lender. Thus if a budgeter pays bills up front and learns to control variable expenses, the budgeter can succeed without formal methods. Our research suggests that failure in intuitive budgeting is one reason consumers shift to the use of more formal methods in an attempt to control expenses.

Preparing for retirement is a one time activity for which an incremental adjustment approach to budgeting is not applicable. We shall discuss this in the next two Chapters.

Up to now we have been focused on the procedures consumers use to solve item searches and budgeting. Now we shift our attention to the consumer performance in these tasks.

Chapter 9

How Close to Optimal?

9.1 Introduction

The main author spent twenty years writing optimization code for which convergence to optimal was asymptotic, for example [Norman (1965)], [Norman and Norman (1973)], [Norman (1976)], and [Norman (1984)]. Based on that experience and the difficulty of the consumer optimization problem relative to what is tractable for an unaided human processor, the author would never ask a Yes/No question regarding whether consumers achieve optimality. Instead he would strongly suggest economists and psychologists should ask how close to optimal is human consumer performance. This question presents a very difficult measurement problem given the ordinal nature of utility theory.

In Section 2, we define the attributes of the reference model we will use to measure performance. We consider a one period model with savings as the variable that connects the periods. We consider both anticipated or decision utility and realized or experienced utility. Next, in Section 3, we review the various measures that have been created to identify mistakes and evaluate performance relative to both anticipated and realized utility.

In Section 4 we consider two experiments that are good approximations to our reference model. These two important studies involving a small number of periods and no long term decisions, such as retirement, are data obtained from an experiment in a psychiatric ward, [Battalio *et al.* (1973)] and [Cox (1997)] and from animal experiments, [Kagel *et al.* (1995)]. In these studies the subjects were presented with few options and quickly learned their preferences. Also, for comparative statics purposes, the consumption decisions were repeated each period. The results demonstrate behavior that closely approximates consumer theory.

In this book we have discussed simplifications that consumers use to solve their consumer optimization problem. In Section 5 we review the literature and present results from our student surveys on the identification of mistakes and performance evaluation in each of these simplifications. We start with the consequences of shifting from bundles to item-by-item searching. Then, before considering the other simplifications we consider psychological limitations to achieving optimal performance. Finally, we consider item searches and budgeting. We include in the item search discussion, decisions involving a component of the bundles a consumer purchases in the marketplace.

In Section 6 we assess the current status of research on consumer performance. It is currently impossible to quantitatively determine how close to optimal is the performance of the typical consumer. Qualitatively we assert two hypotheses. One is that individual differences are an important factor in the magnitude of differences from optimal. Second is that the magnitude of the deviation depends on the magnitude of change taking place in the life of the consumer.

9.2 Reference Model

In this section, we define the model against which we measure performance. In Chapter 2 we presented a single period model. We could measure multiperiod or even lifetime consumer performance against the discounted utility model of [Samuelson (1937)]. How do consumers solve such a model? We assert that to simplify the lifetime consumption problem, they solve each period separately using a sequential process with savings being the variable that connects the periods. This model does not incorporate consumers learning their preferences, which in some cases may be in the form of utility values. In addition, research presented in [Frederick *et al.* (2002)] shows that this model is seriously flawed and attempts to fix it have not been that successful. Instead we shall focus on the accuracy of the one period model and the savings that connect the periods together.

There are two definitions of utility that can be used in the one period model. The first is the *anticipated utility*, which is the judgement of the realized utility at the time of the purchase decision. From early in the 20th century this is the version of utility used in economic theory. The other version is the *realized*, which is the utility experienced during actual consumption. This version is associated with Bentham and 19th century economics, but recently [Kahneman *et al.* (1997)] proposed revising this version of utility theory. A major difference between the two concepts is that anticipated utility is an ordinal concept whereas realized utility is a cardinal concept. We shall not attempt to resolve the conundrum of how an ordinal concept can be a forecast of a cardinal concept.

In [Kahneman *et al.* (1997)] the anticipated utility and realized utility are called decision utility and experienced utility respectively. We prefer the adjective anticipated to decision because it emphasizes the consumer is making a forecast that is a psychological judgement not a scientific forecast. We prefer the adjective realized to experienced in order to emphasize the random elements in many judgments of anticipated utility.

In most cases this anticipated utility is a weighted average of the attributes the consumer considers important. These attributes can have random elements, such as the reliability of a car being evaluated. In most cases the consumer does not have the data or computational ability to obtain an expected value of the random element, but instead has a proxy variable. Consider obtaining a judgment of a car's reliability. The data that is available from a source such as consumer reports is the relative ranking in terms of repairs from previous models. Thus a consumer must make a judgement about expected repair costs from the relative rankings of previous models.

We shall not separate the anticipated utility into subcategories involving zero and one or more random elements. In purchases with random elements a consumer does not maximize the expected (anticipated) utility. Humans tend to focus more on avoiding downside losses than upside gains. In the sequence of decisions leading up to a purchase this bias will be incorporated into the sequence. In addition, a consumer frequently does not have the data to make expected value forecasts as we pointed out in the case of automobile reliability. In repeated purchases with a random element consumers can estimate the anticipated utility, but this estimate is much more likely to have the defects found in anchoring and adjustment heuristics than a basis in good statistical methodology. Computing the expected value from a continuous distribution is not tractable for an unaided human, and so is computing an expected value with a discrete distribution that has many data points. So in item searches involving one or more random elements there is a problem in deciding how the random elements are incorporated into the decision process.

In the next Chapter we will consider improving consumer performance. If anticipated utility is an unbiased estimate of realized utility, it makes no difference which version of utility we use, but if the estimate is biased we should use realized utility. As we shall discuss in the next Chapter, one area of improving consumer performance is to reduce the bias.

The final point concerning this model is to consider the cases where the consumers have learned their anticipated utility. Our criterion is cases where the consumer can make a decision without having to gather and process more data than is necessary to identify the alternatives. This condition constitutes a very strong interpretation of comparative statics. Now let us summarize conditions that are either explicit or implicit in this strong interpretation of comparative statics:

- Consumers have learned their preferences
- Consumer do not seek variety in goods such as food
- The frequency which consumers buy goods corresponds to the budget period
- The costs of solving the problem are negligible.

9.3   The Measurement Problem

As we have pointed out several times, we should measure consumer performance in terms of how close actual performance is to optimal and not ask a Yes/No question about whether consumers optimize their performance. Ideally, we would like to measure the effect of each type of deviation from the stringent assumptions of the theoretical model. For example, how prevalent is variety, such as in choosing restaurant meals, and the magnitude of the affect in terms of overall performance. Also, as decision psychologists and behavioral economists point out an anomaly, we ideally would like to measure its impact on optimal performance.

Measuring consumer performance can be considered a two step process. As a first step we need to demonstrate the existence of an error. As a second step we would like to measure its impact on performance. The second step is much more difficult than the first. Let us first consider measuring performance relative to anticipated utility and then relative to realized utility.

The problem with measuring performance relative to anticipated utility is that given it is an ordinal concept, we can not determine quantitatively how close consumers are to optimal. Suppose we label the optimal as 100 and the actual as 81. It would appear that the consumer is 81% optimal. But if we make a monotonic transformation by taking the square root, the comparison is 9 versus 10 and it would appear that the consumer is 90% optimal.

One approach to revealing the existence of errors might be to consider deviations from axioms defining rationality. For a summary of this literature see [Rieskamp *et al.* (2006)]. Investigators in this area should consider the axiomatic approach of [Fuchs-Seliger and Mayer (2003)] because this approach uses dominance to greatly reduce what consumers must learn in terms of preferences. Preference axioms based on completeness and transitivity are intractable for the unaided human processor. Until economic theorists determine which axiomatic approach requires the least effort to learn, I do not consider this approach useful.

A much better approach to measuring errors is through the concept of revealed preference, [Samuelson (1937)]. This concept has been developed into the generalized axiom of revealed preference, GARP, for example see [Varian (1982)] to test for the existence of errors from optimization. GARP tests are not applicable to all types of item searches. An example is buying a digital camera, where the consumer usually buys a single item and when he buys a new replacement the alternatives have been modified by technological advance.

In addition, GARP tests are yes or no tests. Economists since [Afriat (1967)] have been constructing statistics to measure the deviation in a data set from GARP. In a recent article [Echenique *et al.* (2011b)] construct a new index called a money pump index, MPI, which is similar to Afriat's efficiency indices. The MPI has the desirable feature that it expresses the deviation in a dollar amount.

Now let us consider measuring the existence of realized utility errors. One approach is to ask, using a survey technique, if consumers after or during consumption are self-aware of making an error. They could, of course, have made an error without recognizing the error.

In order to measure the magnitude of performance errors based on realized utility, we need a method of measuring realized utility, a cardinal concept. [Edgeworth (1881)] proposed that psychological developments would make it possible to develop a hedonimeter to measure realized utility. In the 20th century economists switched their focus from realized to anticipated utility. Also, because demand functions could be derived only assuming ordinal utility, there was no need to measure utility theory directly and realized utility could be implied by observing consumer behavior such as by using revealed preference.

In a recent development, [Kahneman *et al.* (1997)] presented a research agenda for measuring cardinal realized (experienced) utility. [Kahneman and Dolan (2008)] propose an application in the field of health. Given the difficulties of implementing this approach it has generated very little interest among economists. As we shall see, economists have employed proxies for utility in order to measure performance.

Our ordering experiment discussed in Chapter 3 suggests that a limited cardinal measure of remembered realized utility may be possible. In the ordering experiments discussed in Chapter 3, the subjects each had to write ABC with each pen before ordering the pen. For most subjects the smoothness with which a pen writes is an important criteria for evaluating the pen and we assume that writing ABC is sufficient experience for subjects to make a reasonably accurate estimate of the realized utility.

In observing several hundred students order pens, I noticed a particular behavior. Students ordered pens on a sheet on which Best was written on one side and on the other side Worst. If the first pen the students evaluated was a very good pen they placed it near the Best sign and a bad pen near the Worst sign. If they had ordered several pens without finding a really good pen, the ordering would be on the Worst side of the sheet. If the next pen they evaluated was a very good pen, they would leave a space between the previously ordered pens and the new pen. In the earliest version of the pen ordering experiment students were asked to order up to 25 pens.

When faced with 20 or more pens, students frequently divided the pens in subsets such as by color. They would then order each subset and merge the subsets. For example, if they preferred black pens to blue pens, they would place all the black pens in a higher position than the blue pens. This heuristic reduced the effort. From my observation of students ordering pens, I claim that they were capable of establishing a utility function with at least 15 levels. We will call such a utility function a n level utility function where n is 15.

Sites on the Internet have developed a 1–5 rating system for restaurants, hotels, and products. For products that a consumer has considerable experience with alternatives such as restaurants, this rating system may well reflect the consumer's rating relative to an ideal good meal. Rating a consumed meal from 1–5 is a 5 level utility measure. As pointed out by [Kahneman et al. (1997)], remembered utility has its defects, but as we shall discuss in the next Chapter, fake reviews are probably a much bigger problem. We believe that for pens a consumer could use a 10 level utility function to measure the gap between the best pen and the pen brought to the experiment. For products for which the consumer has not had much experience with the alternatives, such a rating might well represent the difference between the anticipated and realized utility.

Finally, we need to consider budgeting performance. In Chapter 8 we demonstrated that subjects were self-aware of their budgeting performance, hence we could use a self-aware index of budgeting performance.

9.4 Tests of Utility Theory

Two data samples to test utility theory that approximately satisfy this strong comparative statics condition are the animal experiments presented in [Kagel *et al.* (1995)] and an experiment in a token economy at the Central Islip State Hospital in New York presented in [Battalio *et al.* (1973)].

The animal experiments were conducted using pigeons and rats, in which the subject had a choice of selecting amounts of two goods. In the rat experiments, the rat pressed one lever to obtain a quantity of one good and pressed a second lever to obtain a quantity of the second good. The budget for rats was the total number of lever presses they could make during the experimental session. The price of the good was determined by the amount of the good the rat obtained with one lever press. The pigeons also selected amounts of two goods. The budget for pigeons was the fixed amount of time to obtain goods and the price was determined by the time delay to deliver the selected choice.

There were two experiments. The first was choosing combinations of food and water and the second was choosing combinations of root beer and Tom Collins mix. The purpose of the experiments was to vary the prices to determine if the animal subjects' behavior satisfied the Slutsky compensated demand function. In the case of food and water the animal behavior was consistent 87.5% of the time for rats and 81.3% of the time for pigeons. The chance of these results being obtained by random selection is less than 1% in both cases. In the case of root beer versus Tom Collins mix the results were consistent 100% of the time.

The experimenters took the trouble to eliminate four alternative theories that might explain the results they obtained. They showed that reducing the price of food increases the consumption of both food and water. This is incompatible with the leading psychological theory called the matching law. By demonstrating the existence of a Giffen good and conducting experiments they were able to eliminate Becker's irrational choice model and both the generalized minimum distance hypothesis and the generalized minimum needs hypothesis.

The second experiment that approximately satisfies the strong comparative statics condition was performed with subjects who were patients at the Central Islip State Hospital in New York; see [Battalio *et al.* (1973)]. The 38 patients earned tokens for tasks and could spend them on 16 items. Eight of these items were sold in the token store and consisted of cigarettes and seven food items. They could also rent items such as a private room, attend a dance, or buy items of clothing. The token store had been in operation for 1.5 years and the subjects had been patients for between 1 and 38 years. In this book, we assume consumers learn their preferences. Given the small number of items and time in the hospital we can assume the patients had learned their preferences over the items available to them in the hospital marketplace. The authors made a considerable effort to gather accurate data, collecting two sets of data using two procedures. The budget period in data collection was a week.

The experiment was conducted over 7 weeks to test the patients' responses to price changes that occurred once each week. In the first, third, sixth and seventh periods the prices were the same as before the experiment started. The sixteen goods were divided into three groups. The prices of items in the third group remained the same for all 7 periods. In period 2 the prices of items in the first group were halved and those in the second group doubled. In the fourth and fifth periods the prices of items in the first group were doubled and those in the second group halved. These price changes follow the practice of psychological experiments of baseline, variation, then return to baseline.

In this experiment the authors determined whether the subjects' expenditures satisfied the Slutsky-Hicks conditions. Of the 38 subjects, 19 satisfied these conditions without having to consider the second data set, and 17 of the remainder could be made consistent with the Slutsky-Hicks conditions by considering both data sets. Thus 95% of the time the subjects' behavior was consistent. The authors postulated that two of the subjects did not adjust their expenditure pattern immediately between periods 4 and 6.

[Cox (1997)] provided an alternative analysis of the data collected in this experiment. He extended revealed preference theory to include portfolio choice and labor supply. He selected the data generated by [Battalio *et al.* (1973)] because it met the stringent data requirements for his revealed preference formulation. First, the data must not be aggregated, because conditions imposed on aggregated data confound the testing of disaggregated utility theory, [Sonnenshein (1973a)], [Sonnenshein (1973b)], and

[Shafer and Sonnenshein (1982)]. Second, the data must contain all goods and not be a subset, [Varian (1988)]. Finally, the data must be sufficiently accurate so that the data errors do not confound the results, [Battalio *et al.* (1973)]. In his model, 260 out of 263 observations were not shown to be inconsistent with the utility hypothesis. 38 out of the 39 subjects were consistent with utility maximization without data adjustment. In addition, the data does not support the irrational choice model of [Becker (1962)].

It is possible the [Battalio *et al.* (1973)] data underestimates the effect of variety. In the experiments in the token economy they reported they collected data on the following goods: "Cigarette — various brands available; Penny candy — hard candy of varying flavors; Candy bar — various kinds of 'nickel' candy bars, all with chocolate content; Cookie — vanilla or oatmeal cookie made at C.I. commissary; Soda — 12 oz. can of soda, various flavors." It would appear that each of these goods was considered as one product and not broken down by flavor or brand. In a communication with Professor Kagel, one of the authors, he indicated that each of the goods was probably teated as one product, but given the time lapse, he was not sure. If that is true the Cox results underestimate the magnitude of GARP errors. Nevertheless, it would have been extremely useful to have recorded and processed that data both ways in order to obtain a measure of error that could be attributed to not including variety in the consumer model.

9.5   Simplification Performance

Now let us consider a one period consumer optimization problem faced by consumers in the marketplace. Consumer behavior in the marketplace has much greater deviations from the strong comparative statics model than was the case with the two experiments discussed in the previous section. In buying new goods with a high rate of technological change at infrequent intervals, consumers must learn their preferences. Consumers enjoy variety in goods, such as food and even more in movies. The frequency of many repeat purchases does not correspond to the budget period. In addition, item searches for infrequently purchased goods and budgeting have significant costs. Finally, consumers in the marketplace face a very large number of goods, making the complete solution intractable. Consumers obtain a solution by simplifying the problem they actually solve.

In order to make a qualitative assessment of how close to optimal is human consumer performance in the marketplace, we shall evaluate the consumer performance in the simplifications humans use to solve the consumer problem. We want to identify errors and ideally, measure their magnitude. We divide the discussion into four subsections:

(1) Searching item-by-item instead of by bundles
(2) Item search based on experience.
(3) Item search based on acquiring and analyzing data
(4) Budgeting

We shall include in "Item search based on experience" research on choices involving a small number of alternatives and groceries.

9.5.1   *Item-by-Item*

In Chapter 2 we asserted that switching consumer search from bundles to item-by-item does not necessarily result in errors or require an additive utility function. If at each item search the consumer carefully considers previous purchases, the consumer could evaluate the interaction effects of previous purchases with the current search and avoid error. We shall consider whether this is the case by reviewing the experimental evidence and the results of a questionnaire on consumer mistakes.

Read, Loewenstein and Rabin (2006) create a concept of choice bracketing, which is the number of choices that are grouped together in the decision process. A choice bracketing is narrow if few choices are grouped together in the decision process and broad if a large number are grouped together. They cite an experiment by [Tversky and Kahneman (1981)] involving the choice in two gambles. Subjects make different choices if the two gambles are presented separately than if they are combined into one gamble. Experimental evidence suggests that consumers make mistakes in partitioning the choice bundle into item-by-item searches.

We investigated this possibility in the marketplace using a questionnaire concerning consumer mistakes in 2012. Ninety six students were each paid $5 to answer a three page questionnaire about their mistakes. The question about clothing mistakes is relevant to this discussion. The question is:

III. Clothing Mistakes

A clothing mistake is an article of clothing that you bought that you never or almost never wear. It just sits in your closet or dresser drawer. In the past 3 years how many clothing mistakes have you made? (Check whichever applies)

0: _(10.4%)_, 1-3: _(46.9%)_, 4-6: _(17.7%)_, 7+: _(24.0%)_

Check all reasons that apply:

_(37.2%)_1. I was buying several items of clothing, and it looked good in ads or in the store on a mannequin.

_(44.2%)_2. I forgot to think about what I was going to wear it with or for what occasion, and when I got home I realized I had made a mistake.

_(46.5%)_3. In the store it was presented as a great bargain, and I got caught up into getting a great deal without thinking about when I was going to wear it.

_(22.1%)_4. I was in a hurry and did not have the time to carefully think about the purchase.

_(11.6%)_5. I was under pressure from my peers to buy the item.

The % of the 96 students responding is shown in (), and only 10.4%, which is 10 students, made no mistakes. Of the 86 students making at least one mistake, 85 checked at least one reason that applied and the average number of reasons checked was 1.5. The percents in the "reasons that apply" are in relationship to the 86 students who made at least one mistake. In creating this question various members of the research group pointed out that they had made mistakes in clothing decisions when they failed to consider how the purchase would mesh with their wardrobe. Reasons 2 and 3 reflect this failure to consider previous clothing decisions when making the current clothing decision.

Consumers do make mistakes by failing to carefully consider previous purchases in the current item search.

9.5.2 *Item Searches*

We shall start this section by considering various psychological and economic factors that limit a consumer's ability to achieve optimization. Then we shall consider item searches, which we will divide into two categories. The first are item searches based on past experience. For items searches that are infrequent or for a product that is undergoing rapid technological advance or is new technology, past experience is frequently insufficient to evaluate the alternatives. A consumer must gather and analyze data to evaluate them. We shall call such item searches, data item searches.

9.5.2.1 *Psychological and economic limiting factors*

Psychological factors affect both types of item searches. In some cases, a consumer's anticipated utility may not be a good forecast of realized or experienced utility, even when the consumer has had extensive experience with the alternatives. As [Kahneman and Thaler (2006)] point out, anticipated utility forecasts depend on the emotional and motivational state at the time of the forecast. For example, hungry shoppers tend to buy excessive amount of food to reduce future hunger, [Nisbett and Kanouse (1968)].

[Kahneman and Dolan (2008)] provide another example of the limits of current experience in predicting future realized utility. In this example consumers made hypothetical valuations of health states posed as a gamble between full health and death or certain moderate health. What respondents frequently fail to consider is their ability to adapt, hence such valuations are of questionable value. The authors propose an alternative approach based on realized or experienced utility.

Now let us consider data item searches involving first time, infrequent, or purchases of products undergoing rapid technological change for which the consumer must gather and process data beyond memories of previous experiences. Such searches are likely to have a much larger start set than a frequently conducted search and require several set steps before processing members of the final set individually. At each stage the consumer must gather data to make judgements about alternative sets or individual items.

One economic error is the failure to allocate enough time to gather and analyze data to evaluate alternatives. This error will be discussed in our survey below and is known in the literature. For example, [Hogarth (1987)] gives evidence that trying to solve difficult judgement and choice problems too quickly can lead to a superficial decision process. Related to this insufficient time allocation is the application of the correct decision rule at each stage of the decision process. Non-compensatory decision rules generally require much less data and therefore less effort to execute. Compensatory decision rules generally require more data and more effort to execute. Applying a non-compensatory rule in a case where a compensatory rule is appropriate is likely to result in a less than optimal decision, [Bettman *et al.* (1998)].

Sometimes the desired data is simply not available. For example, modern packaging precludes interaction with the product before purchase and returning a product has costs. Second, in many cases a consumer must use proxies for the desired data. One factor in evaluating alternative automobiles is making a judgment about a car's reliability. The data that is available from a source such as Consumer Reports is the relative ranking in terms of repairs from previous models. Thus a consumer must make a judgement about expected repair costs from the relative rankings of previous models. A consumer must make judgements, which are intuitive, not scientific forecasts, based on the available data.

To simplify the evaluation process, consumers use heuristics to make both judgements and choices. Since about 1970 decision psychologists' studies of human heuristics in judgment and choice, such as [Kahneman *et al.* (1982)], have shown that the use of heuristics is efficient, but not without biases. Some heuristics violate statistical logic. For example, [Tversky and Kahneman (1984)] show that humans violate the conjunctive law. As shown in Chapter 5, human heuristics to update data are not Bayesian. Also, humans tend to regard a small sample as representative of the population as a whole, which is known as the law of small numbers, [Hogarth (1987)].

The leaders in this effort, Daniel Kahneman and Amos Tversky, focused on three heuristics: availability, representativeness, and anchoring and adjustment. The availability heuristic states that a judgement will be biased by the availability of data in memory. For example, subjects, when asked whether there are more words that start with "r" or have "r" as the third letter, respond with the former because it is easier to remember instances of words that start with "r" than have "r" as a third letter.

The representativeness heuristic is making judgments using instances stored in memory considered representative. This can lead to stereotypical thinking. In the anchoring and adjustment heuristic, to make an estimate humans start with an anchor and then make adjustments. The tendency is not to make enough adjustments. These are general heuristics used in making judgments and would also be used in making consumer judgements. The judgment and choice literature can have long lists of heuristics and their biases. For example, in a summary [Hogarth (1987)] lists 38 shortcomings of human judgement and choice heuristics. A recent survey of human behavioral limitations can be found in [DellaVigna (2009)].

The reader unfamiliar with this literature might start with [Kahneman (2011)]. This book gives a very readable discussion with numerous examples. In addition, the reader trained in economics with its emphasis on mathematical models based on broad assumptions should gain an insight into the profound difference between the mind set of a psychologist and an economist. Finally, I found the discussion of the relationship between the prospect function and Daniel Bernoulli's 18th century work very interesting.

[Ariely *et al.* (2003)] present an experiment that shows that subjects can unknowingly use an inappropriate anchor. Subjects in the experiment were asked to bid on 6 items: two bottles of wine, a cordless keyboard, cordless trackball, a design book, and a box of Neuhaus chocolates. Subjects were asked to write the last two digits of their social security number at the top of the page and next to each of the six items in the form of a price before bidding. The subjects bids were significantly correlated with their social security numbers for all six items and the relative preferences were stable. For example, over 95% of the subjects valued the cordless keyboard more than the cordless trackball.

Even where data is available the consumer does not acquire and process it without biases. How data is presented or framed affects how a consumer will process it. Consumers sometimes exhibit confirmation bias that is to only acquire data that supports a hypothesis and reject data that conflicts with the hypothesis. In the case of using relative rankings to predict vehicle reliability, if a consumer has a friend who bought a lemon, the consumer is likely to overweight the concrete experience of the friend in judging the reliability of that make and model.

Consumers must also make judgments about the reliability of the data source. In reading anonymous reviews online, a consumer must judge who wrote the review. A review written by a customer is much more likely to provide an honest evaluation than a review written by a representative of a firm who has an incentive to promote its products and pans its rivals' products. In paying for advertising, the firm's objective is to sell the product. This means that the firm will select the subset of data that could have been provided that presents the product in the most favorable light. Some advertisements provide the consumer with useful information such as the availability of an apartment for rent or house for sale. Some media ads on TV provide a simplistic example of how the product solves the consumer's problem and focus on creating a favorable impression of the product. This leads to the affect heuristic of [Slovic *et al.* (2006a)], in that consumers are inclined to favor products that have positive associations. [Camerer (2006)] points out that sellers exploit behavioral limits of consumers to increase sales.

We accept decades of research by decision psychologists that judgements frequently have biases. But, just because judgements have biases does not necessarily mean a consumer will make a mistake in an item search. In selecting between item A and B, if both forecasts have a bias, but the bias does not alter the relative ranking, no mistake will occur.

To what extent does consumer behavior improve with experience? For example, do the numerous anomalies discovered by behavioral economists and decision psychologists decrease with market experience? Let us consider one such anomaly, the endowment effect, which is the phenomenon that a good's value increases once a consumer owns it, see [Thaler (1980)]. Thus a consumer would require a higher price to sell a good that he owns than to purchase it if he did not own it. This discrepancy invalidates the Coase theorem and is important for public goods such as the environment.

[List (2003)] discusses a field experiment he performed that shows market experience reduces the endowment effect, for which he cites numerous experiments that demonstrate its existence. List examined two sports memorabilia markets comparing the behavior of dealers, consumers with experience, with the behavior of nondealers, consumers with less experience. There is a significant endowment effect in the pooled data, but the endowment effect becomes negligible for dealers and the subset of nondealers with experience. In a follow-up study a year later of the same individuals, he found the endowment effect reduced. All anomalies discovered by behavioral economists and decision psychologists should be subject to a "List" market test to determine the magnitude of the effect under market conditions.

Behavioral economists' and decision psychologists' research has been focused on demonstrating the existence of anomalies, not measuring their impact under market conditions. Until more researchers follow the lead of [List (2003)], it will be impossible to assess the magnitude of their effect on consumer performance.

9.5.2.2 *Item searches based on prior experience*

In this subsection we consider item searches for goods for which prior experience is the most important factor in choice. Let us first look at the experimental evidence and then at sequential trial and error testing.

Now let us consider another question: whether consumer performance in terms of GARP improves with age and market experience. We will briefly discuss the result of two papers by [Harbaugh *et al.* (2001)] and [List and Millimet (2008)] on this topic. In the first paper, the authors use GARP to investigate the consistency of choice behavior of three groups: 2nd graders, 6th graders, and undergraduates. Subjects made 11 choices between combinations of bags of potato chips and boxes of fruit juice. There were 28 combinations and each sheet had between 3 and 7 bundles. The number of bags of chips and boxes of fruit juice varied from 0 to 9 so that 28 combinations included (9,0), (3,3), (2,2), (0,9) and 24 others. The subjects were to circle the bundles they liked best on each page and would be rewarded with one of the selected bundles selected at random. Subjects selected their chosen bundles under three protocols.

As pointed out by [Polisson and Quah (2012)], GARP does not guarantee utility maximization in a discrete consumption space without additional conditions. They impose a condition of cost efficiency. The condition [Harbaugh *et al.* (2001)] impose on the subjects' behavior is 'more is better than less' in the form of "GARP then requires that if a person directly or indirectly reveals that he prefers x^i to x, he can not choice bundle x^i when some alternative x^j with at least as much of every good as in x, and more of at least one, is available". Professor Quah kindly provided me with a proof that this condition is sufficient.

The average number of GARP violations in the 11 choices for the 2nd, 6th, undergraduates, random (uniform), and random (bootstrapping) were 4.3, 2.1, 2.0, 8.91, and 8.29 respectively. The average number of violations for each of the three student groups using a t test were significantly less than each of the two random groups at a 1 percent significance level. In addition, the average number of violations of the 6th graders using a t test was significantly less than the 2nd graders at the 1 percent significance level. The experiment indicates that by 6th grade humans have reached a plateau in rationality.

[List and Millimet (2008)] can be considered an extension of [Harbaugh *et al.* (2001)], testing an additional hypothesis of whether experience in one market leads to more consistent preferences in a second market. [List and Millimet (2008)] conducted field experiments at a mall in Arizona and another mall in Illinois involving 800 children from 6 -18. At each mall there were two tests conducted 7 months apart. They used a format similar to [Harbaugh *et al.* (2001)], using potato chips and fruit juice in the first test, and gum and candy bars in the later test. The subjects were divided into three groups based on their participation in a sportscard market at the mall. The first were children who had come to the mall with no interest in participating in the sportscard market. This group was partitioned into two subgroups. One subgroup at the end of the first test recieved $25 worth of sportscards with the goal of encouraging them to participate in the sportscard market before the gum and candy bar test. The other subgroup received no gift. The third group were children who participated in the sportscard market.

The results of the experiment were:

- On average subjects had 3.6 GARP violations and 69% of subjects had at least one GARP violation
- The number of GARP violations decreased by approximately .5 per year of age
- Subjects who participated frequently in the sportscard market had significantly fewer GARP violations

Now let us consider statistics that measure the deviation from GARP. [Echenique *et al.* (2011b)] tested their money pump index (MPI) on grocery expenditure data for 494 families over 104 weeks ending in June 1993. They limited their study to basic necessities that people buy on a regular basis. This reduces the problem that some foods are bought infrequently such as salt or spices. To obtain a computational DC tractable algorithm they limited their calculations to shopping cycles of 2, 3 and 4. The mean MPI was about 6% of expenditures. They also considered demographic variables and found that the MPI is higher for smaller, older, poorer, and less educated households. Since buying groceries is a frequent expenditure, we can assume that the households have established their preferences over basic necessities and that these results can be interpreted as a small deviation from optimality.

Now let us consider what happens when there are a large number of alternatives, such as types of beer or wine for which the consumer might employ a sequential trial and error testing, STE strategy. Because of modern packaging, a STE strategy is an expensive undertaking because the consumer must purchase the item in order to test it. For example, packaging pens in paper-plastic containers precludes writing with a pen before buying it. From the ordering experiments, we learned that how smoothly a pen writes is an important attribute for most people. In a few cases, customers can taste food before buying it. For example, the sales people in Amy's Ice Cream stores in Austin will provide the customer a sample upon request. But, in almost all cases, the expense and health reasons preclude samples.

The more expensive the item the greater a consumer's strategy is likely to involve acquiring additional information. For example, a customer might not visit a new restaurant without a favorable recommendation from a friend or a favorable review either online or in a newspaper or other media.

Likewise, in buying an expensive wine, a consumer might require a positive review.

Given the prospect function, we argue that for cases involving a large number of alternatives, a STE strategy is likely to stop with a local and not a global maximum. Humans place greater emphasis on avoiding downside losses than achieving upside gains. This means that as a consumer finds items that are better than previously tested items, the incentive to continue a STE strategy decreases to avoid downside losses. We argue that a STE strategy is learned behavior and a consumer learns when to stop from previously conducted STE strategies. The result is a local optimum that may or may not be a global optimum. If items that are actually superior to the tested items are never tested, they would never be revealed as preferred.

A consideration of realized utility is important for another reason, dynamic inconsistency. In food choices an example would be if a consumer chooses an item of food and later regrets eating the item because, for example, it deviates from the consumer's diet. We addressed this issue in our questionnaire about consumer mistakes. The relevant questions are:

II. Food Choices

1. In selecting food on a regular trip to the grocery store, I check:
Number of calories_(51)_, Nutrients _(43)_fat content _(41)_, sugar content _(36)_, salt content_(26)_ nothing_(35)_
2. In a restaurant I consider calories by:
Approximating the number of calories _(30)_, using an app on my phone to tell me the exact number _(03)_, I dont consider calories _(66)_
3. In planning a meal at my residence I consider:
The number of calories _(25)_ whether the meal will be good nutrition _(75)_
4. After eating a second slice of cake, I regret my action because of the affect on my weight:
All the time _(20)_, frequently _(18)_, seldom _(26)_, never _(37)_
5. When I step on the scales and see my weight I regret what I eat recently:
All the time _(9)_, frequently _(20)_, seldom _(32)_, never _(38)_

where the % of the 96 subjects is indicated in the corresponding (). Subjects could respond with more than one answer. For questions 4 and 5, only 26% checked never for both questions indicating that dynamic inconsistency among our subjects was common. Given the rate of obesity in the general population, we believe dynamic inconsistency in food choices is common, in general. We shall consider dynamic inconsistency an example of when anticipated and realized utility can differ.

Many consumers in their food choices place more emphasis on the short-term criterion of taste and less emphasis on the long-term consequences of weight gain and health effects. Dynamic inconsistency illustrates a point about the standard utility model. The model makes no assumption whatsoever that the preferences generated by the consumer are in the consumer's long-term interests such as good health. We shall return to this point again in Chapter 10.

The [Echenique *et al.* (2011b)] analysis of grocery expenditures covers a large component of the consumer problem. Their results demonstrate small deviations from revealed preference. It is entirely possible that if it were possible to measure the results against realized preference, the performance loss would have been larger given that dynamic inconsistency is fairly common concerning food choices. I have no basis to estimate how much larger.

9.5.2.3 *Data item searches*

Let us consider an example of mistakes in data item searches. We addressed these types of mistakes in our questionnaire about consumer mistakes. The relevant questions are:

Please consider the following types of mistakes when purchasing electronic accessories:
(1) Functionality of product: Does product have expected, sought after features?
(2) Compatibility of product: Is product compatible with your current electronics?

In the past 3 years how many electronic mistakes have you made?
(Check whichever applies) 0_(57)_ , 1_(11)_ , 2_(3)_ , 3+_(29)_
Check all reasons that apply:
_(27)_1. I bought the item online and did not fully understand all the products features and specifications.
_(15)_I bought the item in a physical store and did not fully understand all the products features and specifications.
_(15)_I bought the item in a physical store, and the sales associate gave me poor, incorrect advice.
_(63)_I needed to buy the item quickly to satisfy an immediate demand and did not have the time to carefully think about the purchase and compare the alternatives.
_(34)_I should have waited for the new model that had better features.
_(2)_I was influenced by a misleading ad on TV.

In the "Check whichever applies" the number in () is the % of the 95 subjects who answered this question. In "Check all reasons that apply" the number in () is the % of the 41 subjects who made one or more mistakes. In this survey, failure to allocate enough time in the evaluation process was the most important factor.

A consumer can select a product and not be aware that a better choice existed. Testing for this type of mistake is very difficult because of the framing problem. Consumers generally process a small fraction of the available data, so what new fraction of the available data and what organization and questions do you provide consumers to see if they made a mistake?

Even more difficult is measuring the magnitude of a mistake in data item searches where the consumer may have very little experience with the alternatives. One possible measure is consumer satisfaction with the product, but this measure may well reflect the extent to which the realized utility measured up to the anticipated utility, and not how well the purchased product compares to the alternatives, with which the consumer has had no experience.

One approach to measuring the magnitude of mistakes is to use a proxy for utility. One such study is Ketcham, Lucarelli, Miravete and Roebuck (2012) that measures the magnitude of mistakes in purchasing Medicare Part D, the prescription drug program. The authors collected data on 71,399 enrollees during the first two years of the program, 2006 and 2007, who were not subsidized by the federal government. Their data set included some seniors with no drug insurance.

The criterion they used to measure the magnitude of mistakes was the "annual expost out-of-pocket (OOP) costs for insurance and prescription drugs above the cost of the cheapest alternative". The OOP cost reduction from 2006 to 2007 is a good proxy for utility gains because although the various programs have different features, the drugs are either the same or equivalent. The authors found that 81% of the enrollees reduced their OOP in the second year and the average amount was $298. They also determined that their sample overestimated by $12 the reduction in the total senior population.

The primary factor in reducing OOP was switching to a cheaper plan. However, even seniors who stayed with the same plan had some reduction. What would have been helpful for this book would have been data that related the amount of OOP reduction to the details of the data item search strategy used by the seniors. For example, was it related to using an online site with alternative program details? Professor Miravete informed me that such data was not available and that there were no online Part D data sites in 2006.

Our hypothesis is that in repeat purchases with a requirement for extensive effort to understand the technology or details of the alternatives, the magnitude of consumer mistakes decreases with each purchase. In purchasing a digital camera, a first time buyer must spend a considerable effort to learn which features are best suited for the type of pictures he wants to take. With each subsequent buy he only has to focus on changes in technology. But, if the change in technology is significant, it can increase the magnitude of errors. For example, a consumer buying dot matrix printers would increase his item search performance until he switched to ink jet printers. In this new technology he would not likely forecast the high cost of ink jet cartridges based on his experience with low-cost dot matrix ribbon cartridges until he bought his second ink jet printer. At this point he might consider switching to a laser printer.

9.5.3 *Budgeting*

Finally, let us consider an important source of error in budgeting. As we have pointed out, savings connects one-period budgeting. Consumers save to create an emergency fund for unforeseen contingencies, major purchases such as a home, education of children, and retirement. Let us focus on saving for retirement.

[Munnell *et al.* (2012)], using the Federal Reserve 2010 Survey of Consumer Finances, find that more than one half of future retirees will not be able to maintain their current standard of living in retirement. Between the 2007 and 2010 surveys the incidence of this phenomenon climbed from 44% to 53%. The increase can be attributed to the recent recession.

Several reasons might explain this lack of savings. Computing a dynamic optimization problem over a lifetime in order to determine optimal savings is simply not H tractable. Also, in our Chapter on budgeting we found a significant fraction of budgeters were "feast or famine" budgeters. [Thaler and Shefrin (1981)] develop a model of self control based on the resolution of a conflict between a current period doer and a long term planner. Some people lack self control. [Loewenstein *et al.* (2003)] create a model of projection bias which they define as "People exaggerate the degree to which their future tastes will resemble their current tastes". This projection bias leads people "to consume too much early in life and too little late in life relative to what would be optimal".

A basic problem with external criteria such as saving enough to maintain a standard of living in retirement is that they may not agree with a person's subjective desires. A couple could decide to spend more on cruise ship travel before retirement, while they expect to be in good health in order to enjoy such trips and later cut back in retirement. There is a serious measurement problem in trying to measure savings errors from an internal subjective criterion. In the next Chapter on improving consumer performance, we will consider incentives that encourage consumers to save more.

9.6   Overall Assessment

The experiments involving animals, [Kagel *et al.* (1995)], and the token economy at the Central Islip State Hospital in New York, [Battalio *et al.* (1973)] come the closest to satisfying the stringent requirements we imposed on consumer theory. In these controlled experiments there were few alternatives so that computational complexity was not a factor and the cost of solving the consumer problem could be considered small. Also, the subjects had time to learn their preferences, although [Kagel *et al.* (1995)] point out that many of the inconsistencies in food-water choice for rats were in the first period, suggesting they had not learned their preferences. The results indicate that economic consumer theory is a valid approximation of this behavior.

In the marketplace facing consumers, there is insufficient research to make a quantitative assessment of overall consumer performance, either relative to anticipated or realized utility. Economists need to create a better methodology for measuring overall performance.

We make two qualitative assertions concerning consumer performance under market conditions. The first is that there are individual differences in performance. We attribute individual differences in solving the consumer optimization problem to variations in three factors: intelligence, self-control, and market experience. The consumer optimization problem is hard to solve so we would expect intelligence to be a factor in performance. Intelligence was not a factor in performance in the [Harbaugh *et al.* (2001)] experiments, but given the very small number of alternatives considered in the experiment, I do not consider it to be a good test of the affect of intelligence on performance.

Self-control is a factor in saving and food choices. Also, consumers with more experience should have better performance than young people just starting to learn search procedures and budgeting. The authors in [Stanovich and West (2005)] discuss studies that show individual differences in their study. The subjects in the animal and institutional experiments discussed in Section 9.2 showed individual differences in the speed of adjustment.

The second assertion is that the model's accuracy increases under conditions of stable prices and life conditions. For example, if prices are relatively stable, undergraduates would improve their consumer performance over time and seniors would be closer to optimal than sophomores who had just moved into an apartment. A change in life conditions such as graduating and taking a job would decrease performance. This is consistent with our assumption of incremental adjustment budgeting.

In the next Chapter we shall consider improving consumer performance. Improving performance should be considered relative to realized utility because judgments can have biases, and reducing biases is part of improving performance. Also, to improve performance we need to associate performance with choice of search or budget strategy.

Chapter 10

Improving Consumer Performance

10.1 Introduction

Improving consumer performance is important. Since the 1950s the value of adult members of a household has increased. In the typical household of the 50s, the husband earned the paycheck and the wife stayed at home applying her labor to household production procedures such as preparing meals and shopping. In the second half of the 20th century, women have greatly increased their participation in the workforce, which has greatly increased the value of their time. As a consequence household production procedures have less labor input, for example more restaurant or prepared food meals and less home cooked meals from scratch. A working adult couple or a single parent with children has a demand for more efficient item search and budgeting procedures.

Also, at the same time the increasing rate of technological advance has made consumer item search and budgeting more difficult. In international markets, firms compete to be the first to deliver a new product at a reasonable price and reliability so that they can capture a large market share. To support such activity government and firms have created an institutional structure of research universities, government funding for research, corporate R&D, startups, venture capital, and incubators. In addition, technological advances have increased the flexibility of manufacturers and service providers to create goods and services for niche markets. As a result, consumers are faced with an increasing number of alternatives to evaluate. And for many such evaluations, trial and error experience with previous products does not provide then with the ability to accurately forecast the behavior of the new technology in household production processes. Also, as the responsibility for financing retirement is increasingly thrust on the individual, long term budgeting is more difficult.

Consumers need more efficient search procedures that require less time and fewer resources to find a preferred item and budget. Advances in technology, especially the Internet and mobile communications, present opportunities for government, business, and researchers to improve consumer performance by providing consumers with better data and decision aids. We shall consider both near term improvements and the potential for long term improvements.

In the next section we will consider government's role in consumer performance. The federal government created agencies to assure the safety of drugs and improve the safety of autos and products in general. In addition, government at the federal and state levels prosecute fraudulent business practices. The government regulates some aspects of business data collection and has created required disclosures to provide consumers with data that has higher information value. Nevertheless, we will argue that government is likely to be a minor player in improving consumer performance in the near future.

In Section 3 we will discuss five current developments in how firms relate to consumers. The first is the creation of wellness programs. The second is the creation of more effective savings programs for employees. The third is the advance of social media has changed how consumers and firms interact, and the fourth is consumers as inventors. We will argue that, overall, the these four have positive effects. What is much more questionable is the tracking of Internet user online behavior so that sites can present the viewers with targeted ads. Such ads are more efficient for sellers. Given the low information value of ads in discriminating among alternatives and the potential for abuse in the loss of privacy, we argue that the current policy of self regulation on tracking by online sites is not in the public interest, and at some point the government is likely to address the issue.

In Section 4 we discuss possible near term improvements. One of these is a much better approach to measuring body size in order to find clothes that fit. A second is an effort by businesses to improve the quality of consumer reviews of products by reducing fake reviews. In addition, third party review sites should advance. We argue that first time buyers on rapidly changing technological products need to be educated and have a need for decision aids to reduce the start set to the final set for careful review. We present our research on digital cameras to illustrate our points.

In Section 5 we consider the potential for long term improvements. Advances in information technology will create the digital household.

Currently, procedures for buying products using a cell phone are being adopted in the US. This will give the household complete digital records of all transactions and will promote budget tracking by software aids owned by the consumer. The appliances in a household will be interconnected to the household computer system. The slowest product to make the transformation will be food, but in time all aspects of buying and preparing food will be mirrored in the household computer system. A digital household creates numerous new opportunities for second and third parties to provide services. The extent and speed that these potential improvements are realized depends on their profitability.

In Section 6 we discuss future research needed to realize gains in consumer performance in budgeting and item search. We focus on the need for a better computational model of economic agents, a better model of realized utility, so that the gap between real and ideal performance can be measured, and a systematic study of actual consumer strategies to evaluate their relative performance. This will mean the actual economy will more closely reflect that quaint phrase, "consumer sovereignty".

10.2   Government and Consumers

In the 19th century, consumer protection was limited to the advice "Let the buyer beware". In the 20th century, government at various levels passed numerous statutes to establish consumer rights and created numerous agencies to regulate them. At the federal level, the Federal Trade Commission was originally created in 1914 to promote business competition by enforcing the various antitrust laws, and later was given the mandate over consumer rights in 1938. As was pointed out in Chapter 6, one important aspect of consumer rights are government required disclosures for a wide variety of goods and services that provide consumers with data to improve their decisions. We will argue that government is likely to have a minor role in improving consumer performance in the near future.

The FTC and state attorney general offices police markets to stop fraud and deceptive advertising. In order to know where to focus its efforts the FTC has created a Consumer Sentinel database to record and organize the millions of consumer complaints. This database is available to any federal, state, or local law enforcement agency. The FTC uses the courts to seek justice for consumers. For example, the FTC is currently in court to attempt to get the third largest phone billing company (BSG) to return $52 million in bogus charges. In addition, the FTC is attempting to have BSG placed in contempt for failing to abide by a 1999 court order. This year (2012) the FTC ordered five auto dealers to stop deceptive ads claiming the dealers would pay the loan balance on trade-ins.

Now let us consider how the government oversees the collection of credit information. Credit information about consumers is essential to businesses in order to determine the credit worthiness of a customer. From the perspective of customers such information should be accurate so that they are not erroneously denied credit in a major purchase such as a car or house. Starting in 1899, entrepreneurs created a credit reporting agency (CRA) industry that provided merchants with credit information about customers. In 1970, in response to abuses by CRAs, the federal government enacted the Fair Credit Reporting Act (FCRA) to regulate the industry under a mandate to the FTC. This act specified what types of data could and could not be collected. It has been amended several times. For example, the 2003 amendment gave consumers the explicit right to see their credit file once a year. This year the new Consumer Financial Protection Bureau was created to protect consumers in financial transactions and has taken over monitoring the credit reporting industry.

Now let us consider safety. The Federal Pure Food and Drug Administration (FDA) focuses on the safety of drugs for both humans and animals, medical devices, and vaccines as well as the blood supply and the food supply. In addition, the FDA regulates the labeling of cosmetics and tobacco products. The FDA sets the standards for tests of new drugs and medical devices and approves those that meet its standards. If a drug has subsequent negative side effects the FDA can pull the drug from the market. The FDA sets the standards and procedures for vaccines and the blood supply. In conjunction with state agencies the FDA inspects the food supply.

The National Highway Traffic Safety Administration (NHTSA) tests the safety of automobiles and pickups and issues recalls for defects. The agency is active in all aspects of traffic safety, such as distracted driving and car seats for children. Requiring new safety features on vehicles is beyond their authority and requires specific legislation. The Consumer Product Safety Commission (CPSC) is charged with promoting the safety of a wide range of products not under the jurisdiction of other agencies such as the FDA and NHTSA. The CPSC has the authority to issue recalls for products found to be unsafe.

Government acts are a compromise between the agents behind government. As firms make many more contributions to political campaigns and hire many more lobbyists than consumers, who are basically politically un-organized, government compromises tend to favor firms over consumers. For example, under the FCRA consumers lost the right to sue CRAs for damages under common law precedents. Their right to sue was further restricted by the 2003 amendment to the FCRA and in addition, states could not impose higher standards than the federal standards. While government regulates credit data collection, it does not regulate the collection of consumer information by Internet firms.

Government activities improve consumer performance. Federal activity is primarily responsible, although state, and to a lesser extent lower levels of government also contribute. Whether government activities to aid consumers should be expanded or contracted should be determined by a careful cost-benefit analysis. The Tea Party has a simple heuristic to solve this problem: less government is better government. Given the Republican Party's shift to the right, one can forecast less expenditures on any type of government regulation, especially given the budget deficit. In the near future government at any level is not likely to take an active role in improving consumer performance.

10.3   Business and Consumers

In this section we consider the current impact, positive and negative, of business actions on consumer decisions not previously discussed. In Chapter 6 we discussed the information value of data provided by second and third parties. In this section we consider wellness programs, employee savings programs, the impact of the developing social media on the Internet, consumers as inventors, and the impact of tracking viewers by sites on the Internet.

10.3.1   *Wellness Programs*

From an economic perspective, a wellness programs is an incentive system with support services offered to public or private employees in order to change preferences toward a more healthy lifestyle. In this subsection we shall focus primarily on private sector wellness programs. The incentives of a comprehensive program typically encourage employees to give up smoking, choose a healthy diet that reduces excessive weight, and exercise more to promote fitness. Firms monitor the progress of their employees.

Private sector firms have a strong incentive to create a successful wellness program in order to reduce medical costs, absenteeism, and promote a more productive workforce. The rate of return on investment in wellness programs can be very significant. [Baicker *et al.* (2010)] in their study found that for every dollar invested in a wellness program reduced medical and absenteeism costs by six dollars. [Berry *et al.* (2010)] found similar results for comprehensive, well run wellness programs.

Now let us consider an example, see [IBI (2012)], of a successful comprehensive wellness program at Lincoln Industries, which is a metal finishing firm with 550 employees located in Lincoln, NE. In order to measure the status of their wellness program, employees undergo semiannual physical exams to measure health status. Lincoln industries offers social and financial incentives to participate in the wellness program; however, employees are free to decide not to participate.

Participating employees set goals defined in terms of Silver, Gold, and Platinum standards set by the firm. The social aspect of the incentives is gaining status by achieving the highest Platinum standard. Each year Platinum level employees earn a free trip to Leadville, CO, to climb Mount Elbert, the highest mountain in Colorado. Other financial incentives are reduced rates on their medical insurance, 50% subsidy to participate in a Weight Watchers program. Performance in the wellness program is also tied to merit increases and bonuses. The success of the program is reflected in the fact that their employee medical costs are about one half the regional average.

Given the high rate of return on investment in a successful wellness program, they are rapidly being adopted by most firms. The Obama Affordable Health Care Act in 2014 will expand a firm's ability to require employees who do not meet health status goals to pay more for their company health insurance. A consulting industry has arisen promoting the diffusion of these programs. Government will probably create wellness programs for government employees at a slower rate given the financial problems at many levels of government. The adoption of these programs has positive social benefits in reducing medical costs.

Now let us consider participation in a wellness program from the perspective of anticipated and realized utility of the individual. In programs like the one at Lincoln Industries based on free choice to participation, those who participate reveal they prefer to learn preferences for a more healthy lifestyle promoted by the programs incentives. The social and financial rewards plus a reduction in dynamic inconsistency implies a higher rate of realized utility.

Will participation in wellness programs have lasting effects in improved lifestyle choices? Individual dieters frequently regain weight lost and maintaining weight loss is difficult. Wellness programs such as the one at Lincoln offer employees a structured environment that supports maintaining the improved lifestyle choices.

10.3.2 Long Term Savings

In the previous Chapter, we discussed several theories why consumers save too little for retirement. For example, [Thaler and Shefrin (1981)] postulated that individuals frequently lack the self control to postpone immediate consumption for future consumption resulting in insufficient savings for retirement. The problem has become worse as employees shift from defined-benefit programs, such as pensions, to defined-contribution programs, such as 401Ks.

More recently, [Thaler and Benartzi (2004)] created a Save More Tomorrow^{TM} program based on behavioral economics to encourage employees to save more by increasing their savings through automatic transfers from their paycheck. The program has several components. Employees are approached as long as possible before a scheduled pay increase. The increase is scheduled with the first paycheck after the raise. Since the increase in savings is less than the pay increase their is no perception of a loss. Employees continue to increase their savings until they reach the maximum allowed rate. Employees, if they desire, can opt out of the program at any time. Professors Thaler and Benartzi tested their program on three firms and achieved a higher savings rate. Unfortunately, the diffusion of this program will be slower than the diffusion of wellness programs because firms have less incentives.

We discuss this program here because it illustrates how the use of behavioral economics can increase consumer performance. For more private and public sector examples see [Thaler and Sunstein (2009)].

10.3.3 Social Media

Let us start with a definition of *social media* by the online dictionary merriam-webster.com as: "forms of electronic communication (as Web sites for social networking and microblogging) through which users create online communities to share information, ideas, personal messages, and other content (as videos)". It is important to note that there are numerous alternative definitions, for example, [Cohen (2011)] lists 30 social media definitions. What is common in these definitions is the interactive nature of social media that differs from the non-interactive or one way flow of traditional media.

There are a very large number of social media sites. In this section we shall focus on three major sites: Facebook, Twitter, and YouTube. Facebook is a rapidly growing social interaction site, which now has 1 billion users. Twitter is a message service characterized by messages of no more than 140 characters. YouTube allows viewers to post videos that can be viewed by anyone accessing the site.

These and other social media sites are fundamentally changing the interaction of business to consumer firms and their consumers. To explain why, we need to focus on the reach of interactive communication on social media as opposed to the reach prior to the advent of social media. Suppose an individual creates a video and shows it to his friends on his TV. If the video is really interesting, his friends might tell their friends and the number of people who view the video might grow slowly. However, if he uploads the video to YouTube and if it is really interesting, it could "go viral" — that is, attract several hundred thousand viewers in a few days.

Marketers attempt to harness this quick, large number interaction property of social media to sell products. The idea is that these online messages from "friends" are more likely to be trusted than traditional ads. One of Facebook's popular features is that two Facebook users can mutually agree to be Facebook friends to share postings on their respective walls. Users build interlinking communities of friends. Facebook has a 'Like' button that appears on Internet pages both inside and outside Facebook. If a user clicks on a Like button that information is passed on to his Facebook friends when they visit the page. This is one example of mechanisms built into social media sites to promote interactions among large numbers of social media users. Another mechanism in Twitter is the Twitter "follower", a user who received all the messages (or "tweets") of the leader.

Let us consider a successful social media marketing campaign. We start with the Ford Fiesta Movement initiated in 2009 to relaunch the Ford Fiesta into the US market. Ford created a contest to find 100 individuals very active in social media to test drive the Ford Fiesta for six months prior to its US introduction. They reported their experiences on their blogs, Facebook, Twitter, and Flickr, a photo sharing site. The contest winners through their social media efforts created millions of social media interactions including 11,000 videos, which are online at youtube.com/user/FiestaMovement, and

15000 pictures, which are online at flickr.com/photos/fiestamovement. This campaign was very successful in creating Fiesta brand awareness among potential buyers, [Le (2011)].

Many firms have a Facebook page that they use to develop a large number of fans that are viewers who have clicked on the page's Like button. Viewers are likely to click the Like button on an interesting page with pictures, videos, and numerous opportunities to interact with messages to topics presented in boxes on the page. Most pages display the viewers messages. Successful pages are frequently updated. Other enticements to obtain clicks on the Like button are promotions and contests.

Let us consider the September 3, 2012 content of Starbucks' Facebook page, which has 31,603,100 fans — that is, over 30 million viewers at some time clicked the like button on a Starbucks page. On that page the Pumpkin Spice Latte contest announced this years winner. Starbuck fans earn points for their city by various social media activities. The city with the most points will be the one to receive the pumpkin spice latte first. Leavenworth, WA earned 388,180 points and will receive their pumpkin spice lattes first. Also, on the Starbuck page are numerous boxes with pictures and topics encouraging viewer response. The previous comments can be viewed if desired. Some contests offer large prizes. Let us consider one business to business example, the American Express Open on Facebook. The promotion is a national contest for small business owners to compete for a $20,000 prize with a smaller prize for 10 semi-finalists. This contest and American Express's Open Forum are designed to teach small business owners how to use social media to promote their businesses. Indirectly, these efforts create good will and business for American Express from small business owners.

Firms can sell goods and services online through their Facebook page. One example of a large firm is Delta, which has enabled customers to buy tickets through its Facebook page. Most firms currently selling goods and services directly through their Facebook page are much smaller, such as Hallmark and The Baby Grocery Store. An increasing number of small firms are opening storefronts on Facebook, [Zimmerman (2012)]. A more common practice is to use the Facebook page to promote the sale of goods at the firm's online site, [Kessler (2011)]. One example is BabyAndMeGifts.com, which is an online store selling gifts for mothers and babies. The site has a Facebook storefront page that provides an overview of products for sale, but requires a customer to go to the firm's own online site to make a purchase. The owner, Jacquelyn Meyers, attributes about 50% of her online sales to her Facebook page.

Numerous firms use Twitter to promote their business. One of the first was Dell, who in 2008 started using Twitter to provide potential customers with information on the latest items being offered in the Dell Outlet that sells new, dented or scratched, and refurbished Dell products. A second example is Kogi Korean BBQ in the LA area, which has a fleet of mobile trucks offering tacos to its customers. Each truck has a set schedule of where it will stop to sell tacos, but traffic congestion makes achieving exact arrival time at each stop impossible. Kogi uses Twitter to provide customers with expected time of arrival at each stop. Another example is The Coffee Groundz, which uses Twitter to take orders and interact with customers. Firms use Twitter to improve customer service. For example, Comcast Cable uses Twitter to respond to customer service problems.

The most famous use of YouTube videos to promote business has to be by Blendtec, a firm that produces blenders. The CEO, Tom Dickson, tested his blenders by grinding up items seldom ground in blenders and the marketing director realized that videos of these tests would attract a great deal of attention. Starting in 2006 Blendtec made videos of the CEO grinding up unusual products such as an iPhone, garden rake, a Rotisserie Chicken, and an iPad. To see these videos go to YouTube.com and type "Will it blend" as keywords. The videos achieved the desired result. They went viral with over 100 million viewers. Blendtec expanded its social media marketing campaign using Facebook and Twitter. Sales increased 700%.

Social media marketing campaigns can fail miserably, [Curry (2012)]. McDonald's in January 2012, launched a promotion on Twitter encouraging tweets sharing pleasant McDonald memories. It backfired when users tweeted stories of horrible food and service. Social media can also be used by dissatisfied customers to complain about terrible service. In 2008, United airlines baggage handlers broke the singer David Carrol's guitar by throwing the guitar between handlers. After United refused to compensate, David Carrol posted a video on YouTube, use keywords "United breaks guitars", in which he sang a ballad of the breaking of the guitar. This video went viral with over 12 million views.

Marketing on social media is very much in a state of flux as marketing professionals learn by sequential trial and error experiments what works and what to avoid. To avoid a social media backlash firms will need to be more honest than was the case in traditional one way marketing. The future of Facebook in e-commerce is very much in doubt, as most large retailers, after launching catalogue sales through their Facebook pages, discontinued such sales efforts. Although Facebook's ad revenue on mobile devices is climbing,

Facebook is looking for new sources of revenue, [Sengupta (2012a)]. Several business observers have suggested that the e-commerce future of Facebook lies in launching a credit card, for example see [Horton (2012)].

Our forecast is that social media will remain an important factor in the relationship between consumers and sellers. One factor in this new relationship is much more interactive communication between consumers, sellers, and manufacturers.

10.3.4 *Consumers as Inventors*

A major benefit in better communication between consumers and firms is a higher rate of invention in products and innovations in firms' procedures such as customer service. There are numerous media and professional articles describing this development of "consumer-innovation", for example see [Economist (2005)], [Von Hippel *et al.* (2011)], [von Hippel (2005)], and [Luthje *et al.* (2002)].

A major problem in this literature is a failure to carefully define the word 'innovation', which has a large number of alternative media and professional definitions. We shall interpret this literature using the definitions of invention and innovation found in [Norman (1993)] and [Norman (2009)]. An *invention* is a new device or process. To qualify for a patent an invention must pass a test of originality–that is, be sufficiently different from previous inventions. Only a small percent of patented inventions have any economic value. Most inventions are minor improvements on existing inventions which do not qualify for patents.

An *innovation* is an improved procedure for achieving a goal such as profit maximization, providing government services, or achieving a desirable lifestyles. One example would be reorganizing a production process, introducing robots to replace labor and reducing the cost of production. An innovation in government is submitting tax returns to the IRS by email instead of regular mail. An example of an innovation in desirable lifestyles is telecommuting by professionals from Telluride, CO. A simple heuristic definition of an innovation is a better procedure to accomplish a task.

Many current innovations are the result of applying new technology in (1) manufacturing and (2) processing of business and government paperwork. Empirically, better performance is not achieved by using the new technology to improve the performance of the old process. Rather, the manufacturing or paperwork process is redesigned from ground up to make optimal use of the new combination of technology and people. A portion of the performance gain is from carefully analyzing the process to be replaced and asking what really needs to be done to maximize profits.

It is important to distinguish between an invention and an innovation. Spreadsheet software is an invention. A new business application of spreadsheets that increases profits is an innovation. Using these definitions, we interpret the consumer innovation literature. Entrepreneurs are creating an innovation in the production function for profitable inventions through much improved communications among inventive consumers and firms. Let us briefly overview this development.

The traditional model of invention is through corporate research and development. Consumers have no role in the process other than responding to market surveys. What this model ignores is the fact that users make inventions in the form of modifying products to achieve their objectives and in some cases these inventions are completely new products. Let us focus on consumer products. In 1886 Josephine Cochrane invented the dishwasher because servants chipped her china when they washed it by hand. In the early 20th century farmers wanted auto manufacturers to produce a car that had back seats that could be removed. After a ten year delay the auto firms created the pickup truck. Consumers created the skate board, mountain bikes, and foot harnesses for surf boards that led to wind sailing surf boards. The traditional model on invention was never correct.

[Von Hippel *et al.* (2011)] did a study of consumer inventors in the US, UK and Japan. Consumer inventors tend to be males that are highly educated with degrees in science or engineering. The advance of inexpensive CAD programs and now the use of 3-D printing to produce parts has progressively made the task of consumer inventors easier. The amount of money spent by consumers on making inventions is 13%, 33%, and 144% of the amount spent by firms on consumer product R&D in Japan, US, and UK respectively. Most inventions made by consumers are for their own use and do not have market value. However, what is important in the process is that consumer inventors frequently will give away their inventions freely and that a significant portion of these inventions do have market value.

Now let us consider the role of improved communications in the innovation of the production function for profitable inventions. One example is creating communities of interest among consumer inventors. Zach Hoeken and Pre Pettis created an Internet site, Thingiverse.com, a website that allows viewers to upload and share designs. In addition, firms are adopting consumer suggestions for improved products by creating interactive sites for making suggestions, such as FordSocial Your Ideas, which is online at http://social.ford.com/your-ideas/, and, as previously mentioned, the use of Twitter to improve customer service. Proctor and Gamble has a web site called Connect and Develop, which is online at http://www.pg.com/connect_develop/index.shtml, to interact with outside inventors on new or improved products.

Let us consider the role of hackers in the development of the Microsoft product Kinect as discussed by [Torrone (2011)] . After Microsoft released the product on 4 Nov 11, Phil Porrene and Limor Fried at Ada Fruit Industries promised a $3000 reward to the first person to post how they hacked Kinect on GitHub, a public code repository. Microsoft came to realize they should incorporate user innovation into their products. Recently, technology firms have become much more receptive to ideas from product users. Consulting firms are now promoting the diffusion of this innovation, for example see the Deloitte report [Conroy *et al.* (2009)].

Overall, we assert that the impact of the development of social media on consumers has been positive in encouraging a more honest interaction between firms and their customers, and promoting a higher rate of product invention.

10.3.5 *Consumer Tracking*

Now let us consider the development of an infrastructure whose value to the consumer is a more open question — Internet user profiles. These profiles are constructed using several data sources. Sites can track consumer interaction with their website using cookies and spyware. There are three types of cookies: first party, third party, and flash cookies. The Webopedia (Webopedia.com) definition of a cookie is "A message given to a Web browser by a Web server. The browser stores the message in a text file. The message is then sent back to the server each time the browser requests a page from the server". This message can store an ID number for the user, clicking history at the site, and sensitive information such as a credit card number. A first party cookie is one sent by the site, and third party cookie is sent by an entity other than the site. Flash cookies use the Abode flash add on to install themselves on the user's hard drive. Spyware is software that a user unknowingly downloads that can track every keystroke, take over the computer and transmit back sensitive information.

Firms can construct profiles of consumers by combining data from many sources. A site has a history of the user's purchases. A site can also monitor the user history in interacting with the site, such as what pages the user visited, and add this to the profile. Next the firm can add a subset of data available as public information such as births, marriages, and divorces. Sites such as SearchSystems.net offer numerous categories of public data that can be organized by location, such as state, county, or zip code. But a firm can go much further to create a profile. Third party cookies collect data from many sources which is used internally and is sold to interested buyers wishing to create profiles.

One use of these profiles is targeted ads. Currently, the revenue from ads on the Internet now exceeds the revenue of ads on paper media. Consumer profiles offer an Internet ad agency, such as Google's DoubleClick, the opportunity to send the consumer ads most likely to solicit a respond. Google is determined to maximize its profits through targeted advertising. They changed their privacy policy in 2012 so that all sites owned by Google now share consumer data to create better profiles. In addition, because the Android operating system for cell phones and tablets is a Google product, Google can monitor Android users online. Their Map program gives Google the location of the customer at all times. Google is also working on a type of glasses that will project pages on their lenses and enable Google to monitor customers in real time physical space.

The success of generating massive data files on consumers requires using statistical techniques to determine patterns in the data that can be used to select targeted ads or focus a marketing campaign. [Duhigg (2012)] provides an interesting example of a successful marketing campaign by Target based on data analysis of consumer purchasing habits. The goal was to identify pregnant women by the changes in their purchasing patterns alone. A Target market researcher, Andrew Poole, was able to identify changes in the purchases of 25 products and create an index that accurately predicted the delivery date. Why was this research important to the growth of Target? Changes in lifestyle such as leaving school and getting a job, having a child, or taking a job in a new city are times when consumers change the stores in their item searches. By presenting these women with targeted coupons mixed with coupons for products they were unlikely to buy — in order to avoid appearing to spy on the women — Target was able to capture new customers before birth announcements, when the families would be showered with offers. Target is not the only seller developing a successful marketing campaign based on analyzing its customer data. Amazon is successful in making suggestions for additional purchases.

Overall, we assert that the impact of tracking Internet users is negative because ads have a low information value in discriminating among alternatives and the collection of these massive user profiles creates a distinct danger of abuse. Right now Internet tracking is primarily self regulated, meaning very little government regulation. With respect to Internet tracking, the US and EU have taken very different approaches. In the EU a site must ask permission to track a viewer and can not sell data to third parties without explicit permission of the viewer. In the US there is legislation prohibiting spyware and the FTC actively prosecutes spyware use. Nevertheless, Internet tracking in the US is primarily self regulated, which in effect means unregulated. If, or perhaps when, there are major abuses by unscrupulous political or economic agents, the Federal government will enact some of the goals of privacy advocates such as "Do not track".

10.4   Near Term Changes

In the near term we expect many changes in the information value of data available to consumers. In this section we shall discuss near term changes. The first is a new approach to judging how well clothes will fit. The second is a decline in the trust or perceived information value of user reviews. To compensate for products with third party professional reviews, these review sites could present better tools for the initial stages of an item search. We present our research into developing better decision tools, [Norman *et al.* (2008)].

10.4.1   *Clothes Fit*

A new technology that will make consumers, especially women, more efficient in searching for clothes are electromagnetic wave body scanners. Firms, such as Me-Ality have created body scanners that take accurate measurements of the customer's body. These scanners are increasingly being installed in malls. The customer gets a printout with recommended clothes choices. This greatly reduces the labor required for finding clothes that fit well. Stores reduce the required labor of store clerks in placing clothes back on racks. Right now the information is for a subset of the market. In time it will spread to most clothes. Why is this technology important? Online sales of clothes have as much as a 20% return rate for failure to fit. With these measurements a customer could order clothes online with the expectation that they will fit well. The research groups' assessment of the current stage of this technology is that it needs some improvements, such as the ability to designate whether the clothes are to be a loose or a tight fit.

10.4.2 *Fake Review Optimization*

Now let us consider our hypothesis that consumers' perception of the information value of user reviews will decline. Firms have an incentive to promote a positive bias in user reviews of their own goods and a negative bias in reviews of their rivals' goods. [Brokaw (2012)] points out that there is a growing export industry in China to create fictitious people in order to generate fake positive or negative reviews. The term "fake review optimization" (FRO) has been created to study strategies to post positive fake reviews on a firm's products and negative fake reviews on rivals' products. [Ott *et al.* (2012)] estimated that from 2% to 6% of the reviews on Expedia, Hotels.com, Priceline, TripAdvisor and Yelp were fake and the share of fake reviews is rising. In a press release on 17 Sep 2012 on gartner.com, the Gartner firm made an estimate that by 2014, 10-15 percent of social media reviews will be fake.

In the US the FTC has created a fake review policy and has taken steps to enforce the policy. In 2009, the FTC expanded its definition of deceptive advertising to include failure to disclose fake user reviews. In 2011 the FTC fined Legacy Learning Systems, Inc $250,000 for hiring associated marketers to create very positive reviews of their products without making the FTC required disclosures. FTC actions are likely to slow the growth of, but not stop, fake reviews — just as has been the case in deceptive advertising in general.

As fake reviews become more prevalent and consumers become more aware of the problem, firms for which user reviews are an important source of evaluation data have an incentive to reduce the number of fake reviews. One approach to reduce fakes is to restrict writing reviews to actual customers not affiliated with the reviewed firm. [Mayzlin *et al.* (2012)] compared Expedia.com and TripAdvisor.com for the same hotels. Anyone can post a review on TripAdvisor, but a consumer must have booked at least one night to review a hotel on Expedia.com. The incentive to write positive fake reviews for themselves and negative fake reviews for nearby competitors is highest for independent hotels owned by single-unit owners and lowest for chain hotels. The data show more evidence of such behavior on the TripAdvisor data than the Expedia data. As pointed out by [Streitfeld (2012)] a Cornell research team has developed an algorithm that is 90% accurate in detecting fake reviews. The problem is that as defenses against fakes are created, those profiting from fakes will find ways to circumvent the new defenses. Eliminating fake user reviews is a very difficult problem.

We argue that consumers' trust in user reviews will decline and they will place greater reliance on professional reviews from third party sites that develop a reputation for honest, competent reviews. Research to improve the quality of third party tools and reviews has positive social value. The one area in which third party sites could improve the information value of data they present viewers is in better data and tools for making the initial steps in an item search. We shall now present an experiment designed to test software that could improve consumer performance in selecting digital cameras, [Norman *et al.* (2008)]. The type of software presented could be used by most third party review sites. The research was performed from 2003-2007.

10.4.3 *Improving Consumer Selection Procedures*

One aspect that third party Internet data providers could improve is software decision aids. This subsection is from [Norman *et al.* (2008)]. Online sites can improve their software product selection codes. Our survey presented in Chapter 6 indicates that only 9 out of 40 students who bought a digital camera used a selection code, which suggests that consumers are not aware of these codes, or if they are, they do not consider them worth using. Our survey of digital camera sites revealed few examples of digital selection codes.

There are two areas that a selection code for digital cameras can be useful. The first is in the second step of the selection process: finding a small set of cameras with the attributes to take good pictures for the intended use. In digital cameras there are a large number of details about the attributes that a consumer must master if his decision can be said to have been made with perfect information. For example, DPReview.com, a site for serious enthusiasts, lists over 90 attributes of each camera listed while DCResource lists about 30. Our survey showed over half of digital camera buyers were overwhelmed by the number of details. Moreover, asking a friend for advice is not always wise. We also gave the subjects a short quiz about digital cameras and found the average score was 6.7 out of 10. This indicates that even after doing their research to buy a digital camera, subjects were not very knowledgeable. As we shall discuss later, salespersons can have perverse incentives.

Given the time that a consumer has to spend on a search, she can fail to understand the importance of desirable features. Let us consider an auto focus assist light (AFAL), that enables a digital camera to focus quickly and accurately in dim light. Jeff Keller of DCResource.com has frequently argued in his reviews that all digital cameras should have an auto focus assist light, as even a camera for a family of four is likely to encounter situations where it is useful. College students who frequent clubs or parties definitely have a need for an AFAL. We found 6 coeds who did not buy a camera with this feature and took pictures in low light conditions. The 5 coeds who bought a Casio EX Z3 said that on average 86% of these shots turned out with poorer quality than desired. The coed who bought a newer Olympus FE 190 said that 15% of these shots were poorer than desired. The 6 coeds would have been prepared to spend an additional $30, $37, $50, $50, $100, and $250 in order to have obtained a camera with this feature. Subsequently, the coeds who bought the Casio EX Z3, bought digital cameras with an auto focus assist light. If a consumer buys a telephoto camera to take pictures of wildlife including deer at sunset, he would obtain a less than optimal camera if he failed to consider models that incorporated a lens stabilization system that reduces shaking at low light.

The second aspect of a digital selection code is providing consumers better evaluation techniques for the final selection. As the research initiated by Tversky and Kahneman shows, humans use simple heuristics to make decisions. Let us consider three such heuristics. The first is judging the quality of the picture by looking at the picture in the LCD screen. The number of pixels in LCD screens is in the hundreds of thousands and the number used by some firms is one half that used by others. The quality of the picture on the LCD screen is a function of the number of pixels used in the screen and this quality may not be a great indicator of picture quality of the corresponding picture on the memory card.

A second questionable heuristic is using the number of megapixels as a discriminator for quality. The number of pixels in a square inch of picture increases by the square root of the number of pixels, so this heuristic is a gauge of the amount of detail in a picture. But a reading of the reviews over several years at DCResource would inform the reader that the digital camera firms have been engaged in an "arms race" to increase the number of megapixels in their sensors. When firms first come out with digital cameras at the new megapixel frontier, the problem to overcome is picture noise. After a few generations at the frontier the noise problem is overcome and the firms increase the number of megapixels once again. The quality of a picture depends on other factors such as the algorithm to process the sensor data and the quality of the camera lens. One student who bought a digital camera from a firm leaving the digital camera business at Overstock.com choose the maximum megapixels for his budget, but suffered deep regret when he realized that if he dropped down one megapixel, he could have bought a much better camera. A third heuristic is using brand as a discriminator of quality. As was previously pointed out, while Canon makes many quality cameras, their cameras aren't always better than those of their competitors.

A faster way to educate consumers concerning desirable camera features and providing them with better discriminators of quality has positive value.

10.4.3.1 *Selection code development*

In our digital camera selection code the decision process is divided into two components. The first stage is to select a small set of quality cameras within budget with the attributes to take good pictures in the intended photographic conditions. Because consumers are not well informed about digital camera attributes, there is an education module to improve their selection process at this stage. The second component of the decision process is to send the user to online digital camera sites where they can read the reviews and examine photo galleries of the small set selected in the first stage in order to determine the preferred item.

The educational component was the most challenging to develop. To help consumers make better choices a fundamental question is how much data to incorporate into the educational component. Again, the greater the detail, the greater the processing cost for a consumer to master the material. Because our subjects demonstrated little knowledge about digital cameras, our first code, developed in 2004, provided the user with explanations for less than half the detail considered by DPReview.com, the most technologically advanced site. Explanations of each incorporated feature were at least two levels deep: the first was a brief overview, and the other levels provided much greater detail. The code taught the consumer which features were needed for different types of shots. The module also gave them an estimate as to how long it would take them to learn how to use various features such as shutter control. It provided tests the user could perform to decide what size of camera best suited them along with the details about megapixel and sensors. There was an online questionnaire that when filled out gave the user a list of "essential" and "desirable" features for taking the user's desired pictures. The education function consisted of over 40 html pages covering camera attributes that test subjects could not master in an hour, but could master if given a week. The code can be found at http://www.eco.utexas.edu/Homepages/Faculty/Norman/000Cam.

We then refined our code with the goal of subject mastery of the first decision process in 20 minutes. We did so by integrating the education program with the decision structure. The new decision structure began with a decision whether to pick a small or large camera. Subjects were given the tradeoffs between the two groups: small cameras are easier to carry around, but lack the features and picture quality of large cameras. To clarify the difference between the two groups, we provided pictures to illustrate why the external flash hot shoe of a large camera is necessary to take pictures of large groups in dimly lit large spaces. We also explained the concept of optical zoom noting that large cameras have greater optical zoom, and explained why DSLRs are necessary for indoor sports shots.

If the user clicked on large camera, the viewer was provided with a page of pros and cons to decide among a telephoto, a prosumer, or a DSLR digital camera. If they chose the DSLR option, we assumed they had some camera knowledge and we provided them with a table of links to reviews of the DSLR cameras. If the subject selected telephoto, prosumer, or originally chose small camera, the next page educated the subject about digital camera attributes. We shall focus on the small camera page as the telephoto and prosumer pages are similar.

To accomplish the 20 minutes goal, we aggregated the number of defined attributes for a small or tiny camera to ten features: "Best Camera List"; auto focus assist light, video quality, manual controls; "capture the moment", ease of use, camera size, lens, megapixels; and price. A camera on a "Best Camera List" meant that at least one reviewer thought the camera was superior. For nine of the attributes we provided a one sentence explanation and a "More Info" button. For example, the short explanation of the auto focus assist light was "An auto focus assist light, AFAL, enables a camera to focus properly in dim light". The "More Info" explanation is "An auto focus light is highly recommended for taking pictures in low light conditions, such as those at parties for young adults. Without an auto focus assist light, your camera is likely to have difficulty focusing in such conditions. Remember if you want to take pictures of large groups in low light, you also need an external flash. While some small cameras have slave external flashes for mid sized groups, better external flashes are found on large prosumer and DSLR cameras". The first sentence was in bold red letters for emphasis. The short explanation for the other attribute, camera size, was "**Play DEMO video, a must see =>**" in bold red letters. If the subject responded, a short video that demonstrated the difference between small and tiny cameras was shown.

Two attributes that need an explanation to understand the experiment are video quality and capture the moment. We pointed out that video quality on digital cameras in terms of picture size and frames per second has been improving over time and that the best was a picture size of 640 x 480 pixels and 30 frames per second. To capture the moment, you need a short shutter lag. The shutter lag on digital cameras has been decreasing over time and at the time of the experiment 0.1 or less seconds was considered quick. The ten attributes aimed to provide as much discrimination among alternatives as possible. For example, the attribute "Manual Controls" divided cameras into those that did and did not have aperture and shutter priority. The former generally have a complete set of controls, while the latter are point-and-click cameras. For subjects without much digital camera knowledge, this easily understood distinction provides reasonable discrimination capacity.

The next page is a set-selection-by-aspects decision rule, [Norman *et al.* (2004)]. There are so many new digital cameras on the marketplace that a user can specify the characteristics determined by the intended use such as size and features to obtain a much smaller set for detailed study. On the first six attributes we listed the user was given the choice of "Yes" or "Doesn't Matter". For the others the user had a small number of choices. For example, for price the user chose among "Price no more than $200, $300, $400, Doesn't matter". Below the attribute table we had a box listing the number of cameras with the selected criteria. Initially the number of small cameras was 129 and is reduced by each selection of a new criteria. If the number falls to 0 the user is recommended to relax some of the criteria. Because the code works quickly the user can play "what if" scenarios to determine tradeoffs. Once the user has a manageable list, she can click on a button at the bottom to obtain this list of cameras in a table giving their features.

The first stage is to create a small list of digital cameras with the required attributes to take the intended pictures. The reason for obtaining a small list of digital cameras at this stage is that the second stage involves labor intensive operations such as reading reviews and examining picture galleries. To reduce a larger list to a smaller one the attributes included one quality discriminator in a "Best camera list" meaning a third party reviewer recommended the camera. This discriminator was considered superior to the above discussed brand, megapixels, and LCD screen heuristics. Quality of pictures is one aspect of being placed on such a list so that a camera on such a list with the specified attributes is also likely to take superior pictures.

The final page gives the user alternative approaches to selecting the final choice such as reading camera reviews and examining picture galleries that are attached to reviews, which are the alternatives considered most useful in our survey. The user can decide how much time to spend depending on how much detail he wishes to consider. The reader wishing to examine the Oct 2005 version of this code can go to http://www.eco.utexas.edu/Homepages/Faculty/Norman/01Cam/final.html.

We chose this non-compensatory decision rule over a compensatory decision rule code such as the MyProductAdvisor code at http://www.myproductadvisor.com/mpa/camera/inputSummary.do. In the MyProductAdvisor code, consumers choose a point on a sliding scale for each attribute where the value chosen on each sliding scale indicates the importance of that attribute. Our assertion is that consumers who have little knowledge of digital cameras have not formed their preferences over camera attributes. Also, how the code weighs the sliding scales to obtain the outcome is not readily apparent to the user. Thus, to obtain a set of cameras with the attributes needed for a particular type of picture can be a difficult task. As will be discussed later, our experiments show that our approach is superior.

10.4.3.2 *Experiment*

We devised an ANOVA experiment with the Duncan test to evaluate the performance of our code in determining a small set of quality digital cameras for three sets of pictures, the first decision process. We compared four decision aids: (1) our code; (2) having access to the internet, but not our code; (3) asking the advice of a digital camera owner; (4) asking the advice of a digital camera sales clerk.

It should be emphasized that the experiment focuses on the first stage of the decision process, which is selecting a small set of cameras for the stated purpose. It does not involve the more labor intensive second stage process of reading reviews, examining digital camera photo galleries, or physically interacting with the cameras in a store. The question is whether the subjects select a small set of quality cameras with the attributes to take good pictures under the stated scenario. Sales clerks were selected to evaluate their knowledge of digital cameras. From our surveys we found that students frequently ask the advice of a roommate who owns a digital camera, hence subjects who owned a digital camera were selected. As will be discussed, we tested a previous version of our code against an online selection code lacking an education module. This time we had one group of subjects just with access to the Internet without providing them with specific decision aids.

The subjects were asked to find three quality cameras for each of the following scenarios:

(1) A soccer mom has a budget of $300 and wants a camera that fits in her medium sized purse to take pictures of her children in outdoor sports, flowers in her garden and small groups of people outdoors and indoors under artificial light. She wants a camera that will allow her to take the best pictures possible for her budget and she has the time to learn how to use all the features of her camera.

(2) A student who has a budget of $550 wants a camera to take great pictures of birds outdoors, both still and flying, sometimes in the evening before sunset. The student also wants great pictures of UT football games from seats in the upper deck.

(3) if female answer a and if male answer b:
    a. A female student with a budget of $300 wants a camera to fit in her small date purse to take pictures and small videos of small groups of friends at clubs on 6th street at night.
    b. A male student with a budget of $300 wants a camera to fit in his shirt pocket without showing to take pictures and small videos of small groups of friends at clubs on 6th Street at night.

For the experiment there were 52 subjects, evenly divided into four groups. Each had the following resources:

(1) Students with our code. The experiment version of code to be found at http://www.eco.utexas.edu/Homepages/Faculty/Norman/00Cam. The instructions for the second decision stage were removed because the experiment was over after the first stage decision process.

(2) Students who had access to the Internet, but did not have access to our code

(3) Students who owned a digital camera. Students who own digital cameras frequently do not know the model number of their own camera, let alone other cameras. In order to get these students to specify the brand and model number of their choices, they were given pictures of

the various cameras with the name and model number, but no additional data.

(4) Salespeople in stores selling digital cameras. Students and the first author memorized each scenario, went to each store, and acted as consumers, orally requesting the sales clerk's recommendation.

The first three groups had the following instructions:

Objective: You are to use the material provided to find 9 digital cameras: 3 for each of 3 specifications of the type of pictures they should excel in taking. In each category rank the cameras 1, 2, and 3.

(1) Find the best cameras that can take the indicated type of pictures for the price. For each situation there are certain features the camera must have. What are these features? **Do not add features that you might personally like in a camera!!!**

(2) Take the price of the camera in the data as given. **Do not try to find a better price.**

(3) Evaluation criteria: Do the cameras you recommended have the required features? **To earn points you must list the brand and model number of each camera you list. There are up to 5 points per camera.**

For the sales persons, we were interested in what advice they would give to customers, so we pretended to be customers. We went into a store in a group of three. The first member of the group verbally gave the sales person a scenario and asked for three recommendations. After obtaining the recommendations, the next person repeated the process with the next scenario.

The first three groups were given one and a quarter hours to answer a quiz and finish their task. Their incentives were a flat fee of $10 and a chance to win an additional prize: $100 for best performance, $50 for 2nd, or $20 for 3rd, and $10 for each of the three next best performers, and $5 for each of the four next best performers after that. Each of the four groups had $220 in prize money and an expected earnings of $27. Because we wanted to see how salespeople would respond to their store incentives, we did not offer this group any additional incentive, nor did we give them a time limit.

The subjects scored 1 point each for most of the correct attribute selected – a few attributes required a scale. The scoring is shown in Table 10.1 on the next page. The scores were normalized on a 0–10 scale. The term "best video" means a picture size of 640×480 and 30 frames/second. This was the best video available in a digital camera at the time of the

Table 10.1   Camera scoring criteria.

Criteria	Scenario 1	Scenario 2	Scenario 3
auto focus assist light	N/A	N/A	1
best video	N/A	N/A	1
manual controls	1	1	N/A
on "Best Camera List"	1	1	1
price less than budget	1	See a below	1
quick when prefocused	1	1	N/A
small size	1	N/A	1
stabilized lens	N/A	1	N/A
tiny size	N/A	N/A	1
zoom	See b below	See c below	N/A

[1]a means 1 if less than budget, -1 or -2 if more than \$200 or \$1000 over budget, respectively.
[2]b means 0.5 if 2x, 1 if 3x, 1.5 if 4-9x and 2 if 10x.
[3]c means 1 if zoom > 4x and 2 if zoom > 10x.

experiment. The term "on 'Best Camera List'" means one of the sites that the user would be sent to for the stage two selection process if it had the camera on a recommended list. This criteria for quality was considered better than using a brand name such as Canon. In the stage two selection process consumers would read reviews and examine photo galleries. The term "quick when prefocused" refers to the shutter lag. The first digital cameras had a long shutter lag making it difficult to capture the moment in sports or children photography. Over time the shutter lag has decreased with technological advances. A camera in the experiment was considered quick if the shutter lag was less than or equal to 0.1 second. The ANOVA results for four groups, three scenarios, and fifty-two subjects with three observations each are shown in Table 10.2 on the top of the next page. The Duncan test results with an α of 0.05 grouped the performance of the 4 groups into three groups, A, B, and C are shown in Table 10.3 on the top of the next page.

Our code was statistically superior and the Duncan test indicated the differences among the four groups were statistically significant. We tested minor changes in the scoring and determined that small changes considered

Table 10.2 ANOVA results for camera experiment.

Source	DF	Sum of Squares	Mean Square	F Value	Pr > F
Model	11	2093.0	190.3	11.56	<.0001
Error	144	2369.8	16.5		
Corrected Total	155	4462.8			

Table 10.3 Duncan test of four groups in camera experiment.

Grouping	Mean	N	Subjects
A	27.2	39	Our Code
B	22.5	39	Sales Clerks
BC	21.3	39	Own Digital Camera
C	19.9	39	Access to Web

in the scoring resulted in a variation of F value from 9.04 to 11.56. In each of these variations the performance order of the four groups was the same and the Our Code group was significantly better. In some cases, the performance of the Sales Clerks group was not statistically superior to the Own Digital Camera group, and in some cases the performance of the Own Digital Camera group was not significantly better than the performance of the Access to Web group. Also, in an earlier experiment we found that our code was statistically superior to the sliding scale code created by myproductadvisor.com, see [Norman *et al.* (2005)]. Our assessment was that the sliding scale code did not provide the user with any education, so subjects did not know which features were needed for each scenario. The codes at the other sites mentioned also did not have an education module, so were not considered worth testing.

It required several years of effort to create a code that was statistically better than sales people. This fourth version of the code is the first that produced statistically superior performance over sales people. Why did our code perform better than the other groups? The fact that the subjects with our code had access to a "Best Camera List" attribute was not a deciding factor. If the "on Best Camera List" is dropped as a criteria, the F test value drops from 11.56 to 10.54 and the Duncan test of the groups remains the same. Our subjects did not always select cameras on a "Best Camera List" and if subjects chose major brands they were frequently on a "Best Camera List".

The major difficulty is how to educate subjects quickly to make good decisions. The major improvement over the previous version of the code was incorporating the video that made the difference between a tiny and small camera clear. The effect of this video is seen when we consider the three scenarios separately, which have a smaller sample size and more variation in the F values for the cases considered. We considered four alternative scoring criterion of the third scenario, and the corresponding F tests ranged from 12.97 to 18.82. In all four cases the Duncan test revealed that our code group placed first, the subjects who owned a camera placed second, and the other two groups were not significantly different. The video communicated camera size differences effectively so that all our subjects chose a tiny camera. Sales persons recommended a tiny camera less than subjects who owned a digital camera. It is possible that if we had given the sales people the same instructions as the other three groups, their performance would have been better, but this would have negated our effort to solicit their advice as customers.

On the second camera selection scenario the F test values for the four scoring cases ranged from 8.77 to 10.49. In all cases the sales persons placed first and subjects who used our code placed second. The difference was not statistically significant. This is one area where performance decreased with the fourth version of the code versus the third. In the third version of the code there was no initial decision between large and small cameras. Also, in the current version of the code, the html page that showed the relationship between focal length (optical zoom) and magnification was too technical. A simpler, more dramatic explanation probably would have produced better results. In the first camera selection scenario the F test values for the four cases ranged from 5.58 to 9.04. In three cases, the Duncan test revealed that the group that used our code had statistically superior performance.

Now let us consider factors that explain the results. As our surveys showed, subjects who owned a digital camera were not well informed about digital cameras. Subjects who just had access to the Internet had a data source that involved large processing costs. The performance of sales persons was a surprise. The part-time sales persons at Circuit City and other electronic stores generally did better than sale persons at specialized camera stores. We found out that the latter sales persons had questionable incentives. They always recommended a camera well below budget so that they could sell add-on services such as an extended warranty. For example, with a stated budget of $400, a sales person recommended a $330 camera and strongly advised a $130 three-year extended warranty with the purchase. In addition, their recommendations were influenced by the variations in manu-facturers incentives. We were genuinely surprised by their recommendations in the third scenario.

10.4.3.3 *Comments*

The surveyed students took an average of 9.8 hours to find a digital camera. Assuming our code would reduce the search time to four hours and that the subjects valued their time at $8 an hour, the value of such a code would be about $40 per subject. If we were to design this experiment today we would have a choice between using a digital camera on a cell phone or tablet versus buying a separate digital camera.

There are decision support aids for consumers with difficult decisions such as health care. Medicare.gov and Q1Medicare.com provide decision aids for choosing a drug program under Medicare Part D. Assuming "Oba-macare" is not repealed, 22 million will face selecting their health care from health exchanges. Pacific Business Group on Health is performing exper-iments to create decision support rules for selecting a plan from a health exchange, [von Glahn *et al.* (2012)].

The area where the most improvement in decision aid software is needed is in educating consumers in making first time decisions involving consider-able effort to master the details. This is where they are most likely to make a mistake.

10.5   Long Term Improvements

Now let us consider possible long term changes that should positively im-pact consumers. The major technological advance that should positively impact consumers is the creating of an integrated digital household in which all aspects of running a household are supported in mobile communications, the household computer system, and cyberspace. This will provide a frame-work for a major advance in decision tools for the household. Third party sites are likely to combine, resulting in an industry of a few major firms providing a wide array of consumer services and many smaller specialized firms. Also, the greater the variety of goods a seller offers for purchase the higher the information value of the data the seller provides the consumer.

Thus, Amazon will generally provide data with higher information value than a car dealer selling one brand.

In order to create an integrated digital household three developments are necessary: digital purchases using a cell phone, smart appliances that are connected to the household computer system, and integration of food management software. In addition, all household software, such as these and budget software, need to be integrated.

Let us start with technology to create a mobile digital wallet on cell phones, so that the cell phone can be used to pay for transactions. In order for this to take place, the economic agents involved, such as cell phone manufacturers, merchants, credit card companies, and banks must agree on the system specifications, such as how to communicate between the cell phone and merchant and security provisions. Each of the involved agents wants a specification that promotes its interests. In this regard the US is very much behind other countries, such as South Korea, [Sang-Hun (2009)], where an agreement among the involved political economic agents has been reached and the use of cell phones to make purchases is growing quickly.

Currently, the most common technology worldwide enabling the cell phone to communicate with the merchant is the NFC chip, which has a range of a few inches. In the US, Apple has not yet endorsed the NFC approach, as the iPhone 5 did not include a NFC chip. While there are several competing technologies in the US, such as Apple with Bluetooth low energy communications, and Google with the NFC chip, no single approach has gained widespread use. Currently, Apple and Google are engaged in an industrial battle to control the mobile digital wallet, [Rodriquez (2012)]. We expect this struggle will be resolved in the next few years. This technology will give consumers digital records of all their transactions.

Currently, many firms are creating smart appliances, [Martin (2012)]. Being able to connect appliances to the household computer and mobile communication system means that appliances can be controlled remotely by a cell phone or computer. Washing machines can be programmed to run when electric rates are cheaper. Robotic vacuum cleaners are now equipped with a remote-controlled camera. Smart refrigerators present recipes. Smart appliances can also incorporate modules to detect and identify failures needing repairs. To gain efficiency in terms of when to run appliances requires the power companies to provide their customers with a smart grid, with rates that vary depending on the load on the power generators.

This type of grid will take some time before it becomes commonplace, and until it does, consumers will not have an incentive to buy smart appliances to save energy. Also, [Daniels (2012)] discusses a privacy problem with smart home devices that will need to be addressed using the fourth amendment for government intrusion and privacy policy for power companies. The adoption of smart home devices is likely to take some time, but this would not affect the development of other aspects of the integrated digital household.

The area that needs a major technological advance is in home food management based on a device to monitor the flow of food in the kitchen. A requirement for such a monitoring device to be popular is that it requires very little labor input. One possible new kitchen tablet appliance that could achieve success would incorporate a tablet computer, a barcode/RFID reader, and a kitchen weight machine. The device should be separate and not part of a smart refrigerator because the technology of refrigerators advances much more slowly than the technology of such a device, and a replacement should not require buying a new refrigerator. Indeed, all smart capabilities of appliances should be in modules that can easily be updated without having to replace the appliance.

To monitor the flow of food in a kitchen the cook scans the bar code and weighs the package initially and every time a portion of food is removed from the package. These weights allow the food management program to estimate the calories and nutrition in a prepared meal. It also enables the food management program to monitor the inventory of food in the pantry and refrigerator. The tablet computer allows the chef to interact with the food management program and watch videos on how to prepare a selected recipe. The food management program would assist the chef in menu planning consistent with a selected diet plan. Based on the future menu and inventory of food in the household, the program would create a shopping list and determine the total price at competing grocery stores.

The food management program would incorporate all the components of food planning that already exist in an easy to use package. Currently, there are software applications for maintaining a recipe library, creating menus, food shopping lists, and estimating calories. There are apps for estimating the calories in a restaurant meal. The food management program needs to be able to follow a chosen diet plan. Is there a market for an entrepreneur to develop the smart kitchen tablet and integrated food management/lifestyle program?

There definitely are potential buyers, given the trend towards obesity in the US. Households trying to reduce their members weight would be potential buyers. In addition, firms' health costs are increasing from the obesity trend and they are responding with wellness programs. A firm's wellness program would have an incentive to subsidize the purchase of a food management system, especially if it contained a lifestyle component to monitor exercise and the weight of household members.

The importance of integrating all software aspects of running a household is to reduce the labor costs of transferring from one software program to another. A consumer can now transfer transaction data from his credit card account and bank account to his budget program, but this generally still requires labor to specify the category of the transaction, especially in the cases where the consumer bought many items in one transaction. With a digital invoice and rules to interpret the transaction, the categories for each item of a multiple item transaction would be recorded automatically. Consumer Reports asks its customers to manually input data on repair of their autos and appliances. With digital invoices for repairs, this information could be transferred to Consumer Reports automatically resulting in better estimates of product reliability. In an integrated digital household, budget planning would be integrated with item searches.

What the digital household would promote is the consolidation of third party firms providing consumers item search and budgeting services. Historically, new industries begin with startups that tend to consolidate as the market matures. We argue that the market would result in a few large firms, which we will call consumer decision support firms or CDS firms for short, and many smaller more specialized firms. To cover this market a decision support firm would have to offer integrated review services over a wide range of products, a budget program, a food management program, and a household appliance management program.

A CDS firm would obtain revenue through an integrated household software package, monitoring equipment and pass through fees to sellers. The larger the number of clients, and the greater the probability of a sale, the more leverage such a firm would have in negotiating the pass through fee rates. A CDS firm would attract customers by providing helpful services that were easy to use. One factor promoting ease of use is having a common format for the various consumer modules. Another is constantly improving the decision aids incorporated into the integrated package. To do this, the consolidated firm would prefer to have customers run the package in its computer cloud than buy a software package to run on home computers. In order to achieve this goal, the firm needs to gain the trust of its customers by maintaining the security and privacy of the data it collects.

With computing taking place in its cloud, the CDS firm could determine the relationship among relevant variables. For example, what are the budgeting characteristics of a household that was on track to save enough money for retirement? What is the relationship between the amount of data analysis and various types of item searches? Nevertheless, more data is required. In the next section on future research, the type of data and research required to achieve a constant improvement in consumer decision aids is discussed.

10.6 Research

Researchers who find this book interesting should consider three areas of needed research. The first area is the creation of a much better model of what is H tractable for unaided human processors. The second area is the creation of a measure of realized utility or proxies and the third area is applied research to improve data representation and decision aids.

In this book we based H tractable on the limitations of System 2 to perform sequential operations. A much better model of what is tractable needs to be created that incorporates the features of both System 1 and System 2.

Now let us focus on the type of data and applied research required to achieve a constant improvement in consumer decision aids. The focus of such research is identifying superior item search and budget strategies, in the sense that item search strategy A is superior to item search strategy B if it, on average, results in a preferred or equivalent product with fewer resources expended or a preferred product with the same amount of resources.

The ability to discriminate among item strategies and budget strategies requires a measure of the realized utility (or proxy) and budgeting performance respectively. One approach is a consumer survey of recognized errors. It is also possible that the work initiated by [Kahneman *et al.* (1997)] could be applied. Also, without a better measure of consumer utility we can not judge how close actual consumer performance is to optimal. Measures of deviations from revealed preference are useful for frequent purchases, such as food where the consumer faces the same selection each time. But, the longer the time period between purchase, the less useful are deviations from revealed preference because the probability increases that the consumer will face a different set of alternatives. Also, long term budgeting performance needs a better measure.

A focus of research of economists in consumer theory is integrating the prospect function into their models. A neglected area of research is what the psychologists call framing. Research into what data sets have high information value for various types of consumer decisions could greatly improve consumer performance. Again, we need to emphasize how such economic research differs from marketing research. Economic research should focus on how to frame the consumer decision to improve consumer performance and marketing research focuses on how to sell the product, such as how to use the affect heuristic to make the consumer feel good about the product. Economists should focus on what variables are important for the decision and how to educate the consumer on their relative importance. Another factor is how to organize data so that consumers can make comparisons on those variables they consider important.

Such research would be promoted by interaction of university researchers and the consumer decision support industry plus sellers of a large variety of goods whose marketing strategy is reducing the search cost of consumers. The later group would collect a great deal of click data on consumer strategies and their relative performance in order to determine what factors make a difference. In order to comprehensively evaluate alternative strategies, researchers need additional data that they could obtain using independent surveys to supplement the data collected in the consolidated firm's cloud. Let us consider how research in conjunction with a CDS firm might be conducted. The customers of the CDS firm need a reward to participate. If the number of customers of the CDS firm is large, the research could use a $1/k$ sample where k could be as large as 1000 if the firm had 10 million customers. To encourage participation, the CDS firm could offer the sample customers a reduced rate on services or a cash award. The CDS firm could also obtain user reviews with a much lower rate of fakes by requesting reviews from a sample of clients that bought the product being reviewed.

Improving budgeting and item search strategies would be a sequential trial and error improvement process involving proposals by experts and a social media campaign to constantly solicit suggested improvement. Consultants or in house researchers would create decision aids that would be made available in the integrated household software package. An example of a item search decision aid is the code for a digital camera decision search. Codes would vary based on the rate of technological change necessitating the education of consumers. Over time, decision aids would become increasingly sophisticated incorporating ideas from economics, decision psychology, users' input, and artificial intelligence.

The CDS firm would know how popular implemented decision aids were by the number of customers who used them. The CDS should initiate a social media campaign to solicit improvements to the various decision aids based on rewards such as prizes for suggestions that were used. This would create a sequential trial and error approach to improvements based on research and consumer reactions.

The impact of improved decision aids for consumers will have a negative impact on traditional advertising, which will vary by the type of product. In technological products where the consumers uses professional reviews and user reviews, the decrease in the impact of traditional advertising will be the greatest. For products like clothes, where the current style is important, advertising will remain important. Food advertising will decrease in importance for households using an integrated food management system. But, as long as marketing programs succeed, advertising will continue.

Finally, let us briefly mention production. A static profit maximization model with a nonlinear production function is generally not computable. Researchers need to consider how producers achieve performance in repeated production runs using human tractable strategies, which in some cases are aided by computer tractable decision aids.

10.7 Conclusion

In this book we have argued that the traditional consumer optimization model is intractable and discussed the tractable procedures consumers use to solve the problem.

The consumer problem has become more difficult with the increase in research and development and a faster rate of new products entering the marketplace. At the same time, the development of the Internet has created a platform for organizations to provide consumers with better data and decision aids to improve consumer performance. To use a quaint phrase, improving consumer performance means consumer markets will be closer to consumer sovereignty. Will consumer performance ever achieve exact optimality? No!

Appendix A

CC of the Discrete Two-Stage Budgeting Problem

Before restating and proving the main theory, we present some algorithms and prove some needed lemmas. We start by creating the following algorithm:

Block Bundle Search Algorithm, Block-Search

Step 1: Set $s = 0$, Repeat steps 2-5 l times

Step 2: Increment s by 1. Set $k = 1$. $max_{s,r} = 1$ and $r = 1$

Step 3: If $c(k) \leq rI/m$

If $B([\mu(x_{max_{s,r}}), s], [\mu(x_k), s]) \neq [\mu(x_{max_{s,r}}), s] \succeq [\mu(x_k), s]$, then $max_s = k$

Step 4: If $c(k) > rI/m$

Record $([\mu(x_*), s], r)$ and $U(([\mu(x_*), s], r))$

Step 5: If $c(k) \leq I$, $k < q^{n/l}$, and $rI/m < I$ increment k by 1 and r by 1 and perform Steps 3 and 4

END

When the algorithm terminates, a table of $([\mu(x_*), s], rI/m)$ and $U(([\mu(x_*), s], rI/m))$, the preferred bundle and associated utility for each income level for each separable group has been created. This table will be designated the *Opt* table. In the worst case we shall again assume that all bundles are feasible and in the expected case that $\alpha q^{n/l}$ are feasible where $0 < \alpha < 1$.

Lemma 1: If the n categories are divided into l subsets with an equal number of members, the worst and expected computational complexity of determining the *Opt* table is $lq^{n/l}$.

Proof:

a. $O(lq^{n/l})$: The consumer needs to perform no more than $l[q^{\frac{n}{l}} - 1]$ binary comparisons in the worst case and $\alpha l[q^{\frac{n}{l}} - 1]$ in the expected case using the Block-Search algorithm.

b. $\Omega(q^{\frac{n}{l}})$: Each set contains $q^{\frac{n}{l}}$ bundles. Given interactions affects, the consumer must perform at least $q^{\frac{n}{l}} - 1$ binary comparisons in the worse case and $\alpha q^{\frac{n}{l}} - 1$ binary comparisons in the expected case. By definitions D1-D3 of Chapter 2 the computational complexity of determining the *Opt* table is $lq^{\frac{n}{l}}$. END

Now we need to consider how we can create an efficient algorithm using this table to determine the optimal budget allocation among the l disaggregated consumer optimization problems. Let:

(1) $([\mu(x_*), j], rI/m)$ be the preferred bundle in $\{X, j\}$ for rI/m units of income where $1 \leq r \leq m$.

(2) $([\mu(x_*), (1, j)], rI/m)$ be the preferred bundle in the concatenation of separable subgroups $\{X, 1\}$ though $\{X, j\}$ for rI/m units of income.

(3) $U(i, j, rI/m) = U(([\mu(x_*), (1, i-1)], jI/m) + U(([\mu(x_*), i], (r-j)I/m))$.

(4) $U^*(i, rI/m) = \max_j U(i, j, rI/m)$ where $j = 0, 1, 2, \ldots, r$

and recall that I is divided into m equal quantities

The optimal budget allocation algorithm

Step 1: Set i=2

Step 2: Use binary comparison, $>$ to determine and record $U^*(i, I)$ and
$\qquad ([\mu(x_*), (1, i)], I)$ from $U(i, j, rI/m)$ where $r = m$

Step 3: If $i < l$ use binary comparison, $>$ to determine and record:

(1) $U^*(i, rI/m)$ and $([\mu(x_*), (1, i)], rI/m)$ from $U(i, j, rI/m)$
$\qquad$ where $r = m - 1$

(2) $U^*(i, rI/m)$ and $([\mu(x_*), (1, i)], rI/m]$ from $U(i, j, rI/m)$
$\qquad$ where $r = m - 2$

$\qquad \vdots$

(m-1) $U^*(i, rI/m)$ and $([\mu(x_*), (1, i)], rI/m)$ from $U(i, j, rI/m)$
$\qquad$ where $r = 1$

Step 4: Increment i by 1 and if $i \leq l$ repeat steps 2-4

END.

Note that this algorithm determines the optimal budget by concatenating the subgroups together one by one. Step 4 determines the optimal current concatenation for each budget level so that the next subgroup can be added. The operation that characterizes this algorithm is the number of binary comparisons, $>$, we must perform to determine the various $U^*(i, r)$s and $[x_*, (1, i), r]$s. Let us treat this operation, which involves lookup and comparison, as a primitive with cost $c_>$.

Lemma 2: If the n categories are divided into l subsets with an equal number of members, then the real and expected computational complexity of determining the optimal budget given the *Opt* table is lm^2s.

Proof:

a. $O((l)m^2)$: To perform steps 2 and 3 in the Optimal Budget Allocation Algorithm requires $O(m^2) >$ operations. Steps 4 and 5 are repeated $(l-2)$ times.

b. $\Omega((l)m^2)$: By induction: Prop(1) is the case i=3. Given the compensatory definition of the utility function now applied to each block the number of $>$ operations is $\Omega(m^2)$. Prop(t) $\rightarrow$ Prop(t+1). Same number of steps as in the case of Prop(1). END

Theorem: The worst case and expected computational complexity of the optimal budgeting is $\max(lq^{\frac{n}{l}}, lm^2)$.

Proof: By the two lemmas the computational complexity of budgeting $\max(lq^{\frac{n}{l}}, lm^2)$ and is minimized when l is such that $q^{\frac{n}{l}} = m^2$. END

Bibliography

Afriat, S. N. (1967). The construction of a utility function from expenditure data, *International Economic Review* **8**, 1, pp. 67–77.

Aho, A. V., Hopcroft, J. E., and Ullman, J. D. (1974). *The Design and Analysis of Computer Algorithms* (Addison-Wesley, Reading, MA).

Ariely, D. (2008). *Predictably Irrational* (HarperCollins, New York, NY).

Ariely, D., Loewenstein, G., and Prelec, D. (2003). Coherent arbitrariness: Stable demand curves without stable preferences, *International Economic Review* **118**, 1, pp. 73–106.

Ayres, I. (2007). *Super Crunchers* (Bantam Dell Books, New York, NY).

Baicker, K., Cutler, D., and Song, Z. (2010). Workplace wellness programs can generate savings, *Health Affairs* **29**, 2, pp. 304–311.

Barr, V. and Broudy, C. (1986). *Designing to Sell* (McGraw-Hill, New York, NY).

Barr, V. and Field, K. (1997). *Stores: Retail Display and Design* (PBC International, Glen Cove, NY).

Battalio, R., Kagel, J., Winkler, R., Fisher, E., Basmann, R., and Krasner, L. (1973). A test of consumer demand theory using observations of individual consumer purchases, *Western Economic Journal* **11**, pp. 411–428.

Becker, G. (1962). Irrational behavior and economic theory, *Journal of Political Economic* **70**, pp. 1–13.

Berry, L., Mirabito, A., and Baun, W. (2010). Workplace wellness programs can generate savings, *Harvard Business Review*, pp. 2012–2068.

Bettman, J., Luce, M., and Payne, J. (1998). Constructive consumer choice processes, *Journal of Consumer Research* **25**, pp. 187–217.

Bettman, J. R., Luce, M. F., and Payne, J. W. (2006). Constructive consumer choice processes, in S. Lichtenstein and P. Slovic (eds.), *The Construction of Preference* (Cambridge University Press, Cambridge, UK), pp. 323–341.

Blackkorby, C. and Shorrocks, A. F. (eds.) (1995). *Separability and Aggregation: Collected works of W. M. Gorman*, Vol. 1 (Oxford University Press, Oxford and New York).

Breusch, T. S. and Pagan, A. R. (1979). Simple test for heteroscedasticity and random coefficient variation, *Econometrica* **47**, 5, pp. 1287–1294.

Brokaw, L. (2012). The big, insidious business of social network fakes, Posted on January 1, 2012 on sloanreview.mit.edu.

Camber, R. (2007). Clothes shops that take inches off your waistline, Mail*Online*, 448731.

Camerer, C. (2006). Behavioral economics, in R. Blundell, W. K. Newey, and T. Persson (eds.), *Advances in Economics and Econometrics: Theory and Applications, Ninth World Congress, Volume 2* (Cambridge University Press, Cambridge and New York), pp. 181–214.

Cameron, C. (1995). Individual decision making, in J. Kagal and A. Roth (eds.), *Handbook of Experimental Economics* (Princeton University Press, Princeton, NJ), pp. 587–703.

Chow, G. C. (1981). *Econometric Analysis by Control Methods* (John Wiley & Sons, New York, NY).

Cohen, H. (2011). 30 social media definitions, Posted on May 9, 2011 on heidicohen.com.

Conroy, P., Ash, A., and Kutyla, D. (2009). Consumer-centric innovation, Available at http://www.deloitte.com.

Cox, J. C. (1997). On testing the utility hypothesis, *The Economic Journal* **107**, 443, pp. 1054–1078.

Curry, C. (2012). 'mcdialysis? i'm loving it!': Mcdonald's twitter promo fail, Posted on January 24, 2012 on abcnews.go.com/blogs.

Daniels, M. (2012). Are smart appliances spying on you? Posted 16 Mar 12 on www.mobiledia.com/news/13591.html.

Deaton, A. and Muellbauer, J. (1980). *Economics and consumer behavior* (Cambridge University Press, Cambridge, UK).

DellaVigna, S. (2009). Psychology and economics: Evidence from the field, *Journal of Economic Literature* **47**, 2, pp. 315–372.

Duhigg, C. (2012). How companies learn your secrets, *The New York Times Magazine*.

Earl, P. (1986). *Lifestyle Economics* (St. Martin's Press, New York, NY).

Echenique, F., Golovin, D., and Wierman, A. (2011a). A revealed preference approach to computational complexity in economics, Unpublished manuscript, CalTech. For copy contact fede@caltech.edu.

Echenique, F., Sangmok, L., and Shum, M. (2011b). The money pump as a measure of revealed preference violations, *Journal of Political Economy* **119**, 6, pp. 1201–1223.

Economist, S. (2005). The rise of the creative consumer, *The Economist*.

Edgeworth, F. (1881). *Mathematical psychics: an essay on the application of mathematics to the moral sciences* (Augustus M. Kelly 1961, New York, NY).

Encarnacion, J. (1987). Preference paradoxes and lexicographic choice, *Journal of Economic Behavior and Organization* **8**, 2, pp. 231–248.

Evans, J. S. B. T. (2008). Dual-processing accounts of reasoning, judgement, and social cognition, *Annual Review of Psychology* **59**, pp. 255–278.

Fisman, R. (2012). Should you trust online reviews? Posted April 14, 2012 on Slate.com.

Frederick, S., Loewenstein, G., and O'Donoghue, T. (2002). Time discounting and time preference: a critical review, *Journal of Economic Literature* **40**, pp. 351–401.

Friedman, M. and Savage, L. J. (1948). The utility analysis of choices involving risk, *The Journal of Political Economy* **56**, 4, pp. 279–304.

Fuchs-Seliger, S. and Mayer, O. (2003). Rationality without transitivity, *Journal of Economics* **80**, 1, pp. 77–87.

Gigerenzer, G. (2002). The adaptive toolbox, in G. Gigerenzer and R. Selten (eds.), *Bounded Rationality: The Adaptive Toolbox* (MIT Press, Cambridge, MA), pp. 37–50.

Gigerenzer, G. and Selten, R. (2002). Rethinking rationality, in G. Gigerenzer and R. Selten (eds.), *Bounded Rationality: The Adaptive Toolbox*, chap. 1 (MIT Press, Cambridge, MA), pp. 1–12.

Gilboa, I., Postlewaite, A., and Schmeidler, D. (2010). The complexity of the consumer problem and mental accounting, Unpublished manuscript. For copy contact tzachigilboa@gmail.com.

Harbaugh, W. T., Krause, K., and Berry, T. R. (2001). Garp for kids; on the development of rational choice behavior, *American Economic Review* **91**, 5, pp. 1539–1545.

Hazlett, C. (2011). Airbrushed Julia Roberts ad called 'overly perfected' by agency, Posted on July 27, 2011 on scoop.today.msnbc.mcn.com.

Heath, C. and Soll, J. (1996). Mental budgeting and consumer decisions, *Journal of Consumer Research* **23**, pp. 40–52.

Hogarth, R. M. (1987). *Judgement and choice : the psychology of decision*, 2nd edn. (Wiley, Chichester, NY).

Horton, C. (2012). Facebook credit card as your new universal payment solution? Posted on 5 Jul12 on business2community.com.

Huber, O. (1980). The influence of some task variables on cognitive operations in an information-processing decision model, *Acta Psychologica* **45**, pp. 187–196.

IBI, S. (2012). Lincoln industries' wellness program: Roi through innovative programs, aligning incentives and recognizing achievement, Available at www.ibi-nbchforum.com.

Johnson, E. (1988). Deciding how to decide: The effort of making a decision, Unpublished manuscript, The University of Chicago.

Johnson, E., Moe, W., Fader, P., Bellman, S., and Lohse, G. (2004a). On the depth and dynamics of online search behavior, *Management Science* **50**, 3, pp. 299–308.

Johnson, E., Moe, W., Fader, P., Bellman, S., and Lohse, G. (2004b). On the depth and dynamics of online search behavior, *Management Science* **50**, 3, pp. 299–308.

Kagel, J. H., Battalio, R. C., and Green, L. (1995). *Economic choice theory: an experimental analysis of animal behavior* (Cambridge University Press, Cambridge, UK).

Kahneman, D. (2011). *Thinking Fast and Slow* (Farrar, Straus and Giroux, New York, NY).

Kahneman, D. and Dolan, P. (2008). Interpretations of utility and their implications for the valuation of health, *The Economic Journal* **118**, pp. 215–234.

Kahneman, D., Slovic, P., and Tversky, A. (eds.) (1982). *Judgment under Uncertainty Heuristics and Biases* (Cambridge University Press, Cambridge, UK).

Kahneman, D. and Thaler, R. (2006). Anomalies utility maximization and experienced utility, *Journal of Economic Perspectives* **20**, 1, pp. 221–234.

Kahneman, D. and Tversky, A. (1979). Prospect theory: An analysis of decision under risk, *Econometrica* **47**, 2, pp. 263–291.

Kahneman, D., Wakker, P., and Sarin, R. (1997). Back to Bentham? Explorations of experienced utility, *The Quarterly Journal of Economics* **122**, pp. 375–405.

Kessler, S. (2011). 3 Facebook commerce success stories, Posted on February 21, 2011 mashable.com.

Ketcham, J. D., Lucarelli, C., Miravete, E. J., and Roebuck, C. (2012). Sinking, swimming, or learning to swim in medicare Part D, *American Economic Review* **102**, 6, pp. 2639–73.

Klein, G. (2002). The fiction of optimization, in G. Gigerenzer and R. Selten (eds.), *Bounded Rationality: The Adaptive Toolbox* (MIT Press, Cambridge, MA), pp. 103–122.

Knuth, D. E. (1973). *The art of computer programming*, 2nd edn. (Addison-Wesley, Reading, MA).

Kogut, C. (1990). Consumer search theory and sunk costs, *Journal of Economic Behavior and Organization* **14**, pp. 381–392.

Kohn, M. and Shavell, S. (1974). The theory of search, *Journal of Economic Theory* **9**, pp. 93–123.

Kornish, L. (2009). Are user reviews systematically manipulated? Evidence from the helpfulness ratings, Unpublished manuscript Leeds School of Business, University of Colorado at Boulder.

Le, D. (2011). 2011 ford fiesta, Online at http://www.slideshare.net/dmle/ford-fiesta-movement-social-media-campaign-value.

Lichtenstein, S. and Slovic, P. (eds.) (2006). *The Construction of Preference* (Cambridge University Press, Cambridge, UK).

List, J. (2003). Does market experience eliminate market anomalies? *Quarterly Journal of Economics* **118**, 1, pp. 41–71.

List, J. A. and Millimet, D. L. (2008). The market: Catalyst for rationality and filter of irrationality, *The B.E. Journal of Economic Analysis & Policy* **8**, 1, article 47 available at: http://www.bepress.com/bejeap/vol8/iss1/art47.

Loewenstein, G., O'Donoghue, T., and Rabin, M. (2003). Projection bias in predicting future utility, *The Quarterly Journal of Economics* **118**, 4, pp. 1209–1248.

Loomes, G., Starmer, C., and Sugden, R. (1991). Observing violations of transitivity by experimental methods, *Econometrica* **59**, 2, pp. 425–439.

Luca, M. (2011). Reviews, reputation, and revenue: The case of yelp.com, Unpublished manuscript, Harvard Business School.

Luthje, C., Herstatt, C., and von Hippel, E. (2002). The dominant role of "local" information in user innovation: The case of mountain biking, MIT Sloan School of Management Working Paper 4377-02.

Mahnoud, E.-G. and Grether, D. (1995). Are people bayesian? Uncovering behavioral strategies, *Journal of the American Statistical Association* **90**, 432, pp. 1137–1145.

Martin, A. (2012). Not quite smart enough, Posted on January 23, 2012 on nytimes.com.

Mayzlin, D., Dover, Y., and Chevallier, J. (2012). Promotional reviews: An empirical investigation of online review manipulation, Posted August 13, 2012 on the Social Science Research Network, ssrn.com.

McLeod, P. and Dienes, Z. (1996). Do fielders know where to go to catch the ball or only how to get there? *Journal of Experimental Psychology: Human Perception and Performance* **22**, pp. 531–543.

McMillan, j. and Rothschild, M. (1994). Search theory, in R. Aumann and H. S (eds.), *Handbook of Game Theory with Economic Applications*, Vol. 2 (North Holland, Amsterdam, Holland), pp. 905–927.

Mehlhorn, K. (1984). *Data structures and algorithms, EATCS monographs on theoretical computer science*, Vol. 1 (Springer-Verlag, Berlin, Germany).

Montgomery, H. (2006). Decision making and action: The search for a dominance strategy, in S. Lichtenstein and P. Slovic (eds.), *The Construction of Preference* (Cambridge University Press, Cambridge, UK), pp. 342–355.

Munnell, A., Webb, A., and Golub-Sass, F. (2012). The national retirement risk index: An update, Brief Number 12-20 Center for Retirement Research of Boston College.

Myer, J. and Alper, M. (1968). Determinant buying attitudes: Meaning and measurement, *Journal of Marketing* **32**, pp. 31–48.

Nielsen, S. (2012). Global trust in advertising and brand messages, Report available at nielsen.com.

Nisbett, R. E. and Kanouse, D. E. (1968). Obesity, hunger, and supermarket shopping, *Proceedings of the Annual convention of the American Psychological Association* **3**, 2, pp. 683–684.

Norman, A., Aberty, M., DeGroot, M., Gour, S., Govil, C., Hart, J., El Kadiri, G., Keyburn, S., Kulkarni, M., Mehta, N., Sanghai, J., Shah, V., Schieck, J., Sivakumaran, Y., Sussman, J., Tillmanns, C., Yan, K., and Zahradnic, F. (2005). The procedural consumer: The polynomial assist, Available at http://www.eco.utexas.edu/Homepages/Faculty/Norman/research.htm.

Norman, A., Ahmed, A., Chou, J., Dalal, A., Fortson, K., Jindal, M., Kurz, C., Lee, H., Payne, K., Rando, R., Sheppard, K., Sublett, J., Sussman, J., and White, I. (2004). On the computational complexity of consumer decision rules, *Computational Economics* **23**, pp. 173–192.

Norman, A., Ahmed, A., Chou, J., Fortson, K., Kurz, C., Lee, H., Linden, L., Meythaler, K., Rando, R., Sheppard, K., Tantzen, N., I, W., and Ziegler, M. (2003). An ordering experiment, *Journal of Economic Behavior and Organization* **50**, pp. 249–262.

Norman, A., Alberty, M., Brehm, K., Gu, B., Hart, J., El Kadiri, G., Ke, J., Keyburn, S., Kulkarni, M., Mehta, N., Robertson, A., Sanghai, J., Shah, V., Schieck, J., Sivakumaran, Y., Sussman, J., Tillmanns, C., Yan, K., and Zahradnic, F. (2008). Can consumer software selection code for digital cameras improve consumer performance? *Computational Economics* **31**, pp. 363–380.

Norman, A., Berman, J., Brehm, K., Drake, M., Dyer, A., Frisby, J., Govil, C., Hinchey, C., Heuer, L., Ke, J., Kejriwal, S., Kuang, K., Keyburn, S., Ler, S., Powers, K., Robertson, A., Sanghai, J., Schulze, C., Schieck, J., Sussman, J., Tan, L., Tello, A., Wang, R., K, Y., and Zeinullayev, T. (2012). Repeated price search, *Computational Economics* **39**, 3, pp. 243–257.

Norman, A., Brehm, K., Hinchey, C., Kejriwal, S., Kuang, K., Ler, S., Powers, K., Robertson, A., Schieck, J., and Sussman, J. (2007). Sequential consumer model, Unpublished manuscript, The University of Texas at Austin.

Norman, A., Chou, J., Chowdhury, A., Dalal, A., Fortson, K., Jindal, M., Payne, K., and Rajan, M. (2001). Two-stage budgeting: A difficult problem, *Computational Economics* **18**, pp. 259–271.

Norman, A. and Jung, W. S. (1977). Linear quadratic control theory for models with long lags, *Econometrica* **45**, 4, pp. 905–917.

Norman, A., Leonard, G., L, L., Meythaler, K., K, M., Newhouse, H., Tantzen, and Ziegler, M. (1997). Order: Human versus computer, in H. Amman, B. Rustem, and A. Whinston (eds.), *Computational Approaches to Economic Problems*, Advances in computational economics, Vol. 6 (Kluwer Academic Publishers, Boston, MA), pp. 209–225.

Norman, A. and Norman, M. (1973). Behavioral consistency tests of econometric models, *IEEE Transactions on Automatic Control* **18**, 5, pp. 465–472.

Norman, A. L. (1965). Three dimension calculus of variations trajectory and performance analysis manual, Flight Dynamics and Control, Douglas Aircraft Company.

Norman, A. L. (1976). First order dual control, *Annals of Economic and Social Measurement* **5**, 3, pp. 311–321.

Norman, A. L. (1984). Alternative algorithms for the macrae olcv strategy, *Journal of Economic Dynamics and Control* **7**, pp. 21–39.

Norman, A. L. (1987). A theory of monetary exchange, *Review of Economic Studies* **LIV**, pp. 499–517.

Norman, A. L. (1993). *Informational Society: An Economic Theory of Discovery, Invention, and Innovation* (Kluwer Academic Publishers, Boston, MA).

Norman, A. L. (2009). Informational society online, Online at http://www.eco.utexas.edu/Homepages/Faculty/Norman/61N/Text/000IS.html.

Norman, A. L. and Shimer, D. (1994). Risk, uncertainty, and complexity, *Journal of Economic Dynamics and Control* **18**, pp. 231–249.

Ott, M., Cardie, C., and Hancock, J. (2012). Estimating the prevalence of deception in online review communities, WWW 2012, April 16–20, 2012, Lyon, France.

Pagan, F. G. (1981). *Formal specification of programming languages: A panoramic primer* (Prentice-Hall, Englewood Cliffs, NJ).

Parsa, A. (2009). Exclusive: Belkin's development rep is hiring people to write fake positive amazon reviews, Posted January 16, 2009 on TheDailyBackground.com.

Payne, J. W., Bettman, J. R., and Johnson, E. J. (1993). *The Adaptive Decision Maker* (Cambridge University Press, New York, NY).

Polisson, M. and Quah, J. (2012). Revealed preference in a discrete consumption space, IFS working paper W12/03 Institute for Fiscal Studies.

Read, R., Loewenstein, G., and Rabin, M. (2006). Choice braketing, in S. Lichtenstein and P. Slovic (eds.), *The Construction of Preference* (Cambridge University Press, Cambridge, UK), pp. 356–371.

Rieskamp, J., Busemeyer, J., and Mellers, B. (2006). Extending the bounds of rationality: Evidence and theories of preferential choice, *Journal of Economic Literature* **XLIV**, pp. 631–661.

Riewoldt, O. (2000). *Retail Design* (Lawrence King, Hong Kong, China).

Rodriquez, S. (2012). Apple, google gear up for mobile-wallet war, Posted on August 29, 2012 on smh.com.au.

Samuelson, P. (1937). A note on the measurement of utility, *Review of Economic Studies* **4**, pp. 155–161.

Sang-Hun, C. (2009). In South Korea, all of life is mobile, Posted on May 24, 2009 on nytimes.com.

Schwartz, B. (2005). *The Paradox of Choice: Why more is less* (HarperCollins, New York, NY).

Sengupta, S. (2012a). Facebook revenue surpasses forecasts, Posted October 23, 2012 on nytimes.com.

Sengupta, S. (2012b). On facebook, 'likes' become ads, Published May 31, 2012 on NYTimes.com in Business Day Technology.

Shafer, W. and Sonnenshein, H. (1982). Market demand and excess demand functions, in K. Arrow and M. Intrilligator (eds.), *Handbook of Mathematical Economics*, Vol. II (North Holland, New York, NY), pp. 356–371.

Shah, V. (2004). Checking transitivity, Senior Thesis, Department of Economics, (The University of Texas at Austin).

Simon, H. A. (1955). A behavioral model of rational choice, *Quarterly Journal of Economics* **69**, pp. 99–118.

Simon, H. A. (1956). Rational choice and the structure of environments, *Psychological Review* **63**, pp. 129–138.

Simon, H. A. (1976). From substantive to procedural rationality, in S. J. Latsis (ed.), *Method and Appraisal in Economics*, part 3 (Cambridge University Press, New York, NY), pp. 179–183.

Slovic, P., Finucane, M., Peters, E., and MacGregor, D. (2006a). The affect heuristic, in S. Lichtenstein and P. Slovic (eds.), *The Construction of Preference* (Cambridge University Press, Cambridge, UK), pp. 434–453.

Slovic, P., Finucane, M., Peters, E., and MacGregor, D. (2006b). The affect heuristic, in S. Lichtenstein and P. Slovic (eds.), *The Construction of Preference* (Cambridge University Press, Cambridge, UK), pp. 342–355.

Sonnemans, J. (1998). Strategies of search, *Journal of Economic Behavior and Organization* **35**, pp. 309–332.

Sonnenshein, H. (1973a). Do Walras' identity and continuity characterize the class of community excess demand function, *Journal of Economic Theory* **6**, pp. 345–354.

Sonnenshein, H. (1973b). The utility hypothesis and market demand theory, *Western Economic Journal* **11**, pp. 404–410.

Staff (2001). Virgin megastores launching a new design with new store in london, *Design Week* **6**, pp. 281–299.

Stanovich, K. E. and West, R. E. (2005). Individual differences in reasoning: Implications for the rationality debate? in T. Gilovich, D. Griffin, and D. Kahneman (eds.), *Heuristics and Biases The Psychology of Intuitive Judgement* (Cambridge University Press, Cambridge, UK), pp. 421–440.

Streitfeld, D. (2012). In a race to out-rave, 5-star web reviews go for $5, Published August 19, 2011 on NYTimes.com in Business Day Technology.

Strotz, R. H. (1957). The empirical implications of a utility tree, *Econometrica* **25**, pp. 269–280.

Svenson, O. (2006). Pre- and post-decision construction of preferences: Differentiation and consolidation, in S. Lichtenstein and P. Slovic (eds.), *The Construction of Preference* (Cambridge University Press, Cambridge, UK), pp. 356–371.

Thaler, R. (1980). Toward a positive theory of consumer choice, *Economic Behavior and Organization* **1**, pp. 39–60.

Thaler, R. and Benartzi, S. (2004). Save more tomorrow: Using behavioral economics to increase empolyee saving, *Journal of Political Economy* **122**, pp. S164–S187.

Thaler, R. and Shefrin, H. (1981). An economic theory of self control, *Journal of Political Economy* **89**, pp. 392–406.

Thaler, R. and Sunstein, C. (2009). *Nudge: Improving Decisions about Health, Wealth, and Happiness* (Penguin Books, Ltd, London, England).

Thaler, R. H. (1991). *Quasi-rational economics* (Russell Sage Foundation, New York, NY).

Torrone, P. (2011). This week in "user innovations", Posted February 18, 2011 on blog.makezine.com.

Traub, J. F., Wasilkowski, G. W., and Wozniakowski, H. (1988). *Information-based complexity* (Academic Press, Boston, MA).

Tversky, A. (1969). Intransitivity of preferences, *Psychological Review* **76**, 1, pp. 31–48.

Tversky, A. (1972). Elimination by aspects: A theory of choice, *Psychological Review* **79**, 4, pp. 281–299.

Tversky, A. and Kahneman, D. (1981). The framing of decisions and the psychology of choice, *Science* **211**, pp. 453–458.

Tversky, A. and Kahneman, D. (1984). Extensional versus intuitive reasoning: the conjunction fallacy in probability judgment, *Psychological Review* **91**, pp. 293–315.

Varian, H. (1988). Revealed preference with a subset of goods, *Journal of Economic Theory* **46**, pp. 179–185.

Varian, H. R. (1982). The nonparametric approach to demand analysis, *Econometrica* **50**, 4, pp. 9456–973.

Velupillai, K. (2000). *Computable Economics* (Oxford University Press, New York, NY).

Velupillai, K. (ed.) (2005). *Computability, Complexity and Constructivity in Economic Analysis* (Blackwell Publishing, Oxford, UK).

Velupillai, K. (2010). *Computable Foundations for Economics* (Routledge, London, UK).

von Glahn, T., Ketchel, A., Johnson, R., Eric andHarin, and Baker, T. (2012). *Consumer choice of health plan: Decision support rules for health exchanges*, PBGH report available at http://www.pbgh.org/news-and-publications/pbgh-articles-a-publications.

von Hippel, E. (2005). *Democratizing innovation* (MIT Press, Cambridge, MA).

Von Hippel, E., Ogawa, S., and de Jong, J. P. (2011). The age of the consumer-innovator, *MIT Sloan Management Review*.

White, H. (1980). A heteroscedasticity-consistent covariance matrix estimator and a direct test for heteroskecasticity, *Econometrica* **48**, 4, pp. 817–838.

Zimmerman, E. (2012). Small retailers open up storefronts on facebook pages, Posted on July 25, 2012 on nytimes.com.

Index

Printed in the United States
By Bookmasters